# TRANSNATIONAL CORPORATIONS AND INDUSTRIAL TRANSFORMATION IN LATIN AMERICA

Few issues in contemporary political economy arouse such feelings as the transnational corporation (TNC). For some it is the modern embodiment of imperialism playing a crucial role in perpetuating underdevelopment in the third world. For others it can play a major part in eliminating international inequalities as a result of its global vision. Such views are, however, often based on inadequate theoretical conceptions and insufficient empirical information.

This book fills an important gap. It draws on a mass of detailed empirical research carried out in Latin America over the last decade to give a comprehensive picture of the recent expansion by industrial TNCs in the region. It also deepens the analysis through specific case-studies of two key industries, motor-vehicles and pharmaceuticals, which have been major areas of transnational penetration. The relationship between TNCs, local class structure and the state is also discussed.

The analytical framework of the book emphasises the internationalisation of capital, seeing the growth of TNCs as an aspect of competitive capital accumulation. It stresses that, despite the growth of large oligopolies, TNCs remain subject to market forces and competitive pressures.

**Rhys Jenkins** has been Lecturer in the School of Development Studies at the University of East Anglia since the School was set up in 1973. He was a Visiting Research Fellow at the Centro de Investigacion y Docencia Economicas, Mexico City, in 1976 and worked with the Instituto Latinoamericano de Estudios Transnacionales, Mexico City, in 1980. He has carried out research in Argentina, Chile and Mexico and travelled widely in Latin America. He is the author of *Dependent Industrialization in Latin America*.

LATIN AMERICAN STUDIES SERIES
General Editors: Philip O'Brien and Peter Flynn

The series is a new initiative designed to give a comprehensive
analysis of some of the many complex problems facing contemporary Latin America and individual Latin American
countries.

*Published*

David Booth and Bernardo Sorj (*editors*)
MILITARY REFORMISM AND SOCIAL CLASSES: The
Peruvian Experience, 1968–80

Rhys Jenkins
TRANSNATIONAL CORPORATIONS AND INDUSTRIAL
TRANSFORMATION IN LATIN AMERICA

*Forthcoming*

Christian Anglade and Carlos Fortin (*editors*)
THE STATE AND CAPITAL ACCUMULATION IN LATIN
AMERICA

Jean Carrière (*editor*)
POLITICS, INDUSTRIAL RELATIONS AND THE LABOUR
MOVEMENT IN LATIN AMERICA, 1860–1980 (*two volumes*)

Joe Foweraker
CLASS DOMINATION AND THE AUTHORITARIAN
STATE: A Political Economy of Latin America

# TRANSNATIONAL CORPORATIONS AND INDUSTRIAL TRANSFORMATION IN LATIN AMERICA

Owen

Rhys Jenkins

MACMILLAN

*First published 1984 by*
THE MACMILLAN PRESS LTD
*London and Basingstoke*
*Companies and representatives*
*throughout the world*

ISBN 0 333 28449 6√

*Printed in Hong Kong*

# Contents

# Preface

This book reflects more than ten years' work studying the impact of transnational corporations (TNCs) in Latin America. As the bibliography bears witness, when I first started taking an interest in this theme in the late 1960s, the literature was extremely limited. The importance of TNCs had only recently been recognised and little empirical work had been undertaken. In the 1970s there was a great flood of studies which substantially increased our knowledge of the role of TNCs in the region. Unfortunately for English readers much of the work is relatively inaccessible either because it is available only in Spanish or Portuguese or because it is in the form of government documents, reports for international organisations or unpublished monographs or dissertations.

The purpose of this book is twofold. First, it attempts to analyse the implications of TNC operations for the process of economic and social change in Latin America. In doing so, alternative theoretical and policy approaches to TNCs are considered, and one such approach, the internationalisation of capital, provides the thread around which the study is organised. Second, I have also attempted to present in a synthetic form a considerable amount of empirical data on TNCs in Latin America which is not otherwise readily available. While this information is used to support the general argument, it has been provided in some detail, together with the results of many individual studies of TNCs in Latin America, in the hope that it will be useful for others who wish to undertake further analyses of TNCs in the region.

Any book such as this which represents a prolonged period of work on a single theme will inevitably have been influenced over time by a large number of people. It would be impossible to name all the friends and colleagues in Britain, Latin America and North America who have in some way contributed to the ideas presented in this book. I am, however, particularly grateful to Andre Gunder Frank, Gary Gereffi, Nigel Haworth, John Humphrey, Richard Newfarmer, Ruth Pearson, Ian Roxborough, Chris Scott and Peter

West, who commented on all or part of the original draft. My thanks also to Barbara Wraight, who produced a typescript from a chaotic manuscript.

R.O.J.

# List of Tables

# Part I
# The Internationalisation
# of Latin American
# Industry

# 1 The Internationalisation of Latin American Industry: Alternative Views

Private investment as a carrier of technology, of trade opportunities, and of capital itself . . . becomes a major factor in promoting industrial and agricultural development. Further, a significant flow of private capital stimulates the mobilization and formation of domestic capital within the recipient country.

Richard Nixon (1972)

This is not the first time in economic history that a new structure of business, such as the multinational corporations, has evolved. The difference is that we had institutional structures in national government that could cope with previous changes to align private interest with the greater public welfare. The international nature of the MNC limits the capability of present institutional structures to guide and direct them in a manner perceived as maximizing the public good.

Senator Frank Church, Foreword to Newfarmer and<br>Mueller (1975)

At the third UNCTAD I was able to discuss the phenomenon of the transnational corporations. I mentioned the great growth in their economic power, political influence and corrupting action . . . They make huge profits and drain off tremendous resources from the developing countries.

Salvador Allende (1972)

3

The effects of TNCs on development in third world countries has been a major issue of debate for the past decade or more. As the most important region of TNC activity in the third world, Latin America has been a particular focus for this debate. At the same time as foreign capital withdrew or was taken over in its traditional preserves, the public utilities and extractive industries, the effects of foreign investment in manufacturing became a central concern. The debate has not been restricted to academic scribbling but has had major consequences in terms both of national government policies and international relations.

The different positions adopted towards TNCs have at their roots different implicit theoretical frameworks for the analysis of their impact. Before embarking on the empirical analysis of this book, it seems appropriate therefore to highlight the most influential approaches to the analysis of TNCs in Latin American industry. The first approach which predominated in Latin America in the 1950s and early 1960s was developmentalism ('desarrollismo') with its emphasis on the benefits which TNCs' investment in manufacturing brought. Two alternative views developed in the late 1960s, both more critical of the TNCs. Economic nationalists emphasised the existence of monopoly rents and questioned the distribution of the returns between host countries and the foreign investor. Dependency theorists attacked developmentalism, pointing to the emergence of a 'new dependence' in which significant sectors of industry had come under the control of the transnationals. While these three approaches have been selected because they represent influential positions in the debate on foreign investment in Latin America, they also correspond to theoretical distinctions which have been made in the context of trade and development.[1] However none offer an entirely satisfactory framework for analysing the impact of the TNCs in Latin America. In the last section of this Chapter an alternative approach based on the internationalisation of capital is therefore presented.

## 1 DEVELOPMENTALISM

The mainstream of thinking on problems of economic development in the 1950s and 1960s, both in Latin America and elsewhere, emphasised the positive effects of direct foreign investment. This derived from a view of development which considered low levels of savings and inadequate foreign exchange earnings as major obstacles to growth, and considered industrialisation as a prerequisite for breaking out of this vicious circle. Consequently the contribution of foreign capital was usually classified under three main headings. First, capital inflows permitted an increase in the rate of accumulation over and above what would have been possible on the basis of local savings. Second, it permitted imports of machinery and equipment which could not have been financed from export earnings. Finally, foreign firms brought in new technology and management techniques, and provided external economies through training the local labour force (ECLA, 1969, p. 33).

It is not entirely surprising, in view of their general analysis of development problems in Latin America, that the Economic Commission for Latin American should also have adopted this position in the 1950s. ECLA stressed the persistent balance of payments problems of the Latin American economies as a result of their deteriorating terms of trade, and saw import-substituting industrialisation as a mechanism for restructuring the international division of labour, which was at the root of the problem of the uneven distribution of the fruits of technical progress.[2] Foreign investment in manufacturing, it was believed, could make an important contribution to both these objectives, as well as supplementing domestic savings kept low by the low level of productivity. A sharp distinction was therefore drawn between two kinds of foreign capital, the traditional type related to the development of export enclaves which had reinforced the existing international division of labour, and the new kind of manufacturing investment (Prebisch 1969).

With the extensive penetration of industry by the TNCs in the late 1950s and 1960s, ECLA and its associated economists came to adopt a more qualified view of the benefits of foreign investment. They now recognised the possible adverse consequences of foreign investment in manufacturing and the need to take measures to guard against such effects. Nevertheless the underlying view continued to be that, for the present, reliance on international firms was inevitable and that with suitable controls their effects in Latin America could be beneficial (Prebisch, 1969; and Urquidi, 1965).

By the 1970s, unqualified support for foreign investment in Latin America was largely confined to the TNCs themselves and their spokesmen. The fundamental arguments deployed remained unchanged, although they were elaborated to rebut some of the

criticisms made of TNC operations. Amongst the clearest examples
of studies adopting this position are those prepared for the Council
of the Americas, an organisation representing US TNCs active in
Latin America.[3]

A crucial assumption that is made in these studies is that TNC
operations in Latin America supplement local resources rather than
replace them. This of course leads to the maximum estimation of the
beneficial impact of foreign investment in the empirical analysis.
The problem of development is again seen in terms of inadequate
domestic savings and local technological and managerial skills. The
contribution of TNCs to income and employment in Latin
America, it is argued, consists not only of the value added and
employment directly generated by foreign subsidiaries, but also of
an increased demand for locally purchased goods and services
(backward linkages). In fact the full contribution should also take
account of forward linkages and the Keynesian multiplier effects of
foreign investment.

The implications of considering foreign investment as entirely
supplementing local resources can be seen very clearly in the
analysis that is made of the balance of payments impact of TNC
operations. These balance of payments effects consist not only of the
new inflows of capital minus remitted earnings, royalties and so on,
but also include exports by TNC subsidiaries and, crucially, the
import-substituting effects of their activities. It is this last that item
which accounts for the bulk of the estimated balance of payments
contribution of the TNCs.[4] The calculation of this import substitution effect assumes that in the absence of foreign investment, there
would have been no local production and the same goods would
have had to be imported. It also assumes that those resources which
were devoted to supplying goods and services to the TNCs, would
not have been used in the absence of TNCs. It is not surprising in
view of these assumptions that TNCs appear to make a major
contribution to the balance of payments of the Latin American
countries.[5]

A further theme in this literature is to indicate that the declared
profits of TNCs abroad are not very high and that direct foreign
investment is a cheap way of obtaining access to capital and
technology. The data usually presented in support of this argument
is that on US foreign investment collected by the Department of
Commerce. This shows that, over a long period of time, the rate of
return earned on US investment in Latin American manufacturing

industry has been of the order of 11 per cent, increasing to 13 per cent or 14 per cent if royalties and technical assistance payments are included. The conclusion that can then be drawn is that not only do TNCs provide substantial benefits to the Latin American economies, but they do so for a minimal return.[6]

The developmentalist view of the benefits of foreign investment underlay the policies adopted to attract foreign capital in a number of Latin American countries in the late 1950s and early 1960s (see Chapter 7). The influence of developmentalist ideas on these policies can be illustrated by the message which accompanied the foreign investment law of 1958, proposed by Frondizi in Argentina. This recognised that the fundamental reason for the law was the insufficiency of local savings to finance the required level of economic growth. It was further argued that the constantly declining import capacity of the country was also an obstacle to development because of the need to obtain raw materials and equipment from abroad (Sourrouille, 1976, appendix 1). As will be seen in the next Chapter, these laws contributed to the substantial growth of TNC activities in Latin American industry in the late 1950s and 1960s. This proved to be a severe test for the developmentalists' optimism about the contribution of foreign investment to Latin American development.

## 2 ECONOMIC NATIONALISM

From a developmentalist standpoint, nationalist opposition to foreign capital could only be conceived of as a political factor with no economic rationale, in view of the mutual benefits derived from foreign investment. Theoretical developments in the analysis of TNC operations in the 1960s, however, provided an economic basis for nationalist policies towards foreign capital. It was no coincidence that the seminal contribution to the development of a new, critical approach to foreign investment was made by an economist from Canada, a country in which extensive foreign penetration had aroused considerable nationalist concern (Hymer, 1976).[7]

A central element in Hymer's analysis was the link between industrial concentration and direct foreign investment. The view that direct foreign investment should be seen as an aspect of the economics of industrial structure rather than of international factor movements was subsequently developed by Kindleberger (1969),

Caves (1971) and others. It was established that TNCs tended to be
located in the most concentrated sectors of their home economies,
and that they tended to be large oligopolistic firms.

A second aspect of the break with the neoclassical view of direct
foreign investment as an international factor movement was to stress
the package nature of direct foreign investment. The package
consisted not only of capital, but also technology, brand names,
trademarks and management techniques. Recognition of the package nature of investment led to the conclusion that some components of the package might be competitive with local factors and
tend to displace rather than supplement local efforts (Hirschman,
1969). This undermined any *a priori* arguments about the benefits of
foreign investment.

As far as the Latin American host countries were concerned, these
theoretical developments permitted a more critical appraisal of the
operations of TNCs than was possible while they were viewed in
purely neoclassical terms. Recognition of the oligopolistic nature of
TNCs and the packaged nature of their investment focussed
attention on the market power of foreign firms and the distribution
of monopoly (or oligopoly) rents between TNCs and host countries.
In contrast to the developmentalist view, which evaluated foreign
investment on a 'take it or leave it' basis, this approach led to an
emphasis on bargaining between the state and the TNCs over the
terms on which foreign investment should be permitted. It also led to
concern over the effects of TNCs on accumulation by domestic
capital, and their use of market power resulting in the denationalisation (that is, foreign take-over) of locally owned firms.

Recognition of the oligopolistic nature of the corporations
responsible for most direct foreign investment raised a number of
issues which had been ignored, or whose importance had been
denied, by the prevailing developmentalist view. A crucial area was
that of the profitability of TNC subsidiaries operating in Latin
America. The advocates of foreign investment, as has already been
indicated, had long argued that the profits earned by TNCs in the
region, especially in manufacturing, were relatively low and that
direct foreign investment was a cheap way of obtaining access to
foreign capital and technology. This apparently contradicted the
view that such companies enjoyed considerable market power and
were able to appropriate a large share of the monopoly rents which
were generated by their activities.

Against this, it was argued that the declared profits of foreign subsidiaries in Latin America were a poor indicator of their true profitability. As part of an integrated global operation, the relevant concept of profitability is the contribution made by the subsidiary to the overall earnings of the TNCs rather than the profits declared in the host country. These may diverge for a number of reasons. In the first place, royalty and technical assistance payments may not correspond to the true cost of providing technology (which has already been generated) to a subsidiary, and should therefore be included in the profit figures. Secondly, where there is a considerable amount of trade between the subsidiary and the parent company or its affiliates in other countries, the existence of transfer prices (as opposed to 'arm's length' prices determined on the open market) enables the TNCs to disguise profit remission from a host country by overpricing imported inputs or underpricing exports. Finally the *rate* of profit earned by a subsidiary depends on the valuation put on the firm's investment. Since this is often provided in the form of machinery and equipment by the parent company (sometimes including second-hand machinery) there is a possibility of overvaluing the capital contribution of the TNC and thus artificially reducing the declared rate of profit of the subsidiary.

Detailed empirical investigation revealed the importance of these mechanisms for disguising the true profitability of TNCs operating in Latin America, and cast doubts on the validity of the figures declared by the companies. The first major study of transfer pricing in a third world country was carried out by Vaitsos in Colombia (Vaitsos, 1974). He found that imports were overpriced in all the sectors which he studied; by 25 per cent in chemicals, 16–60 per cent in the electronics industry, 155 per cent in pharmaceuticals and 40 per cent in rubber (Vaitsos, 1974, table 4.3). As a result he estimated that declared profits in the pharmaceutical industry accounted for only 3.4 per cent of total earnings, while 14 per cent was accounted for by royalties and the remaining 82.6 per cent by overpricing. Similar studies in other countries produced parallel results, particularly in the pharmaceutical industry. Another study of thirteen firms in the Colombian pharmaceutical, electrical and rubber industries found that the average profit rate of these firms increased sharply from 15.8 per cent to 52 per cent when account was taken of transfer pricing (Chudnovsky, 1974, p. 77).

Concern over the market power of TNCs in Latin America was not confined to the question of profitability. Another major area of interest was the use of restrictive business practices of various kinds to protect monopoly rents, in order to maximise profits world-wide. Investigation of these issues focussed especially on the technology contracts between TNCs and their local subsidiaries or licensees. Time and again it was found that such contracts imposed restrictions on the operations of the subsidiary or licensee. One of the most common types of restriction was a prohibition on exports, taking the form either of an outright ban or the limitation of exports to certain countries. Studies in a number of Latin American countries found that a majority of the contracts examined had some kind of restriction on exports (Vaitsos, 1971, tables 2 and 4; INTI, 1974; UNCTAD, 1974, table 7; Cassialato and Fung, 1976, table 4.30). A second type of restriction was to require the local producer to buy its inputs from the foreign technology supplier. Particularly in the case of local licensees, this was a necessary precaution in order to permit overpricing of such inputs, since otherwise the local firm might choose to shop around for lower cost sources of supply.

The emphasis on the market power of TNCs in Latin America also opened the way to consideration of their demand-creating activities, in sharp contrast to the developmentalists unquestioning acceptance of the existing profile of demand. It has been argued that important changes have taken place in consumer preferences because of the heavy advertising carried out by foreign firms (Vaitsos, 1976, p. 38). This, under certain economists' assumptions, can lead to the poorer sections of the population being made even worse off.[8] The TNCs are seen as transferring 'consumption technology' as well as production technology to Latin America, devoting substantial sums to the promotion of their own products and brand names. This is reflected in the rapid expansion of transnational (especially US based) advertising agencies into the continent in the wake of the manufacturing TNCs.

Examining the oligopolistic nature of foreign investment suggests that the relationship between host countries and TNCs may be conflictual (although not necessarily involving a zero-sum game), in contrast to the developmentalist emphasis on the mutual benefits to be derived from foreign investment. Such a view provided the basis for a bargaining model of the relations between the host country and the TNC, which has been applied primarily in two main areas where rents are particularly important, namely extractive industries and the commercialisation of technology. Clearly rent of particularly important in natural resource industries and is analagous to Ricardo's differential rent on land. In fact there is a long history of struggle over the distribution of this rent between foreign companies and the state in a number of Latin American countries.[9] As far as manufacturing is concerned, the main discussion of bargaining has occurred in the area of technology transfer (Vaitsos, 1971). Monopoly rents arise in this context because of a divergence between the minimum price which the supplier is prepared to accept for his technology (reflecting the relatively low cost of supplying existing technology), and the maximum price which the buyer is prepared to pay for the same technology, reflecting the benefits from its use and the cost of alternatives. Within this range, the price ultimately paid will depend on the bargaining power of the two parties and this provides an opportunity for the Latin American state to intervene on the part of the buyer.

Emphasis on the market power of TNCs suggested that increasing control of Latin American industry by foreign capital did not necessarily simply reflect the greater productive efficiency of foreign firms. In many cases foreign penetration was increased through the acquisition of existing locally owned firms, a practise which accounted for a growing proportion of the new subsidiaries being set up in the region. Concern over denationalisation was heightened by a belief that in some ways the behaviour of local firms was more conducive to national economic development than that of foreign subsidiaries. Thus, comparisons of a number of aspects of the behaviour of TNC and nationally owned firms were made, such as their balance of payments effects, capital-intensity and local technological efforts. Whereas for the developmentalist writers discussed earlier, the 'alternative situation' used in evaluating the impact of TNCs was implicitly (and often explicitly) that of importing, for some economic nationalists the standard of comparison was local production by a national firm.[10]

In the late 1960s and early 1970s, this type of analysis came to provide a rationale for more restrictive policies towards foreign capital in Latin America (see Chapter 7). Two distinct aspects of such policies emerge. One is the need for the state to intervene to control and regulate the TNCs operating within its borders. The other is the emphasis on supporting and protecting local capital in its relations with the TNCs. Put another way, one set of policies emphasises behavioural controls on TNCs while the other emphasises ownership controls. Both of these have been applied in Latin America at different times and to different degrees.[11]

Behavioural controls on TNCs in Latin America included limits on profit repatriation, and the prohibition of restrictive clauses in technology contracts. In a number of countries new government departments were created with responsibility for screening and monitoring foreign investment. Ownership controls included divestment requirements such as the 'fade-out joint ventures' of the Andean Pact, measures to exclude foreign capital (or majority owned foreign firms) from certain sectors, and preferential access to credit for locally owned firms.

The emphasis on the oligopolistic structure of direct foreign investment and the market power of TNCs provides important theoretical insights, and has been the origin of valuable empirical research. The fundamental issues raised are central to any study of TNCs in Latin America. Nevertheless the nationalist approach also has its limits. A major limitation is the view of the state as the embodiment of the national interest which underlies the bargaining model of state–TNC relations and the view that the state should intervene to control the operations of the TNCs. There is little room here for class conflict or contradictory state policies reflecting the interests of different class fractions.

A second limitation is the use of the behaviour of locally owned firms as a standard of comparison for TNC behaviour. Both the limitations reflect an implicit acceptance of capitalist relations of production. Locally owned firms are encouraged because they promote capitalist development more effectively, while state intervention to control the TNCs is conceived of within the general framework of the rights of private property (cf. Rowthorn, 1979, on Hymer's early writings).

## 3 DEPENDENCY

The question of foreign investment in manufacturing was one of the major issues which led to the dependency critique of ECLA developmentalism in the late 1960s (Booth, 1975). The TNCs played a central role in the characterisation of the 'New Dependence' by writers such as Dos Santos. One of the key features of the new phase of dependence was the shift in the structure of foreign investment away from the traditional sectors, the extractive industries and public utilities, towards manufacturing (Dos Santos, 1968a). This led to the intensified dependence of the Latin American countries, as their industrial sectors became increasingly integrated into the international operations of the TNCs. At the same time, there was a growing outflow of foreign exchange associated with the operations of the TNCs in the form of profits, interest, royalties and technical assistance payments, which absorbed an increasing share of the foreign exchange earnings of the Latin American economies and reinforced their dependence on the traditional export sectors. Thus, far from import-substituting industrialisation reducing the external vulnerability of the Latin American economies this was heightened by the nature of the industrialisation process, and in particular the role assigned to the TNCs.

Given the central role ascribed to foreign investment in manufacturing in the 'New Dependence', it is paradoxical that the dependency analysis of the impact of TNCs has on the whole been somewhat superficial. Much of the writing on foreign investment from a dependency perspective has merely consisted of standing some of the central propositions of the developmentalist approach on their heads, and has done little to advance the analysis of the dynamic of transnational corporate behaviour and its consequences in Latin America.

The critique of the developmentalist concept of foreign investment is therefore the most appropriate starting point for a discussion of dependency views on the TNCs. As had already been mentioned, three major contributions of foreign investment were stressed by its advocates: additional foreign exchange; additional savings; and better technology and management techniques. The dependency critique focussed particularly on the first two of these contributions, and also stressed that reliance on foreign capital could not be transitory as ECLA assumed (Caputo and Pizarro, 1970).

In part, the dependency critique re-emphasised Baran's view of foreign capital leading to a 'drain of surplus' from the third world, in direct opposition to the argument that foreign capital supplemented foreign exchange earnings and local savings (Baran, 1973, pp. 324–5). It was pointed out that Latin America enjoyed a persistent surplus in its trade in goods in the 1950s and 1960s and the sources of its balance of payments deficit were in services such as freight and insurance and the servicing of foreign capital. Thus, far from financing an external disequilibrium resulting from inadequate export expansion, foreign investment was required to finance the servicing of previous foreign capital inflows. Between 1946 and 1967, new inflows of US capital to Latin America totalled $5415

million, whereas profits repatriated to the United States came to
$14 775 million (Caputo and Pizarro, 1970, table 3).

One of the main reasons for this pattern is the extent to which
TNCs finance their investments from re-invested profits and
depreciation and locally raised capital, rather than from new
inflows of capital from the parent company. Between 1958 and
1968, funds from the United States accounted for only 20 per cent of
the total sources of investment by US manufacturing affiliates in
Latin America, whereas internal funds of the subsidiaries and
foreign sources of funds accounted for roughly 40 per cent each
(Newfarmer and Mueller, 1975, table 1.5). Thus foreign capital, far
from supplementing local savings, appropriates a significant proportion of such savings to finance its own expansion. Finally, far
from being a transitory phenomenon, reliance on foreign capital
tends to continually reproduce itself, as more new investment is
needed in order to meet the increasing requirements of profit,
dividend, royalty and technical assistance payments.

While most of the empirical analysis of foreign investment by
dependency writers has concentrated on capital outflows from
Latin America, it has been suggested that the main authors consider
this to be less important than the restructuring of the internal
productive structure by the TNCs (O'Brien, 1975, p. 18). One
aspect which has been stressed by some writers, and parallels the
discussion of the previous section, is the monopolisation of the
national economy associated with penetration by foreign
capital (Dos Santos, 1968b on Brazil; Caputo and Pizarro, 1970,
ch. 2.5 on Chile). There is also stress on the denationalisation
of Latin American industry, and the transfer of decision
centres abroad which this implies (Furtado, 1976, ch. 18; Sunkel,
1971).

The economic implications of the twin processes of concentration
and centralisation of capital and denationalisation, however, are
only discussed in the most general terms. The consequences of
decision making being governed by the global rationality of the
TNCs is not analysed in any detail. It is asserted that a structure of
production is created which corresponds to the interests of the TNCs
and that this implies a failure to create employment, increased
concentration of income and the growth of luxury consumption
(Sunkel, 1972). However little empirical data is presented in
support of any of these propositions, and O'Brien's comment that
'the actual mechanisms of dependency are seldom spelt out in

detail' (O'Brien, 1975, p. 23), is particularly apposite in the context of dependency analyses of the TNCs.

One area on which more detailed research was focussed was the implications of the new phase of dependence for class structure, and particularly the question of the existence of a national bourgeoisie of the classical type within Latin America. It was argued that the local industrial bourgeoisie in the region was not opposed to foreign capital, as the classical model supposed. Surveys of industrialists in Latin America confirmed this, finding that far from being opposed to foreign capital, they were generally in favour of foreign investment (Johnson, 1972 on Chile; Petras and Cook, 1973 on Argentina).

Most dependency writers concluded from this analysis that national capitalist development was not viable in Latin America[12]. The alternative posed was, of course, socialism. In some respects socialism for the dependency writers, is a standard of comparison in the evaluation of TNC-induced development. This is most clearly the case in the work of Baran, from whom a number of dependency writers draw their inspiration. His concept of the potential economic surplus, which is so central to his analysis of under-development, refers to the surplus that would be available in a more rationally ordered (that is, socialist) society (Baran, 1973, pp. 133–4). However, there is also an analysis of the tendencies of the system, and the contradictions which these generate in Latin America, which seeks to pose socialism not simply as an intellectual alternative, but also as a concrete possibility emerging from the development of the productive forces and class struggle (Bambirra, 1974).

Some of the more recent dependency writings on TNCs in Latin America have moved away from the totally negative evaluation of the earlier critics. The simple 'drain of surplus' approach has been replaced by a new emphasis on the classical Marxist view of the contradictory nature of capitalist development and the inter-nationalisation of capital in particular. Drawing particularly on recent Brazilian experience, it has been argued that dependence and development are not contradictions in terms. Indeed, the growth of direct foreign investment in manufacturing has qualitatively changed the nature of imperialism so that '*to some extent*, the interests of the foreign corporations become compatible with the internal prosperity of the dependent countries. In this sense, they help promote development' (Cardoso, 1973, p. 149). This has been described as 'associated-dependent development' (Cardoso), or simply 'dependent development' (Evans, 1979). This more nuanced view of the impact of TNCs in Latin America has been accompanied by a greater interest in the complex relationships between TNCs, local capital and the state. Further research in this direction will permit a fuller development of the dependency analysis.

## 4 THE INTERNATIONALISATION OF CAPITAL AND THE TNCs

In the course of reviewing the three views of TNCs discussed in this chapter, a number of weaknesses of each approach have been brought out. By way of conclusion, two main criticisms will be levelled at all three approaches, and it will be argued that an approach based on a broader concept of the internationalisation of capital provides a more adequate framework within which to analyse the impact of TNCs in Latin America.

The first defect of the above approaches is the illegitimate isolation of TNC activities. Although the causes of the international expansion of TNCs in Latin America were not discussed, the tendency to see it in isolation begins here. TNC expansion tends to be analysed either directly in terms of the declared motives of individual firms in entering foreign markets, such as entry into large or fast growing markets, avoidance of tariff barriers, favourable investment climate, cheap labour and so on, or through cross-section analyses of data, which seek to identify the specific characteristics of firms or industries which tend to be transnational (research and development intensity, differentiated products, high levels of concentration, large size of firms). While such approaches can provide some useful insights, the very focus on TNCs *per se* disqualifies them from analysing the tendencies of the capitalist system over time, and the context within which the expansion of TNCs developed.

The illegitimate isolation of TNC activities extends to the analysis of their impact within Latin America. In the case of the developmentalist approach, the assumption that foreign capital is a supplement to domestic capital means that it is impossible to raise questions about the effect of foreign investment on accumulation by local capital. The TNCs are simply filling a pre-existing gap between demand and supply, and do not affect the levels of either. In contrast, the economic nationalists tend to counterpose foreign capital and local capital, but again in doing so are guilty of isolating foreign capital. Dependency theory operates at two levels. On the one hand, in considering the outflow of capital associated with TNCs it is also isolating foreign capital, while on the other hand when the broader effects of TNCs are considered the level of generality is so high that the mechanisms of dependency remain unspecified.

Although the internationalisation of capital approach developed particularly by Palloix (1975, 1978) does not offer a detailed theory of TNC expansion and its effects, it does provide a number of valuable insights into many of the questions posed by an analysis of TNCs. The internationalisation of capital is seen as a tendency of the capitalist system towards an ever more integrated world economy. This tendency has existed since the earliest days of capitalism, with the growth of international trade and subsequently in the nineteenth century the export of capital. In the twentieth century the integration of international production within TNCs has been a major form taken by the internationalisation of capital. It is important to stress, however, that the growth of foreign operations by TNCs is not itself the internationalisation of capital but merely one, albeit a very important, form in which internationalisation is reflected.

Concentration and centralisation of capital, and developments in the fields of transport and communications, have tended to make the world smaller in economic terms. Thus capital has been able to realise its inherently international nature to an increasing degree. Internal organisational developments of large firms have meant that the institutional form adopted by the internationalisation of capital has often been the TNC (cf. Hymer, 1979, ch. 2). However this should not lead to an exclusive focus on the TNCs in isolation from those broader tendencies of which they constitute a part.

The driving force of the internationalisation of capital, which is in turn an aspect of capital accumulation, is the competition of capitals (cf. Cypher, 1979). It is important to stress that despite concentration and centralisation of capital, the TNCs remain subject to the compulsion of competition. The forms of competition may be modified, and at times or in certain places competition may be restrained, as for example through the formation of cartels, but the essentially competitive nature of the accumulation process remains.

It is necessary to stress this point to avoid the tendency which is sometimes found of suggesting that the monopolistic nature of TNCs renders them free of market forces.[13]

The creation of a unified, capitalist world economy which the internationalisation of capital brings about is reflected in the standardisation of commodities and production processes at the international level. National idiosyncracies in the products consumed in different countries tend to be eliminated. In the case of consumer goods there is a tendency for similar products to be consumed world wide, while in intermediate and capital goods international standards are often established. Similarly, production processes also tend to conform to an international pattern, irrespective of specific national conditions. Adjustment to local circumstances, whether in terms of particular consumption or production conditions are relatively minor, while the main direction of change is established at an international level (Vernon, 1977, pp. 3–5).

Competition however implies not only standardisation of products and processes internationally, but also a simultaneous process of differentiation, as individual capitals seek to gain a competitive advantage through a temporary technological monopoly by the introduction of a new product or production technique. The internationalisation of capital implies the international extension of the process of simultaneous standardisation and differentiation. Although clearly an aspect of competition between TNCs, it takes place even in sectors such as steel where overseas production by TNCs is rare (Palloix, 1978, pp. 134–52). In other words, the internationalisation of capital involves not only the overseas expansion of TNCs but also the incorporation of local capital in the international processes of standardisation and differentiation.

This has important implications for the analysis of the position of local capital in Latin America. It is no longer possible to counterpose TNCs and local firms in the way that economic nationalists do. If TNCs are merely one institutional form adopted by the internationalisation of capital, there is no reason necessarily to contrast them with local firms, some of which may reflect the same tendency. Often, local firms competing with TNCs are forced to behave in similar ways in order to survive, adjusting both the products which they manufacture and the techniques which they use to international norms. In some cases, even where there is little or no direct competition from TNCs, large local firms may adopt similar products, techniques and competitive strategies to those employed by TNCs elsewhere.[14]

Consequently, the impact of the internationalisation of capital on the Latin American economies is far more extensive than the figures on foreign ownership in the region would imply, substantial though these certainly are. This point also has the important methodological implication that comparisons between foreign owned and locally owned firms should be treated with extreme caution, and cannot necessarily throw much light on the effects of TNC investment in Latin America.

The internationalisation of capital leads, as has already been indicated, to the creation of a single capitalist world economy. So far, the emphasis has been on the unity of this economy, but its capitalist nature should not be forgotten. Thus pre-capitalist modes of production within its ambit tend either to be transformed through the extension of capitalist relations of production, or subordinated to the dynamic of capital accumulation. An obvious example of this is the expansion of transnational agribusiness, for example, the food processing industry, and the resulting social transformations in rural areas of Latin America.

A second major defect of the three previous approaches is their inadequate conceptualisation of the state. The emphasis of developmentalism is on the harmony of interests between host countries and TNCs, reflecting the underlying, mutually beneficial nature of foreign investment. Tensions, when they do arise, are the result of misplaced criticism of TNCs. It is emphasised that TNCs enter underdeveloped countries 'by invitation' from host governments, and this fact is used to support the view of a harmonious relationship. The nationalist approach, as mentioned above, stresses the conflict between the global profit-maximising behaviour of TNCs and the national interest of the host country. The state, as representative of the national interest, is then seen as playing a regulatory role over TNCs and sometimes involving itself in direct bargaining with TNCs. The relationship between state and TNC is therefore essentially conflictual. Both approaches however share a common view of the state in which the conflict of interest between groups or classes is ignored, the former by its emphasis on harmonious relations at all levels, the latter because of its stress on national rather than class conflicts.

Dependency theory does, contrary to some critics, concern itself with the internal class structure of the Latin American economies.

As far as the relationship of the state and TNCs is concerned, however, it tends to be assumed that there is a coincidence of interests between local dominant classes which control the state and international dominant classes. Since, in the post-war period, the TNCs have been a major element of the international dominant classes, this theory again points to a harmony of interest between the state (but not this time the 'nation') and the TNCs.

The internationalisation of capital poses the contradictory nature of the state in two important respects. In the first place, there is the contradiction between the increasingly international nature of capital and the continuing national basis of the state, modified in political terms by the incorporation of international capital amongst the local dominant classes. Secondly, there are the internal class conflicts within the nation which the state is required to mediate. Caught between the pressures of the internationalisation of capital and its own restricted national base within which it has some power to affect the rate and direction of accumulation, the actions of the state in relation to the TNCs are likely themselves to be contradictory. Thus, simple formulations in terms of either harmony or conflict are unlikely to prove adequate in the analysis of concrete situations.

· An approach based on the internationalisation of capital is not without problems, particularly as it involves a high level of abstraction which makes it difficult to concretise. A fruitful way of attempting concrete analysis of the internationalisation of capital is through the study of individual branches of industry (Palloix, 1975). This is a particularly appropriate level of analysis because international competition takes place primarily at the level of individual branches, and the internationalisation of products and production processes (that is the process of simultaneous standardisation and differentiation) also occurs at this level. The specific ways in which the dynamic of capital accumulation require the internationalisation of capital can be spelt out in some detail through historical analyses of individual branches. It also makes possible a detailed analysis of the articulation between the international industry and its operation in Latin America. Thus, the way in which production techniques and consumption patterns are adjusted to international norms can be analysed. The ways in which patterns of industrial structure and competitive strategies are transferred can also be examined. In doing so, much of the analysis of oligopolistic behaviour discussed above will prove extremely useful.

Part II of the book contains case studies of two branches of particular interest. The motor industry, because of its strategic importance in Latin American industrialisation, and the pharmaceutical industry, because of its high degree of internationalisation of production, are in different ways leading sectors in the internationalisation of capital. The third chapter in this Part is of a somewhat different nature, focussing as it does on the export activities of TNCs in Latin America, although here again (in Section 3), attention is focussed on two branches, garments and electronics. Unfortunately, within the confines of a relatively short book, it is impossible to present further detailed studies of individual branches. However, in the course of the work, reference will frequently be made to the experience of other branches of production in which TNCs play an important role (for a collection of industry case studies see Newfarmer, forthcoming).

At the same time, a focus on particular branches does not permit a comprehensive analysis of certain developments which are essentially nationally rather than sectorally based. Two particularly important areas here are the relation of the internationalisation of capital to both class structure and the state. While these can be studied partly at the level of individual industries, they can only be understood in their totality by transcending the industry approach. Part III therefore consists of two chapters on TNCs and class structure and the state respectively. Part 4 brings together the various strands which emerge from both the study of individual branches and the analysis of TNCs, class structure and the state in a more comprehensive discussion of the implications of the TNCs in Latin American industry.

## NOTES

1. See Smith and Toye (1979). They distinguish 'the story of mutually beneficial trade', 'the story of structurally biased gains from trade', 'the story of trade-induced global polarity'. Our own classification could be rewritten by simply substituting investment for trade in the above.
2. For a comprehensive analysis of ECLA's theories, see Rodriguez (1980). The classic presentation is Prebisch (1950).
3. For example May (1970); May and Fernandez Arena (1970); May (1975).
4. For US manufacturing affiliates in Latin America, import substitution accounted for over 90 per cent of the balance of payments impact in both 1966 and 1972 according to May (1975, table 12).

5. This conclusion is not supported by a number of micro studies of foreign investment. See for instance Streeten and Lall (1977, ch. 9).

6. This is certainly not as obvious as the writers claim. Vernon, who is relatively favourably disposed towards the TNCs has stated that 'the conscientious analyst . . . cannot establish a universal preference between the multinational enterprises and the unbundling alternative' on the basis of this kind of analysis (Vernon, 1977, p. 161).

7. Hymer's thesis was completed in 1960 and was eventually published posthumously in 1976.

8. See Helleiner (1975) for the theoretical elaboration of this argument.

9. The best documented case is that of Chilean copper; see for instance Moran (1974).

10. Streeten and Lall (1977) in their studies attempt to resolve this problem on an 'ad hoc' basis by guessing the most likely alternative for each of the firms which they studied.

11. For a comparison of Brazil emphasising behavioural control and Mexico emphasising ownership controls, and the tendency of policies to converge, see Evans and Gereffi (1979).

12. Sunkel (1969) is an exception arguing that socialism is an improbable historic event in the near future in Latin America and that the real option is a truly national development policy.

13. This is facilitated by the tendency of orthodox economists to see market structure as a continuum from perfect competition to pure monopoly. Thus, the fewer the number of firms in an industry, the closer it is to pure monopoly and therefore the less competition there will be. In practice however, there may be very intense competition between a small number of firms, although the forms of competition may differ from those found in industries with a large number of firms.

14. An example of this is the Mexican-owned bakery product firm Bimbo which produces along typical TNC lines, although there is no significant TNC presence in this sector of the Mexican food processing industry.

# 2 Foreign Penetration of Latin American Industry: An Overview

## 1 THE PRE-WAR ORIGINS

Although the spectacular expansion of TNCs in Latin America occurred after the Second World War, the origins of this penetration can be traced back to the inter-war years and in some cases even earlier. The extent to which industry in Latin America was born under the hegemony of international capital, or was in its origins predominantly national, is a matter of academic and political debate in the region. Some authors have argued that in those Latin American countries which began their industrialisation at a relatively early date, Argentina, Brazil, Chile, Colombia, Mexico and Uruguay, a national bourgeoisie was able to develop industry in the period before the Second World War because, among other reasons, foreign capital was mainly interested in the primary sector (Bambirra, 1974, p. 65). On the other hand, it has been claimed that extensive sectors of industry in these countries were controlled by foreign capital even in the inter-war period and that there is no justification for the view that local industrialists constitute a class opposed to foreign capital and imperialism (for example, Polit, 1968, on Argentina).

It is certainly true that only a small part of foreign investment in Latin America before the Second World War went into the manufacturing sector. In 1914 only 7.4 per cent of foreign private investment in the region was in manufacturing (ECLA, 1965, table 18). In part, of course, this reflected the limited development of industry in the region at the time. But even with the considerable import-substituting industrialisation of the inter-war years in a number of countries, manufacturing accounted for only 7.8 per cent of US direct foreign investment in Latin America in 1940, well behind railroads and public utilities, petroleum, mining and agriculture (*ibid*, table 31). In Mexico in the same year 7.1 per cent of all foreign capital in the country was in manufacturing (Sepulveda and Chumacero, 1973, appendix table 1).

On the other hand, the world's leading TNCs (both US and European) had already set up as many as 200 subsidiaries in Latin America before 1939. US firms such as Ford, General Motors, Goodyear, Firestone, National Cash Register, General Electric, ITT, Singer, Abbott and Parke Davis, and European firms such as Philips, Siemens, Lever, Roche, Nestlé, Pirelli and Olivetti established themselves on the continent in this period. Even more suggestive of the significance of this foreign penetration is the fragmentary data available on the extent of foreign control over industry in some Latin American countries. In Argentina, Dorfman estimated that half of the capital invested in industry was foreign in 1935 (Dorfman, 1970). Prior to and during the Second World War, foreign capital accounted for 18 per cent of total manufacturing capital in Brazil and 25 per cent in Chile (Weaver, 1980, p. 130). Another estimate for Brazil put the figure as high as 40 per cent in 1940 (Baklanoff, 1966, p. 112). In Argentina, foreign capital dominated, among other sectors, meat packing, auto assembly, rubber products and artificial silk, and was significant in tobacco, petroleum, electric conductors, radio telephonic equipment, pharmaceuticals and lifts. In Mexico, auto assembly, tyres, cement, paper and pharmaceuticals were industries with important foreign shares.

Before accepting the view that industry in Latin America has always been dominated by foreign capital and that the expansion of TNCs in the region in the period after the Second World War is not a qualitatively new phenomenon, it is necessary to introduce a number of qualifications. First, the vast majority of industrial enterprises in Latin America in the inter-war period were artesan-type operations, and the coverage of the industrial censuses on these firms may well have been deficient. Second, even if the coverage had been complete, the share of foreign controlled firms in capital would have tended to be higher than their share in production and employment because of the tendency for such firms to be more capital-intensive than industry as a whole, particularly when the artesan sector is taken into account. Third, it is worth recalling that industry in Latin America was primarily producing non-durable consumer goods and that a few sectors such as food, drink, textiles, clothing, wood and leather products accounted for the bulk of industrial output. These sectors were not generally dominated by the TNCs (with the exception of industries linked to the export sector such as meat-packing in Argentina). Foreign investment in manufacturing in the 1920s and 1930s were concentrated in certain assembly industries such as vehicles, electrical products and lifts and in other chemically based industries using imported raw materials such as tyres and pharmaceuticals.

The role of foreign capital in the industrialisation process of the 1920s and 1930s in Latin America was qualitatively different from that which it played in the 1950s and 1960s. In the earlier period, the sectors which played the leading role in industrialisation were predominantly under the control of local firms (set up by immigrants, it is true, in some countries). TNCs were involved in new, rapidly growing industrial sectors, but their contribution to the industrialisation process was less central since often they were merely introducing the final stage of the production process into Latin America in order to hop tariffs or save on transport costs, and consequently the extent to which their activities were integrated into the industrial structure of the host country was extremely limited. The classic example of this was, of course, the US motor manufacturers who set up assembly plants all over Latin America.

Where foreign firms were important in the production of non-durable consumer goods they tended to compete as one more industrial firm in the local market, rather than setting the pace in terms of type of product, competitive strategy and the direction of industrial development. The case of the tobacco industry is a good illustration of this point. Although the British American Tobacco Company entered the industry in a number of Latin American countries in the early twentieth century, it followed a 'national brand' policy, manufacturing dark tobacco cigarettes of the kind produced by local firms. A similar pattern seems to have existed in the food industry.[1] Thus, the pre-war expansion of TNCs in the consumer goods industries did not lead to the same internationalisation of consumption patterns as was to develop after the Second World War.

In the post-war period, the extension of the internationalisation of capital and the changing nature of industrialisation in Latin America, particularly from the mid 1950s, qualitatively altered the role of foreign capital in the region. Increasingly, TNCs came to occupy centre stage, stamping their mark on the entire pattern of industrial development with implications that extended far beyond the manufacturing sector.


## 2 POST-WAR EXPANSION

The expansion of TNC manufacturing activity in Latin America can only be understood in the context of the intense inter-imperialist rivalry of the post-war period. In the early post-war years, US capital enjoyed a pre-eminent position internationally as much of Europe lay in ruins. European recovery in the 1950s and the establishment of the EEC led to an upsurge of US investment in Western Europe as American capital attempted to penetrate this market, which was growing much faster than the US market. The response of European capital to this American penetration was an offensive strategy of overseas expansion in order to offset the inroads being made by US firms in its domestic markets (Rowthorn, 1975). The stage was thus set for an intensified struggle for world markets between US and European TNCs.

In the early post-war years, US capital enjoyed a dominant position in Latin America. In 1955, when the process of import substitution was beginning to get under way, the United States accounted for over half of Latin America's imports of manufactured goods, and almost 60 per cent in the two key categories of chemicals, and machinery and transport equipment. In terms of direct foreign investment in manufacturing in the region, the position of US capital was almost certainly even more dominant in the early 1950s.


### International competition in Latin America

From the mid-1950s, Latin America became an important area of international competition, first between US and European capital, and later in the 1970s with Japanese capital as well. As far as European capital was concerned, particularly German and Italian capital which did not have an established position in ex-colonial markets, Latin America offered an attractive area for accumulation. In terms of an offensive strategy of international expansion to counter the 'American challenge', Latin America possessed a sufficiently large high-income sector of the population to create an attractive market (a condition that tended not to be met in other third world countries to the same extent). It was also much easier to enter the Latin American markets, where a new phase of import substitution was just getting under way and new industries were in the process of being established, than to dispute the control of US TNCs in North America with its well established oligopolistic structures and high barriers to entry of new firms.

The policies of import substitution followed in Latin America from the 1950s were a further crucial factor in the expansion of manufacturing TNCs in the region. In the first place, quotas and tariffs meant that overseas expansion could not take place through exports but would have to involve setting up local manufacturing activities. Second, trade restrictions, disrupting normal sources of supply and in some cases creating acute shortages, facilitated the entry of new firms. There was thus a two-way relationship between international competition and import substitution policies. European capital, anxious to expand overseas, was more willing to undertake large scale import substitution than US capital had been in the inter-war period, ensuring the effectiveness of government policies. At the same time these policies, by disrupting the existing market supply conditions, made it possible for European capital to effectively challenge the US TNCs in Latin America.

A classic illustration of this process was the entry of Volkswagen into the Brazilian motor industry. Before the Second World War, US capital dominated the industry and the major firms operated local assembly plants. Germany was the second most important source of supply but accounted for only some 10 per cent of all cars sold in Brazil. In 1956, when the government set up the Grupo Ejecutivo de la Industria Automovilistica to develop a local vehicle industry, Volkswagen was one of the first companies to submit plans to produce cars locally. Ford and General Motors were at first reluctant to build cars in Brazil and concentrated on lorries, enabling Volkswagen to gain a dominant position in the market, which it has held ever since. Similar examples can be given from other industries in this period. The first firm to begin production of tractors in Argentina in the 1950s was Fiat, while in the Brazilian electrical industry four of the five firms which made major investments in the late 1950s were European, (Newfarmer, 1980, p. 139).

These developments had two important consequences for the structure of direct foreign investment in Latin America in the post-war period. First, manufacturing, from being a relatively unimportant sector from the point of view of total investment in the region, became the most dynamic area for TNC expansion. The share of manufacturing in the total value of US investment in the region increased from 13.3 per cent in 1946 to 17.1 per cent in 1957, and then rose sharply to 32.2 per cent in 1967 and 50.5 per cent by 1976 (US Department of Commerce, *Survey of Current Business*, various issues). Foreign investment from other developed countries has been even more heavily oriented towards the manufacturing sector. In 1967, 54 per cent of the total investment in Latin America of OECD countries other than the United States was in manufacturing (ECLA, 1978, appendix, table 12).

The second trend has been for US capital to lose ground *vis-à-vis* European and Japanese capital in the manufacturing sector. By 1967 the United States accounted for 54 per cent of the total value of investment by OECD countries in Latin American manufacturing (ECLA, 1978, appendix, table 2). Data for individual countries confirm that European capital is at least matching US capital in terms of its penetration of industry. In Brazil, Western Europe accounts for almost 50 per cent of industrial investment, compared to less than 40 per cent owned by the United States and Canada in 1973 (von Doellinger and Cavalcanti, 1975, table 3.15). In Argentina in 1969, just over half of industrial production by foreign companies was by US owned firms and the remainder was mainly by European firms (Sourrouille, 1976, table 2). Of the three major Latin American countries, the United States only maintains a clear predominance over European capital in Mexico, and even here the share of US capital has been declining.[2]

The corollary of inter-imperialist rivalry to control international markets was the denationalisation of Latin American industry which accompanied the process of import substitution, particularly in the largest Latin American countries, where the local bourgeoisie had developed most in the inter-war and immediate post-war period and where the new wave of TNC expansion was now concentrated. In Argentina, the share of industrial output controlled by foreign capital rose from 18 per cent in the late 1950s to around 30 per cent by the early 1970s (Sourrouille, 1976, table 2.1). In Mexico there was a similar increase, from 19 per cent in 1962 to 28 per cent by 1970 (Chumacero and Sepulveda, 1973), while in Brazil during a somewhat later period, the share of foreign capital in the total capital in industry rose from 19 per cent to 29 per cent between 1965 and 1975, (Luiz Possas, 1979, table 28). Comparison of the value added of US manufacturing subsidiaries in Latin

America with the total industrial value added produced in the region reveals the same pattern. The share of US firms in industrial production increased rapidly between 1957 and 1966, and continued to increase at a more gradual rate to the mid–1970s despite the adoption of more restrictive policies by a number of countries in this period.[3] Increased penetration of industry has been particularly marked in Brazil and Venezuela. Moreover, in view of the increased importance of non-US TNCs in Latin America in this period, the share of all foreign firms in the region's output is likely to have increased at an even faster rate.

## Modes of penetration

The increased penetration of foreign capital in industry came about in three different ways . The first, which generated the strongest political reaction among certain groups and received most publicity, was the acquisition of local firms by TNCs. In Brazil, a Parliamentary Commission of Inquiry into denationalisation was set up, and in a number of countries lists were published of important firms bought out by foreign capital. As Table 2.1 indicates, this concern was not unfounded. Over time, an increasing proportion of the new subsidiaries being set up in Latin America were through acquisitions, and the proportion was particularly high

TABLE 2.1    *% of new manufacturing subsidiaries of US TNCs in Latin America acquired through takeover*

|  | *Pre-1946* | *1946–57* | *1958–67* |
|---|---|---|---|
| Latin America |  |  |  |
| Total | 206 | 340 | 750 |
| % acquisition | 23 | 29 | 44 |
| Argentina |  |  |  |
| Total | 45 | 34 | 79 |
| % acquisition | 24 | 38 | 53 |
| Brazil |  |  |  |
| Total | 34 | 70 | 94 |
| % acquisition | 26 | 27 | 46 |
| Mexico |  |  |  |
| Total | 46 | 90 | 216 |
| % acquision | 20 | 34 | 54 |

SOURCE    Vaupel and Curhan (1969, table 4.1.3).

in the most industrialised countries of the region. In the pharmaceutical and tobacco industries for instance, the acquisition of well established local firms was an important mechanism through which these industries came to be almost totally foreign owned in a number of countries.

A second way in which local capital was displaced in certain sectors was through direct competition in their markets from TNC subsidiaries. In many cases, the advantages of the TNCs in terms of technology, access to finance, brand names or management techniques were too much for their local competitors. These were then either forced out of business, taken over or continued to operate with reduced market shares. This pattern has characterised the motor industry in most Latin American countries where initially several locally owned firms began production under license from foreign companies.

The third factor which contributed to the denationalisation of industry as a whole was the changing structure of manufacturing production. The fact that TNCs tended to be concentrated in the fastest growing sectors of industry meant that even if their share of output in each sector remained constant, their overall share would increase as a result of the changing composition of output. A rough estimate of the relative importance of each of these three factors in explaining the denationalisation of Mexican industry in the 1960s indicated that over half of the increased market share of foreign firms could be explained by takeovers, while the competitiveness of foreign firms within sectors and the faster growth of foreign-dominated sectors were each responsible for slightly less than a quarter (Jenkins, 1979, p. 174).

The growing penetration of foreign capital in this period was made possible by the combination of policies on trade and foreign investment introduced by most Latin American governments in the 1950s and 1960s. The deteriorating balance-of-payments situation of Latin America after the Korean War boom made both protection to encourage further import substitution and the attraction of foreign capital priority concerns for the ruling regimes. For the more industrialised countries, imports of traditional non-durable consumer goods such as food, furniture, clothing and footwear had already been reduced to negligible levels during the Depression and the Second World War. Further import substitution would involve local production of consumer durables and intermediate inputs, industries in which established brand names and/or high technology were important and in which TNCs were prominent. As a result, the tariffs and quotas usually justified in terms of providing 'infant industry' protection came to protect firms which were anything but infantile. That this occurred was a result of the paradox that while highly restrictive trade regimes were introduced, the policies adopted towards foreign capital were extremely liberal.[4] In most cases, foreign capital was guaranteed equal treatment with local capital and freedom to repatriate profits without any restrictions. In some cases, the TNCs were assured of preferential treatment compared to their local competitors. The most notorious case of this was Sumoc Instruction 113 in Brazil (the 1955 legislation under which foreign firms set up in Brazil), which permitted foreign firms to import machinery for capitalisation in a subsidiary without having to go through the foreign exchange markets, whereas a Brazilian firm would be forced to buy dollars at an unfavourable exchange rate in order to import the same machinery (Newfarmer, 1980, p. 139, quoting Bergsman). Clearly the TNCs did not thrust themselves upon unwilling host governments in Latin America, but once established in key positions within the host countries the trend towards denationalisation would require conscious decisions to reverse.

## 3 THE STRUCTURE AND NATURE OF TNC PENETRATION

It is clear that by the 1970s, in the major Latin American countries a situation had developed in which the TNCs were key actors in the determination of the pattern of development of the local economies. The internationalisation of capital in the late 1950s and 1960s created a qualitatively different form of integration of Latin American industry into the world economy, whose implications extended far beyond manufacturing production. A third or more of the entire manufacturing sector of most Latin American countries was controlled by the TNCs by around 1970 (see Table 2.2).

Such aggregate figures, however, are a poor indicator of the nature of the qualitative changes that had taken place in industry. The power of capital (both economic and political) is related to the mass of means of production and workers which it controls. The TNCs in Latin America represent large concentrations of capital whereas local capital is often fragmented into many small units. In

TABLE 2.2    *Share of manufacturing industry controlled by foreign firms c. 1970*

| Country | Year | Foreign share (%) | Basis of calculation |
|---|---|---|---|
| Argentina | 1972 | 31.0 | Manufacturing production |
| Brazil | 1969 | 41.6 | Manufacturing assets |
| Central America | 1968 | 30 | Manufacturing production |
| Chile | 1968 | 29.9 | Capital and reserves of manufacturing limited liability companies |
| Colombia | 1974 | 43.4 | Manufacturing production |
| Ecuador | 1971–3 | 66.1 | Assets of public corporations |
| Mexico | 1970 | 34.9 | Manufacturing production |
| Peru | 1969 | 44.0 | Manufacturing production |
| Venezuela | 1975 | 35.9 | Manufacturing value added |

SOURCES    Argentina   Sourrouille (1976, table II.1), Brazil   Newfarmer and Mueller (1975, table 5.7); Central America   Wilmore (1976, p. 501); Chile   Gassic (1971, table 38); Colombia   ECLA/UNCTC (1979, table 19); Ecuador   Mytelka (1979, table 1.6); Mexico   Fajnzylber and Tarrago (1975, p. 256); Peru   Anaya Franco (1974, table 13); Venezuela   Bitar and Troncoso (1981, table 7).

Mexico for instance, foreign subsidiaries were on average almost nine times as large as locally owned firms in terms of sales (Fajnzylber and Tarrago, 1975, ch. 3, table 2), while in Brazil they were more than three times larger,[5] and in Peru seven times larger (calculated from Anaya Franco, 1974, table 13). This size differentiation is also apparent when the ownership of the largest firms within each country is considered (see Table 2.3). In Argentina, Brazil, Mexico and Peru, the largest foreign owned companies accounted for a greater share of output or assets than private national firms included amongst the largest firms, and in Argentina and Peru they accounted for a greater share of output than all local firms including state enterprises. Table 2.3 also shows that foreign firms generally account for a greater share of the output of the largest firms than they do of industrial output as a whole.[6]

The position of TNCs as leading firms in the industrial sector is confirmed by their presence among the four largest firms in each industry (defined at the four-digit level of industrial classification). In Mexico, almost 80 per cent and in Brazil, over 70 per cent of total industrial production comes from sectors in which at least one of the four largest firms is a foreign subsidiary (Newfarmer and Mueller, 1975, Tables 3.10 and 5.10). Even in Chile, with a lower level of

TABLE 2.3   *Share of foreign, national and state firms among largest industrial firms**

| Country | Date | No. of firms | Foreign | Private national | State |
|---------|------|--------------|---------|------------------|-------|
| Argentina | 1971 | 100 | 79 | 16 | 4 |
| Brazil | 1972 | 287 | 50 | 35 | 15 |
| Chile | 1968 | 100 | 40 | 60 | |
| Colombia | 1968 | 100 | 32 | 68 | |
| Mexico | 1965 | 100 | 47 | 40 | 13 |
| Peru† | 1973 | 200 | 53 | 28 | 15 |

* Table refers to the share of production accounted for by each group of firms in all countries except Brazil, where it refers to assets, and Chile where it refers to the number of firms.
† Total does not add up to 100% because of the existence of 8 cooperatives amongst the largest 200 firms.
SOURCES   Argentina   CICSO (n.d., p. 83); Brazil   Newfarmer and Mueller (1975, table 5.5); Chile   Bitar (1977, p. 90); Colombia   Misas (1973, p. 93); Mexico   Cinta (1972, table 10); Peru   INP (1976, table 25).

foreign penetration and a less advanced industrial structure, more than half of output is accounted for by industries in which at least one of the leaders is foreign (own calculations from CORFO, 1971).

It is these firms, in a position of leadership both in the economy as a whole and within individual sectors, which are able to structure the pattern of industrial development, consumption and distribution. Their ability to do so is, of course, by no means absolute and may require the establishment of links with the state and local capital which can act as constraints on their corporate strategies. However, to ignore the influences which these positions of economic power imply would be to gravely misinterpret the tendencies of the system.

## Level of penetration

A further aspect of the penetration of Latin American industry by the TNCs is its uneven distribution between sectors. This reflects the tendency for TNCs to be largely concentrated in a number of key sectors within the advanced countries, while they are largely absent in others. Over 60 per cent of the world-wide stock of overseas manufacturing investment of both the United States and West Germany in the mid-1970s was accounted for by chemicals, machinery and transport equipment (mainly the motor industry) (Nakase, 1981, chart 1). These also tend to be the sectors with the highest level of TNC penetration in Latin America.

TABLE 2.4  *Foreign shares by industry in seven countries c. 1970 (%)*

| Country | Argentina | Brazil | Chile | Colombia | Mexico | Peru | Venezuela |
|---|---|---|---|---|---|---|---|
| Year | 1963 | 1970 | 1968 | 1974 | 1970 | 1969 | 1971 |
| Food | 15.3 | 42.1 | 23.2 | 22.0 | 21.5 | 33.1 | 10.0 |
| Drink | 24.1 | 30.9 | 20.3 | 3.1 | 30.0 | 18.0 | 5.5 |
| Tobacco | 93.4 | 98.7 | 100.0 | 1.1 | 96.8 | 87.6 | 71.5 |
| Textiles | 14.2 | 34.2 | 22.9 | 61.9 | 15.3 | 39.7 | 12.9 |
| Clothing and footwear | 10.4 | 29.5 | 24.2 | 11.4 | 6.2 | 21.5 | 2.1 |
| Wood | 0.5 | 23.2 | 5.2 | 33.5 | 7.9 | 29.0 | 2.5 |
| Furniture | 1.2 | 16.0 | 6.4 | 6.0 | 3.8 | 19.0 | 11.5 |
| Paper | 25.7 | 22.3 | 7.9 | 79.3 | 32.9 | 64.8 | 20.1 |
| Printing and publishing | 1.5 | 3.5 | 19.6 | 6.0 | 7.9 | 2.6 | 5.3 |
| Leather | 1.5 | 37.9 | 4.0 | 18.4 | 3.7 | 9.4 | 0.7 |
| Rubber | 72.1 | 81.1 | 78.5 | 82.0 | 63.9 | 87.5 | 24.9 |
| Chemicals | 34.9 | 49.0 | 61.9 | 66.9 | 50.7 | 66.7 | 16.5 |
| Petroleum products | 31.2 | NA | 11.4 | 22.1 | 48.7 | 17.7 | 0 |
| Non-metallic minerals | 9.2 | 44.0 | 48.0 | 58.4 | 20.8 | 46.7 | 12.4 |
| Basic metals | 21.1 | | 16.9 | 54.7 | 46.6 | 82.7 | 7.2 |
| Metal products | 8.9 | 33.0 | 30.5 | 42.7 | 20.6 | 35.2 | 20.9 |
| Non-electrical machinery | 35.6 | 70.0 | 6.7 | 29.6 | 52.1 | 24.8 | 12.8 |
| Electrical machinery | 27.6 | 83.7 | 48.6 | 67.2 | 50.1 | 60.7 | 23.2 |
| Transport equipment | 44.4 | 88.2 | 64.5 | 79.7 | 64.0 | 72.9 | 31.1 |
| Other industries | 2.4 | 40.9 | 18.0 | 26.6 | 33.1 | 15.0 | 5.2 |
| All Manufacturing | 23.8 | 50.1 | 29.9 | 43.4 | 34.9 | 44.0 | 13.8 |

SOURCES Argentina  Peralta Ramos (1972, table 13, value of production); Brazil  Luiz Possas (1979, table 24, value of production of largest 4 plants); Chile  Gassic (1971, table 38, capital plus reserves); Colombia  ECLA/CTC (1979, table 19, value of production); Mexico  Fajnzylber and Tarrago (1975, p. 313, value of production); Peru  Anaya Franco (1974, table 13, value of production); Venezuela  CORDIPLAN (1971, tables 18 and 19, subscribed capital).

Table 2.4 indicates the extent of foreign ownership by sector for the seven Latin American countries with the most important manufacturing sectors, which between them account for over 90 per cent of the region's industrial output. The share of production controlled by foreign firms ranges from 100 per cent in the case of the Chilean tobacco industry to negligible levels in industries such as wood and furniture. The same sectors tend to appear in each country with the highest levels of foreign ownership. These include rubber, transport equipment, tobacco (which has the highest level of foreign ownership in all the Latin American countries, except Colombia where it is controlled by a locally owned monopoly), chemicals and electrical machinery. At the other end of the scale wood products, furniture, printing and publishing and leather products usually have a very low level of foreign ownership. In fact, the similarity in the ranking of sectors across the seven countries was highly significant in statistical terms,[7] indicating the existence of a common pattern of foreign penetration despite differences in the level of foreign ownership, the degree of industrial development and government policies towards foreign investment between the countries.

The differential levels of penetration by sector is related to the tendency for TNCs to be concentrated in the production of certain types of goods. The highest levels of foreign penetration is usually to be found in the manufacture of consumer durable goods such as cars, refrigerators, televisions and washing machines, while foreign ownership is below average in non-durable consumer goods (see Fajnzylber and Tarrago, 1975, p. 264, on Mexico and Luiz Possas, 1979, table 26 on Brazil). Even within the non-durable consumer goods industries average figures hide variation, with high levels of foreign penetration in the production of differentiated consumer goods such as processed foods, tobacco and pharmaceuticals and low levels of foreign penetration in undifferentiated goods. TNCs also have an important presence in some sectors producing intermediate goods, particularly chemicals where their penetration is based not so much on product differentiation as on their technological developments. In intermediate products generally however, the level of foreign penetration tends to be below average partly because this is the area where state enterprises have been most significant.

These sectoral differences imply that a close relationship exists between the type of development strategy followed in a particular country and the role played by TNCs in the industrial sector. The strategy of import-substituting industrialisation embarked upon since the 1950s, with its emphasis on local production of consumer durables, has been a crucial factor in establishing the present position of TNCs within the Latin American economies.

The sectors which have been most heavily penetrated by foreign capital have tended to grow faster than manufacturing industry as a whole. Table 2.5 indicates the growth rates of the five industries in which TNCs account for the highest share of production in each of the seven main Latin American countries. In two countries, all five grew faster than the average, while in four more countries four of the five sectors had above average growth, the only exception being tobacco. Finally, in Peru, three sectors grew faster than the average, with tobacco and basic metals as the two exceptions. The tobacco industry is in many ways an anomalous case since health scares in the advanced countries, which adversely affected demand, led to substantial overseas investment in the 1960s and resulted in a rapid

TABLE 2.5  *Growth rates of the five industries with the highest share of foreign capital*

| | Foreign dominated industries with | |
| | Above Average Growth Rates | Below Average Growth Rates |
| --- | --- | --- |
| Argentina (1963–9) | Rubber, Transport Equipment, Non-electrical Machinery, Chemicals | Tobacco |
| Brazil (1963–9) | Transport Equipment, Rubber, Non-electrical Machinery, Electrical Machinery | Tobacco |
| Chile (1960–70) | Rubber, Transport Equipment, Chemicals, Electrical Machinery | Tobacco |
| Colombia (1958–69) | Chemicals, Transport Equipment, Paper, Electrical Machinery, Rubber | |
| Mexico (1963–72) | Rubber, Chemicals, Transport Equipment, Non-electrical Machinery | Tobacco |
| Peru (1963–72) | Rubber, Transport Equipment, Chemicals | Tobacco, Basic Metals |
| Venezuela (1963–72) | Tobacco, Transport Equipment, Rubber, Electrical Machinery, Metal Products | |

SOURCES   Table 2.4; UN, *Growth of World Industry*; CORFO (1971a); Matter (1976).

denationalisation of the industry in a number of Latin American countries. Despite low overall growth rates in the region, these are considerably higher than in advanced countries where sales are stagnant or declining. Moreover, the denationalisation of the industry in a number of countries in the 1960s enabled the tobacco TNCs to achieve growth rates similar to those of manufacturing as a whole.

## *The TNCs and concentrated markets*

The role of TNCs in orienting industrial development in Latin America derives not only from their location in the most dynamic branches of industry but also from the fact that they tend to operate in highly concentrated markets in which the bulk of production is accounted for by a small number of firms.[8] The ranking of industries according to the levels of foreign penetration and concentration is similar in Brazil, Chile and Mexico[9] and studies in other countries have also suggested an association between TNC presence and concentration (see Matter, 1976, on Colombia; Wilmore, 1976, on Gautemala).

On a more detailed examination, significant differences exist between the level of foreign penetration in highly concentrated industries and more competitive sectors. In Argentina, foreign firms accounted for 39.3 per cent of production in sectors of high concentration (eight firms making up more than 50 per cent of production) compared to only 3.5 per cent in those sectors where the share of the largest eight firms was less than 25 per cent (CICSO, n.d., p. 24). Similarly in Mexico, foreign firms accounted for 53.1 per cent of output in the most concentrated sectors (defined this time as those in which four firms accounted for 50 per cent of production) and only 12.8 per cent in the least concentrated sectors (four firms having less than 25 per cent of production) (Fajnzylber and Tarrago, 1975, pp. 292, 303).

An alternative indicator of the relationship between concentration and the presence of TNCs is the average share of the largest four firms or plants in the output of an industry according to the number of TNCs amongst the first four firms. Data for Brazil, Chile and Mexico indicate that sectors where three or four of the largest firms or plants are foreign owned tend to have the highest levels of concentration, and that those industries which are dominated entirely by local firms tend to have below average levels of concentration (see Table 2.6).

TABLE 2.6    *Average four-firm concentration ratio according to number of TNCs amongst largest four firms*

|  | Brazil | Chile | Mexico |
|---|---|---|---|
| Four largest firms TNCs | 54% | 67% | 55% |
| Three of four largest firms TNCs | | | 49% |
| Two of four largest firms TNCs | 37% | 60% | 46% |
| One of four largest firms TNCs | | 55% | 39% |
| None of four largest firms TNCs | 39% | 30% | 28% |

SOURCES    Brazil  Fajnzylber (1970, table 3.8); Chile  Own elaboration from CORFO (1971); Mexico  Fajnzylber and Tavares (1974, table 3).

The tendency for foreign capital to enjoy dominant positions and operate in concentrated market structures is further supported by studies of the subsidiaries of individual TNCs. In Brazil, 50 per cent of a sample of 119 US subsidiaries controlled more than 25 per cent of the principal product market in which they sold, while the corresponding figure for 183 US firms in Mexico was 47 per cent (Newfarmer and Mueller, 1975, tables 4.13 and 6.13). In another Mexican study, 55 per cent of a sample of 212 firms, mainly US-owned, reported market penetration in excess of 25 per cent (Robinson and Smith, 1976, table 35). A study of the 22 major foreign investors in Chilean manufacturing industries found that all but three had market shares in excess of 25 per cent (CORFO, 1970). The correlation between the presence of TNCs and highly concentrated market structures which has been noted within the United States and in other developed countries such as Britain, Canada and Australia is clearly present in Latin America.

*Standardisation of product*

The presence of TNCs as leading firms in the most dynamic sectors of Latin American manufacturing is an important indicator of the internationalisation of capital in the post-war period. It does not however capture the totality of this phenomenon. The increasingly integrated nature of global production by the TNCs has qualitatively altered the significance of a given level of TNC penetration compared to the period before the Second World War. One of the manifestations of this has been a tendency for increasingly similar products to be manufactured in different countries. Where foreign expansion is associated with product differentiation it is not surprising to find that the same product form is being supplied to different national markets. An example of this occurs in the cigarette industry where, particularly since US tobacco TNCs began entering the Latin American industry in the 1960s, there has been a rapid shift in consumption patterns towards light tobacco brands produced by the TNCs in their domestic market at the expense of local dark tobacco (Shepherd, forthcoming). This illustrates the tendency of the TNCs to create a 'consumption community – a bond transcending race, geography and tradition based on eating, drinking, smoking, wearing and driving identical things' (Barnet and Muller, 1974, p. 33). The need to produce a particular product form often determines the kind of technology to be used. The internationalisation of consumption patterns and production structures are therefore closely linked. This extends well beyond the direct penetration of TNC subsidiaries in Latin America. Coca Cola, the example *par excellence* of the international spread of US consumption patterns to the remotest corners of Latin America, is often produced under licence by locally owned firms. Where local capital competes with the TNCs in particular industries it frequently does so on the basis of imported technology. Similarly, where local firms develop as suppliers for TNCs they are also often obliged to acquire foreign technology. In Brazil and Colombia, almost two-thirds of all technology contracts are with national firms (Almeida Biato et al., 1973, table 4.21 and Junta del Acuerdo de Cartagena, 1979, table 2) and in Argentina almost 45 per cent (INTI, 1974, p. 17). These contracts involve not only technical assistance and the licensing of patents but also permission to use trademarks which may be an essential element in an imitative strategy on the part of local capital.

## 4 CONCLUSION

Despite the early involvement of TNCs in Latin American industry prior to the Second World War, the post-war internationalisation of capital represents an important qualitative change. Pre-war foreign investment was mainly an extension of trade operations involving both Latin American exports, such as the meat packing plants in Argentina, and imports, such as the setting up of local plants to assemble finished products imported from abroad. The key sectors which accounted for the bulk of industrial expansion in the period, mainly producing non-durable consumer goods for the internal market, were controlled by local capital. Where foreign capital was important in the production of non-durable consumer goods, it did so more on the basis of being one more industrial firm rather than setting the pace in terms of type of product, competitive strategy and the direction of industrial development.

In the post-war period, TNCs came to occupy a central position in the accumulation process. They are now located in the leading sectors of the industrialisation strategy pursued by the Latin American countries. They occupy leadership positions within the sectors in which they operate and within manufacturing as a whole. The question that needs to be posed therefore is not so much, what are the consequences of having a third of industrial production controlled by foreign capital, but what are the implications of a process of capital accumulation in which the leading firms within the most dynamic sectors are the spearheads of the internationalisation of capital? By putting the question in these terms it is possible to avoid a narrow focus on TNCs *per se* and a misleading preoccupation with the relative performance of foreign and nationally owned firms.

NOTES

1. See Horst (1974, p. 41) on the way in which Quaker Oats varied its product in different markets, in accordance with local tastes and customs in the inter-war period.
2. The share of US firms in total sales by foreign firms in Mexico declined from 83 per cent in 1962 to 78 per cent in 1970. Calculated from Newfarmer and Mueller (1975, table 3.7).
3. May (1975, table 5) and ECLA (1978, appendix, table 30). The absolute figures given in these two sources differ but the trends which they show are consistent.
4. These will be discussed in more detail in Chapter 7.
5. Calculated from ECLA (1977, table 4). The original data refers to over 5000 large firms and the size difference would be even greater if all firms were included.
6. The only apparent exception is Colombia but this is probably accounted for by the fact that only those firms with a foreign shareholding of over 40 per cent have been classified as foreign in Table 2.3 whereas all firms with foreign ownership are included in Table 2.2.
7. The value for Kendall's coefficient of concordance W calculated for 18 of the 20 industry groups was 0.6819. The calculated $X^2$ value was 81.150 which was significant at the 0.1 per cent level. Sectors 32 (petroleum and coal derivatives)

and 39 (other industries) are excluded because it was believed that these were likely to be difficult to compare across the countries.

8. At this stage the direction of causation in the relationship between foreign penetration and concentration will not be discussed.

9. Spearman's rank correlation coefficient between the share of foreign firms in production and the weighted average four-firm concentration ratio for each two digit industry was 0.74 for Brazil (18 industries), 0.60 for Chile (17 industries) and 0.82 for Mexico (20 industries), all of which were significant at the 1 per cent level. (Fajnzylber and Tarrago, 1975, p. 313; Luiz Possas, 1979, table 16; CORFO, 1971, and Table 2.4 above).

# Part II
# Case-studies

# 3 Wheels of Change? The Latin American Motor Industry

## 1 THE INTERNATIONAL MOTOR INDUSTRY

The motor industry has been a centrepiece of capitalist development for the greater part of the twentieth century. It is therefore a particularly appropriate branch with which to begin an analysis of the internationalisation of capital and its implication for Latin America. In the advanced capitalist countries, this industry has not only directly affected a large number of other industries through its backward and forward linkages, but it has also pioneered new forms of the labour process and transformed every-day life, giving rise to new patterns of consumption and of urbanisation. The major TNCs such as General Motors, Ford, Toyota, Volkswagen, Renault and Fiat are household names and rank amongst the world's largest companies. In Latin America, particularly in Argentina, Brazil and Mexico, the establishment and promotion of this industry has been a major element in the development strategy of governments since the late 1950s or early 1960s.

The motor industry is one of the most concentrated of all international industries in the world today. Certainly, when its large absolute size is taken into account, there can be few branches to rival it. Ten firms account for 85 per cent of all the vehicles produced in the capitalist world. This structure has been the outcome of a prolonged period of concentration and centralisation of capital at the national and the international level.

### International competition

After an initial period of experimentation in the late nineteenth and early twentieth centuries, the international motor industry began to

45

take its present shape around the First World War. The introduction of mass production techniques by Ford, and the combination of Taylorist methods of work study and increased control over the pace of work which the assembly line made possible, gave US capital a huge advantage over European competition. European states responded by imposing protectionist measures and discriminatory taxation in order to defend the industry against US competition. This had two main consequences for the internationalisation of capital in the industry. First, both Ford and General Motors responded by investing in Britain and Germany, and second, international trade in vehicles tended to consist almost exclusively of exports to non-producing countries, with the United States dominating world markets but with Europe enjoying preferential access to certain areas, particularly in the colonies. Both Ford and General Motors set up assembly plants in a number of countries to which they exported, including Australia, New Zealand, South Africa, India, Argentina, Brazil, Chile and Mexico in the inter-war years; however they did not engage in manufacturing outside of Europe.

The dominance of the United States in the international motor industry continued through the immediate period after the Second World War, as a result of the disruption of Europe's motor manufacturing capacity by the war. By the mid-1950s, however, the recovery of Europe had been largely completed and the stage was set for a new phase in the development of the international motor industry in which European capital challenged the hegemony of the United States. The much more rapid growth of production in Europe in the 1950s was accompanied by the introduction of automatic transfer lines and the addition of control devices to standard engineering machines. The result was a substantial narrowing in the productivity differential between the United States and Europe from between 3 and 6:1 in 1950 to 2:1 in 1959 (Silberston, 1965, tables 5–8).

Intensified competition took place not only for the European market, particularly with the formation of the EEC in 1958, but also in the United States and in third markets. US firms, faced with falling profits and a much slower expansion in their domestic market, began to pay growing attention to overseas expansion, particularly in Europe. At the same time European firms, led by VW began an aggressive overseas expansion both through exports to the United States and to other markets which did not have a local motor industry. This latter expansion led to the breakdown of the old 'colonial' division of markets which had characterised the inter-war years, and more specifically the dominance of US capital within Latin America. This intensification of international competition coincided with, and as will be seen below facilitated, government policies to establish motor manufacturing in a number of countries, and to create assembly plants with an increasing local content over time. In the 1950s and early 1960s, vehicle manufacturing was established in Argentina, Brazil, Mexico, Spain, India, Australia and South Africa, while more than fifty countries began assembly operations in the 1950s and 1960s (UNIDO, 1972, p. 39).

In the past decade, the international motor industry has undergone further major changes of which three stand out. First, a new competitive element has been introduced into the industry with the international expansion of Japanese capital. Second, there has been a growing international integration of the industry most vividly illustrated by the so-called 'world cars' produced by General Motors and Ford, but also characterised by growing market interpenetration by the major companies, and increasing standardisation of both product design and production techniques around common international norms. Finally, of course, the industry has been in a severe crisis during the 1970s, precipitated by major increases in the price of oil in 1973 and 1979, but with even more deep-seated causes related to the slowing down in the growth of demand in the advanced capitalist countries and increasing difficulties in labour relations.

Faced with this crisis, the dominant tendency in the industry has been towards greater internationalisation of capital, further extending the developments of the 1950s and 1960s. The three major producing blocks of the motor industry, North America, Western Europe and Japan, which were consolidated in the late 1950s and 1960s, are becoming much more closely integrated. This is reflected both in increasing trade flows, particularly Japanese exports to North America and Europe, and increasing cross investment and joint production agreements. The major transnationals are also increasingly treating their global operations as an integrated whole and developing 'world component supply strategies'. It is within this context that certain semi-industrialised countries such as Argentina, Brazil, Mexico, Spain and Yugoslavia have substantially increased their exports from the motor industry.

*Internationalisation of capital*

The internationalisation of capital in the motor industry in the post-war period is reflected in a number of ways. In the 1950s and 1960s, there was a substantial expansion of international trade in vehicles, which increased from a tenth of world production in 1950 to more than a quarter by the 1970s. Increasingly, however, the emphasis has moved towards overseas production of vehicles by TNC subsidiaries. By the late 1970s, a fifth of the production of the world's leading motor manufacturers took place outside their home countries (Lall, 1980a, table 3), although this figure hides substantial differences between firms. Exports and overseas production together accounted for around half or more of the total production of the leading European and Japanese TNCs, and more than a quarter for US manufacturers. Increasing international integration of production through the sourcing of components in different countries is a further manifestation of the same process, as is the standardisation of models implied by the 'world car' concept.

The growing emphasis on producing a wide range of models and frequent model changes which has characterised competition in the car industry in the post-war period has substantially increased the design and development costs which need to be met before production is started up. The costs of launching a new model

TABLE 3.1    *Distribution of output between domestic sales, exports and production by foreign subsidiaries for major car TNCs in 1978 (%)[1]*

|  | Domestic Sales | Exports | Foreign Subsidiaries |
|---|---|---|---|
| General Motors | 73 | – | 27 |
| Ford | 63 | – | 37 |
| Chrysler | 73 | – | 27 |
| VW | 30 | 36 | 34 |
| Daimler-Benz[2] | 49 | 35 | 16 |
| Renault[2] | 55 | 10 | 35 |
| Peugeot-Citroën[3] | 40 | 43 | 17 |
| Fiat[4] | 42 | 30 | 28 |
| Toyota | 51 | 45 | 4 |
| Nissan | 42 | 51 | 7 |

[1] Refers to number of vehicles produced unless otherwise specified.
[2] Calculated on the basis of value of sales.
[3] Includes Chrysler-Europe.
[4] Cars and car derivatives only.
SOURCE  Own elaboration from company reports.

around 1970 was in the region of $40–60 million (Jenkins, 1977, p. 33), while by 1980 the corresponding figure was of the order of $500 million, rising to $1,000 million for the 'world cars' being produced by Ford and General Motors. As a result, it has become increasingly important for the motor manufacturers to find the widest possible international market in order to recoup the substantial pre-production expenses involved. At the same time, to prolong the life of these models they must continue their production in peripheral markets, after they have been superseded by new models in the advanced capitalist countries. These factors, together with the slowing down of market growth, first in the United States and then in Western Europe, have made it increasingly important for capital to secure a foothold in other markets. Moreover, with the emphasis moving increasingly towards the need to cover the costs of developing new models, rather than increasing the scale of production in the home countries of the manufacturers, there has been a growing trend towards local *manufacture* as opposed to CKD assembly, in a number of countries.

The intensification of competition in the international industry since the mid–1950s has also contributed to the internationalisation of capital, with the breakdown of US hegemony. The threat of competition which was only evident within Europe in the inter-war period, has, with the international expansion of European capital, extended to parts of the globe which were previously the exclusive preserves of US capital. This considerably increased the bargaining power of local states which wished to promote the local manufacture of cars and lorries. As T. A. Murphy, Vice-President of General Motors put it:

There is no question that if General Motors or other US automotive firms were to turn their backs on market participation through overseas facilities, multinational firms based in other countries would be alert and quick to act to fill the need. (US Senate, 1973)

The pattern of internationalisation which characterised the industry from the mid–1950s, corresponds to the model of 'oligopolistic reaction' (Knickerbocker, 1973). In an oligopolistic industry which is either sufficiently stable or insufficiently concentrated for collusive strategies to be employed, interdependence will tend to lead to the major firms exhibiting a 'follow my leader' pattern of

behaviour in establishing subsidiaries overseas. Thus, a decision by
one TNC to enter a particular country will create a bandwagon
effect, and its major competitors will also attempt to set up a
subsidiary in that country. This, of course, is particularly likely to be
the case where the host government is expected to intervene in
favour of those firms which establish local subsidiaries. The result of
such oligopolistic strategies is a tendency for a number of firms from
the international oligopoly to enter the market, irrespective of its
size and the number of plants which could be efficiently
accommodated.

   Clearly, in the case of the international motor industry, the entry
first of the major European TNSs and more recently of the Japanese
has been a major destabilising factor, leading to a high level of
oligopolistic reaction in the industry. This is reflected in the large
number of firms which set up in most of the countries which have
embarked on vehicle production since the mid–1950s, and more
recently the large number of firms which have expressed interest in
establishing in new markets where the state has announced a tender
for local vehicle production–for example in the case of the Andean
Pact countries and Algeria.

   The increasingly integrated international design, production and
supply strategies of the major TNCs in the 1970s, pioneered within
Europe by Ford in the 1960s, is a further reflection of the increased
costs of developing new models and intensified international
competition. It is increasingly uneconomical to produce different
models for each market, and General Motors and Ford have moved
away from the strategy to the 'world car' concept involving a
unified basic model range with adaptations to local market
conditions. As will be argued below, it is this new strategy of
international integration which has made possible the growth of
exports of automotive products from a number of underdeveloped
countries in the 1970s, rather than any effort to take advantage of
cheap labour in those countries.


## 2 THE DEVELOPMENT OF THE LATIN AMERICAN MOTOR INDUSTRY

The motor industry is in many ways the spearhead of TNC
penetration of Latin American industry. By the early 1970s, the
transport equipment industry, of which by far the most important

component is the motor industry, accounted for almost a fifth of the accumulated foreign investment in Brazilian industry (Luis Possas, 1979, table 27) and over a quarter of the authorised foreign investment in Argentina since 1954 (Sourrouille, 1976, table 4). In Mexico, the other country of the region which had gone furthest in developing the industry, it accounted for more than 10 per cent of direct investment in manufacturing (Sepulveda and Chumacero, 1973, appendix, tables 3 and 4). In each case, the only branch with more foreign capital invested was chemicals, a much more diversified sector in terms of the firms involved and products manufactured. Similarly, transport equipment accounted for almost a fifth of sales by US majority-owned subsidiaries in Latin America in the mid 1970s (US Department of Commerce, *Survey of Current Business*) and almost a third of employment by German TNCs in the region (Fröbel *et al.*, 1980, table 11.12).

In the larger Latin American countries the motor industry is also significant because of the central role which it has played in the overall strategy of industrialisation since the mid-1950s. In the 1970s, it accounted for 12 per cent of industrial output in Brazil, almost 10 per cent in Argentina and around 6 per cent in Mexico. In each of these countries, the motor TNCs rank amongst the largest manufacturing firms and have an influence which spreads well beyond their own production through their network of suppliers and dealers. The impact of the industry is also indirectly illustrated by the growing traffic congestion of the Latin American cities and the expanding network of roads and motorways.

The origins of the industry in Latin America date back to the inter-war years when General Motors, Ford and Chrysler set up a number of local assembly plants. The domination of US capital in the region was virtually complete in this period. In Brazil, Germany, the second most important source of vehicles, accounted for only 10 per cent of cars sold in the late 1930s while in Argentina, the United States controlled 85 per cent of the market followed by Germany with 7 per cent and Britain 3 per cent (PEP, 1950, p. 102). The lack of international competition for the Latin American market, together with the companies' objective of obtaining the largest possible market for US produced parts and components, militated against any move towards greater integration of the industry locally through a move towards manufacturing as opposed to pure assembly.

In the period after the Second World War, there was a distinct move away from the United States as a source of supply so that by the early 1950s, in both Brazil and Argentina, only about 60 per cent of car imports came from the USA (Guimaraes, 1981, table 2; Jenkins, 1977, p. 49). Whereas in the pre-war period, only the US firms had set up assembly plants in Latin America, after the war and particularly after 1950, a number of European firms set up subsidiaries or licenced local assemblers in Brazil, Mexico and Argentina. These included Volkswagen, Mercedes-Benz, DKW, Fiat and BMC. A similar trend away from the dominant position enjoyed by US capital was clearly evident in other Latin American countries in the 1950s, so that by 1960 the United States accounted for less than half the cars imported into Colombia and Venezuela, less than a third in Peru and less than a sixth in Chile (Society of Motor Manufacturers and Traders, 1961).

### The development of a local manufacturing industry

Although in the larger Latin American countries the parts industry had experienced considerable development during the Depression and the Second World War, production was mainly for the replacement market and the terminal firms continued to operate primarily as assemblers of imported CKD kits. In the 1950s, however, host governments faced with serious balance of payments difficulties began to pressurise the terminals to incorporate a greater proportion of local parts. Of the larger Latin American countries, first Brazil in 1956, then Argentina in 1959 and finally Mexico in 1962 introduced legislation requiring companies to manufacture vehicles locally within a few years. Local content requirements were set at over 90 per cent in Brazil and Argentina and 60 per cent in Mexico. In the smaller Latin American countries, Chile, Venezuela, Peru, Colombia and Uruguay, efforts were made during the 1960s to develop an assembly industry which would make increasing use of locally produced parts, although the aim was not to promote full manufacturing operations locally.

The successful implementation of these programmes and the establishment of a substantial number of TNC subsidiaries in Latin America in the late 1950s and early 1960s must be seen in the context of the developments in the international motor industry in this period described above. It was in fact the international situation which made such moves feasible. In Brazil and Argentina, the firms which were most active in the development of a local manufacturing industry were not the previously dominant US Big Three (General Motors, Ford and Chrysler), but the Europeans and particularly the Germans. Volkswagen and Daimler Benz, which had built assembly plants in Brazil in the early 1950s became the leading manufacturers of cars and commercial vehicles respectively under the GEIA programme. Other German firms including Borgward, NSU, BMW and Auto-Union also submitted investment proposals although only the last of these, in association with a local assembler Vemag, was actually implemented. The French firms, Simca and Renault (the latter in association with Willys) were also involved. Initially, the US Big Three decided only to produce lorries in Brazil and it was not until the late 1960s that they began to produce cars on a significant scale (Guimaraes, 1981).

The same situation emerged in Argentina where the early development of the industry was undertaken by Kaiser, which had gone out of the car business in the United States in the early 1950s, and Mercedes-Benz. With the introduction of a comprehensive promotion policy in 1959 the lead in car production was taken by Kaiser, Fiat, Citroen and the local licensees of BMC, Peugeot and BMW. As in Brazil, the US Big Three initially decided to concentrate on lorries and only entered the car market in 1962.

These two cases point in the same direction. The firms which until the 1950s had dominated the Latin American market were clearly reluctant to move towards full-scale manufacturing. Faced with government policies to promote the development of the industry, they sought a risk-minimising strategy. This meant initially avoiding car production, in which production costs were likely to be high because of a lack of economies of scale and future demand trends were uncertain, but at the same time establishing a foothold in the industry through producing lorries whose manufacture is less subject to large economies of scale and where the future expansion of demand with the growth of the economy was more predictable. Lorry production could then provide a base for diversification into the car industry at a later date if this proved desirable. The European producers, on the other hand, were anxious to further penetrate the US preserves in Latin America as part of their strategy of international expansion. Clearly, one way of doing so was to anticipate the US firms in entering local production and thus consolidate the position of their own models and trademarks.

When Mexico began developing a policy towards the motor industry in the early 1960s, the strategy of the US TNCs was somewhat different. By then, the experience of Brazil and Argentina had made it clear that car production in the region was viable and that if the US manufacturers were not prepared to undertake it, their European competitors certainly were. Thus, rather than standing back as they had done in Brazil and Argentina, the US Big Three became involved at an early stage, pressurising for the type of policy which would be most in their interest. The firms brought pressure to bear on the Mexican government to make important modifications to the initial draft decree which had been drawn up. An overriding fear of the companies by this time was that they would find themselves excluded from the Mexican market by a policy of restricting the number of firms permitted to operate (Bennett and Sharpe, 1979a). A 'wait and see' policy of the type adopted in Brazil and Argentina would therefore have been extremely dangerous for the companies.

What all three cases illustrate is the importance of the changes in the international competitive environment in the transition to full-scale manufacturing in the Latin American motor industry. Had US capital continued to enjoy the same dominant position as it had in the inter-war years, it would have been much more difficult to push the industry in Latin America much beyond the stage of final assembly, and to give it such a pivotal role in the import substituting strategies of the 1950s and 1960s.

In the assembly phase and the early years of the development of motor manufacturing in Latin America, a number of the firms involved were locally owned, operating under licence from a foreign manufacturer. During the 1960s the major auto TNCs extended their hold over the Latin American market, taking over licensees, acquiring independent national firms and driving out national competitors (Jenkins, 1976). By the late 1970s, foreign capital dominated the entire Latin American motor industry as Table 3.2 indicates. The only apparent exception, Uruguay, where such firms accounted for less than half the vehicles produced locally, in fact confirms the above observation, as the country only began to develop a local assembly industry recently. It is therefore still at that early stage when a significant local capital participation has traditionally been found. In the countries with a higher level of local content (Argentina, Brazil and Mexico) national firms account for less than 5 per cent of the total output of the industry and the only significant local firms are the state-owned IME in Argentina and DINA in Mexico.

TABLE 3.2   *Foreign firms' share of vehicle production in Latin America, 1978*

|  | Majority foreign owned | Minority foreign owned | Nationally owned |
|---|---|---|---|
| Argentina | 95.4 | – | 4.6 |
| Brazil | 99.7 | – | 0.3 |
| Chile | 85.7 | 14.3 | – |
| Colombia | 45.0 | 55.0 | – |
| Mexico | 86.0 | 9.9 | 4.1 |
| Peru | 75.0 | 25.0 | – |
| Venezuela | 77.9 | 22.1 | – |
| Uruguay* | 41.8 | – | 58.2 |

\* 1977

SOURCE   UN Centre on Transnational Corporations, *Transnational Corporations in the International Auto Industry* (New York: UNCTC, 1982) table 25.

## New patterns of international integration

The intensification of international competition in the motor industry in the 1970s and the increasing world-wide integration of the industry, has created a new context for the development of the Latin American motor industry. The stagnation of demand and production in the major developed countries (except Japan) in the 1970s has given a new significance to the Latin American market from the point of view of the TNCs. Since 1973, the region has been one of the three most important areas in terms of production growth, together with Japan and the COMECON countries, between them accounting for the bulk of the increase in world production of cars. The major TNCs are concentrating more and more on the Latin American market, as is illustrated by the decision of Fiat to enter Brazil in the early 1970s.

At the same time, the new strategies of international integration in the motor industry have opened up certain opportunities for the Latin American countries. Until the 1970s, the Latin American countries' integration into the international industry was almost exclusively as a market for the export of parts, components and capital equipment from the advanced capitalist countries. In the 1970s, the industry's integration came to acquire a much more complex pattern. Latin American countries, particularly Brazil and Mexico, are now used by the TNCs as a source of parts and components for assembly plants in other countries and in some cases as a source of supply for particular models to other markets. Latin American operations are also becoming more integrated into the international industry on the supply side, as a result of reduced local content requirements in Brazil and Argentina, and a decision in Mexico not to raise local content substantially. The development is being actively promoted by the TNCs themselves, particularly Ford and General Motors, who see considerable advantages in being able to rationalise their international component production and hold out the prospect for host countries of lower vehicle costs as a result of more efficient local production (*The Economist*, 22 Dec 1979).

While the increasing international integration of the motor industry has made a new export-oriented development possible, governments in Latin America have taken advantage of international competition in order to require firms to increase their exports if they wish to expand their sales on the domestic market (see Chapter 5 for a discussion of these policies). They have also offered substantial fiscal incentives to companies which export. The growth of motor vehicle exports in this context are an extension of the drive to control expanding markets by the TNCs rather than to exploit cheap labour, as is the case in the electronics industry.

The experience of the Latin American motor industry since the 1920s provides a clear illustration of the way in which the structure of the international industry has conditioned developments within the region. This should not be interpreted to mean that developments in Latin America are a direct reflection of what happens at an international level, but rather that the latter determines the limits of possible developments within Latin America. It is difficult to believe that the transition to manufacturing could have been effected had the US Big Three continued to hold a firm grip over the market and had not been faced with increased European competition in the 1950s. Nevertheless, changes at the international level alone would not necessarily have led to manufacturing without active government policies within Latin America. Similarly, the rapid expansion of exports of automotive products from the region in the 1970s would not have been possible without the changes that took place at the international level, but also required the implementation of new policies by host governments.

# 3 CONCENTRATION IN THE LATIN AMERICAN MOTOR INDUSTRY

One of the most striking features of the structure of the Latin American motor industry is that, although clearly oligopolistic, the concentration of production is on the whole lower than in the advanced capitalist countries. In the United States and Western Europe the industry has been characterised by high barriers to entry as a result of economies of scale in production, large absolute capital requirements and product differentiation. These barriers to entry have resulted in high levels of concentration in each of the major producing countries. The situation in Latin America is clearly different because the major entrants or prospective entrants are the motor TNCs from other countries. For these firms which are already established at the international level and who only need devote a small proportion of their total resources to entering any Latin American market, there are no very high entry barriers to be overcome. Where firms form part of the global operations of a TNC, the 'deep pocket' of the parent company makes entry relatively easy and forcing firms to leave the market through prolonged losses more difficult.

## Proliferation of entrants

As already mentioned, 'oligopolistic reaction' in the international motor industry has tended to lead to a proliferation of firms wishing to enter in new countries which establish this branch of production. Latin America provides a classic example of this phenomenon. Generally speaking, all the firms which met the requirements of the promotional legislation had their investment plans approved and no attempt was made to limit the number of firms entering the industry. In Argentina, 23 firms submitted proposals of which 21 actually produced some vehicles. In Brazil 17 proposals were accepted by GEIA of which 11 began production, while in Mexico 10 firms received government approval of which 2 subsequently withdrew. The situation in countries which promoted assembly operations with a certain level of local content was worse, if anything. 20 companies set up in Chile, 16 in Venezuela and 13 in Peru during the early-and mid-1960s. Thus, the characteristic fragmentation of the Latin American motor industries between a large number of manufacturers was established at the outset, through a combination of intense oligopolistic rivalry between the leading transnationals in the industry and a failure on the part of the Latin American states to intervene to control entry into the industry.

The lack of state intervention to control the number of entrants in the industry raises some interesting questions. In view of the large minimum-efficient scale of plant in the industry and the relatively small size of Latin American markets, there was clearly only room for a very small number of firms in each country, if the industry was to be efficient in cost terms. The official justification for a policy which permitted free entry to allcomers was that this encouraged competition, which would benefit consumers through reduced prices and eliminate the least efficient firms without need for arbitrary choices imposed by government officials (see Sourrouille, 1980, p. 51 on Argentina and Bueno, 1971, p. 95 on Mexico). In view of the pattern of oligopolistic competition in the industry this seems a peculiary naïve view. Moreover, it was not one that was shared by all government advisors involved in designing policies to promote the development of the industry. In Mexico, at least, a strong case was made for controlling the number of firms permitted to operate in the industry and the number of models which they produced (NAFINSA, 1960). The failure to do so was the result of organised pressure by the auto TNCs themselves and their home states to ensure that they would not be excluded from the Mexican market (for a detailed examination of the Mexican case, see Bennett and Sharpe, 1979a). In general, a universal preoccupation seems to have been the possible adverse effects on the 'climate for foreign investment'. Since Latin American governments in the late 1950s and early 1960s were basing their development strategies on the attraction of foreign capital to promote industrialisation, policies to control TNC entry tended to contradict this aim.

*Changes in market structure*

Although the number of firms was reduced considerably during the 1960s, the overall fragmentation of the market and lack of concentration was largely unaltered. In 1970s, only Brazil and Colombia had four-firm concentration levels of over 90 per cent, characteristic of all the major motor manufacturing countries in the developed world in both car and commercial vehicle production (see Table 3.3). Of these two countries, Colombia had never adopted the type of liberal promotional legislation characteristic of

T ABLE 3.3   *Concentration in the Latin American motor industry, 1970*

| | Cars | | CVs | |
|---|---|---|---|---|
| | Four-firm concentration | No. of firms | Four-firm concentration | No. of firms |
| Argentina | 75 | 7 | 61 | 10 |
| Brazil | 99 | 6 | 96 | 9 |
| Chile | 67 | 10 | 100 | 2 |
| Colombia | 100 | 3 | 100 | 2 |
| Mexico | 73 | 7 | 87 | 8 |
| Peru | 64 | 9 | 83 | 7 |
| Venezuela* | 80 | 8 | 66 | 13 |

\* 1972
SOURCE   As for Table 3.2 (table 2.4).

all the other Latin American countries, while Brazil was the only country in which the reduction in the number of firms in the 1960s led to a significant increase in concentration. This arose because two important producers, Willys and Vemag were taken over by two of the market leaders, VW and Ford.

In the 1970s, there was some further concentration of production in certain countries of the region. This came about in one of two ways. In Chile and Peru, the state intervened to rationalise the structure of the industry by calling an international tender which would result in only a small number of firms continuing to produce in those countries. As a result, the number of firms was reduced from ten to four in Chile and from thirteen to five in Peru in the 1970s. Significantly, these policies to rationalise the local industry were undertaken by governments which were much less concerned to provide a favourable climate for foreign investment than those of the 1950s and 1960s (Popular Unity in Chile and the Velasco regime in Peru),within a general context which emphasised the need to control the operation of TNCs (as in the case of Decision 24 of the Andean Pact).

The second way in which important structural changes in the industry within Latin America has been brought about is as a result of changes at the international level. The merger of Peugeot and Citröen in France led, a few years later, to the withdrawal of Citröen from the Argentinian market where both firms had subsidiaries. The crisis in the international motor industry has also had an effect on industrial structure in Latin America, most noticeably through the withdrawal of Chrysler, which in the face of financial difficulties was forced to sell its subsidiaries in Argentina and Brazil to Volkswagen, and in Colombia and Venezuela to General Motors. In both Brazil and Venezuela, where VW and General Motors already had subsidiaries this contributed to increased concentration in the local industry.

In contrast to the advanced capitalist countries, where historically concentration and centralisation of capital was primarily the result of the internal dynamic of the competitive struggle within each country, in Latin America this process has been conditioned primarily by developments external to the national industry, either as a result of developments at the international level or of state intervention.

## 4 COMPETITIVE STRATEGIES

Since the 1920s in the United States and the 1950s in Western Europe, competitive strategies in the car industry have been dominated by model competition (that is, styling changes and the production of a 'full line' of models), large scale advertising and consumer credit. Price leadership rather than price competition has been the norm, as in the case of General Motors in the United States (White, 1971, 1977; Rhys, 1972; Jenkins, 1977, ch. 2). During the 1960s, the motor industry in Latin America came to be increasingly characterised by these forms of oligopolistic competition. This tendency was particularly marked in the two countries with the highest level of local integration, Brazil and Argentina. It was associated with three other important developments in the industry, namely the end of the initial boom in car production based on the pent-up demand built up during the period of restricted supply prior to the commencement of local manufacture, the entry of the US Big Three into car production, and the elimination of locally owned producers.

In the late 1950s and early 1960s, the number of models produced in both Brazil and Argentina was relatively small, fewer than two per firm, and in so far as there was an excessive proliferation of models this was the result of a large number of firms in production (Lenicov, 1973; Guimaraes, 1981). The major problems facing firms in this early period were technical, financial and organisational difficulties in getting vehicles produced, rather than marketing. By the mid–

1960s however, in both Argentina and Brazil, competition between capitals came to rely increasingly on the traditional oligopolistic methods of increasing demand. The most clear evidence of this is the proliferation in the number of models produced and the rate at which new models were introduced within a short space of time (Table 3.4). More than twice as many new models were introduced in the period 1966–70 as in 1961–5 in both countries. This is all the more spectacular when it is remembered that in Argentina there was a sharp reduction in the number of firms producing cars in the early 1960s.

TABLE 3.4   *Model proliferation and model changes in Argentina and Brazil, 1961–71*

|      | Argentina | | Brazil | |
|------|-------------------------|------------------------|-------------------------|------------------------|
|      | *New models introduced* | *Total models produced* | *New models introduced* | *Total models produced* |
| 1961 | 2  | 20 | 1  | 9  |
| 1962 | 9  | 26 | 5  | 14 |
| 1963 | 5  | 27 | 4  | 16 |
| 1964 | 4  | 26 | 6  | 21 |
| 1965 | 5  | 27 | 6  | 23 |
| 1966 | 15 | 40 | 11 | 25 |
| 1967 | 10 | 42 | 10 | 25 |
| 1968 | 6  | 36 | 2  | 14 |
| 1969 | 16 | 53 | 20 | 31 |
| 1970 | 14 | 53 | 11 | 32 |
| 1971 | 6  | 49 | 16 | 42 |

SOURCE   ADEFA; Guimaraes, (1981, table 14).

As demand for new cars came increasingly to rely on persuading existing owners to replace their vehicles, the twin strategies of providing a range of models and of introducing new models at frequent intervals gained in importance. Moreover, both the entry of the US Big Three with their emphasis on product differentiation and the disappearance of the locally owned firms, which had often produced a limited range of models, accentuated this tendency.

The Latin American countries which developed assembly industries during the 1960s were similarly characterised by a large number of models in production. Despite moves to rationalise the industry in a number of countries in the 1970s, most are still characterised by substantial model diversity. Thus, in 1978 Argentina produced 47 models of passenger cars, Brazil 68 models of

TABLE 3.5    *Car models produced and average output per model, 1978*

|            | Number of models* | Output per model |
|------------|-------------------|------------------|
| Argentina  | 47                | 2 854            |
| Brazil     | 68                | 13 528           |
| Chile      | 13                | 1 317            |
| Colombia   | 12                | 2 650            |
| Mexico     | 37                | 6 555            |
| Peru       | 10                | 705              |
| Venezuela  | 43                | 2 406            |

\* Models include variations in body style (saloon, hatchback, estate) and engine capacity.
SOURCE   Based on Motor Vehicle Manufacturing Association, *World Motor Vehicle Data* (Detroit, 1979).

passenger cars and multiple-usage light vehicles, Mexico 37 car models and Venezuela 43. Chile and Peru, where government-imposed rationalisation of the industry had reduced the number of firms, had 13 and 10 models respectively and Colombia, where only three firms had been set up, 12 (Table 3. 5). The variety of models produced, together with the low levels of national production in all countries except Brazil, led to levels of output per model which averaged from 700 in Peru to 6 500 in Mexico. Brazil, with an average output per model of 13 500 and two VW models produced in volumes of over 100 000 was an exception within this general picture.

## Advertising

The introduction of new models as a competitive strategy in Latin America, as elsewhere in the motor industry, is supported by large-scale advertising. Although advertising accounts for only about 1 per cent of the total value of sales in the industry in Latin America (Jenkins, 1977, pp. 185–6, 194; Connor and Mueller, 1977, table 2. 6), a level that was slightly lower than in the USA but higher than in the UK, in absolute terms the industry is an extremely important advertiser because of the value of sales. Moreover, because of the higher prices of cars in Latin America, a lower ratio of advertising to sales gives rise to quite similar levels of advertising expenditure per car sold to that of the United States.

*Consumer credit*

Consumer credit has been another important element in the competitive strategies of the auto TNCs, providing a means of expanding the market for their product and also often a profitable business in its own right. In 1973, it was reported that in Argentina sales on credit accounted for 85 per cent of total new car sales, while the corresponding figures in other Latin American countries were 96 per cent in Brazil, 45 per cent in Mexico and 70 per cent in Venezuela (AMDA, 1973). In Argentina, the vehicle manufacturers were able to obtain access to bank credit at negative real rates of interest which were then used to provide financing for sales to the public which were always made at positive real rates of interest (Sourrouille, 1980, pp. 199–200). There has been a massive growth in consumer credit in the Latin American countries since the 1960s, the bulk of it directed to the financing of automotive sales.

As has been found to be the case in the advanced capitalist countries, price competition has not been a major competitive weapon in the Latin American motor industry. If anything the price elasticity of demand is lower in the Latin American countries than in the United States or Britain. In Argentina in the 1960s, it was estimated that the elasticity of demand was only −0.3 while in Brazil estimates in the region of −0.5 were obtained (Jenkins, 1977, p. 133; Guimaraes, 1981, p. 27).

## 5 STRATEGY AND STRUCTURE–SOME IMPLICATIONS

The structure of industry created and the competitive strategies employed by the TNCs in Latin America are at the root of a number of problems which have plagued the Latin American motor industry since the 1960s. The most commented upon of these problems was the high level of costs and prices of locally produced vehicles in comparison with international standards. Table 3. 6 illustrates the extent of this differential both for production costs and for prices for a number of Latin American countries, including both those which had established manufacturing operations and those which were still in the assembly phase.

In much of the orthodox economic literature on the Latin American motor industry, this problem is seen primarily in technical terms, as the outcome of high levels of local content

TABLE 3.6   *Production costs and price to the public of vehicles, 1970*
*(country of origin = 100)*

|            | Production costs | Price to public |
|------------|------------------|-----------------|
| Argentina  | 194.9            | 209.0           |
| Brazil     | 134.6            | 196.4           |
| Chile      | 263.9            | 305.0           |
| Colombia   | 193.8            | 373.3           |
| Mexico     | 152.6            | 152.1           |
| Peru       | 163.8            | 175.3           |
| Venezuela  | 145.0            | 140.6           |

SOURCE   ECLA (1973, table 1.25).

requirements in small protected markets in an industry subject to important economies of scale (Baranson, 1969; Munk, 1969). However, while it is true that market size and local content requirements place a limit on the economies of scale which could be achieved on the basis of import substitution, the fragmentation of the industry and the strategies of model proliferation and model changes adopted by the TNCs created a situation in which actual economies of scale were far below this potential level (this argument is developed in greater detail in Jenkins, 1976a). Seeing the question in these purely technical terms led to the conclusion that the only way in which the cost problem could be resolved was by a more open development strategy, in which import content was reduced and a larger market obtained either regionally or through exports to international markets. Such recommendations avoided a direct challenge to the TNCs which would be implied by government-imposed rationalisation or measures to control the competitive strategies of the companies.

Because of the high levels of tariff protection granted to the industry and its oligopolistic structure, the TNCs were able to pass the high costs of production on to consumers in the form of higher prices. This further limited the internal market by restricting car demand to the highest income groups. Whereas in Germany in the mid-1960s, the price of the most popular car was equivalent to a motor industry worker's earnings over five months, in Brazil the equivalent figure was 16½ months and in Argentina 28 months (Baranson, 1969, p. 106).

A further factor contributing to high costs in the industry was the competitive investments undertaken by the TNCs. This created a situation in which the output capacity of the industry was far in excess of existing volumes of production, and the resulting un-utilised capacity increased production costs. In the late 1960s or early 1970s, levels of excess capacity of 40 per cent or more were to be found in Argentina, Brazil, Chile and Mexico (Jenkins, 1977, pp. 208–11; Mericle, forthcoming, table 3). In the case of Argentina, it was estimated that full utilisation of capacity could have reduced prices by 10 per cent (DNEI, 1969, p. 38). While the strategy of building capacity in excess of demand may in part have reflected technical indivisibilities in production, a more important motive is likely to have been the need felt by individual capitals to get ahead of existing competitors and to forestal the entry of new firms (Guimaraes, 1981, pp. 39–40). The investment strategies of the auto TNCs therefore not only created a highly fragmented market but also one in which installed capacity bore little relation to prospective demand, at considerable cost in terms of foreign exchange to import capital goods.

A further way in which the competitive behaviour of the TNCs diverted resources was through the massive expansion of consumer credit. In Brazil, the proportion of the total loans to the private sector accounted for by finance houses (the bulk of which went to finance car purchases) increased from 3.3 per cent in 1963 to 15.1 per cent a decade later (De Oliveira and Travolo Popoutchi, 1979, table 86). Thus, a growing proportion of savings was being channeled into purchases of consumer durables. The importance of consumer credit for car sales in other Latin American countries leaves little doubt that a similar situation existed elsewhere. In Argentina in the early 1960s, for example, a spokesman for local industrialists described the growth of finance companies providing consumer credit for car purchases as a 'cancer of the Argentine economy' (IKA, 1963, p. 61).

# 6 LOCAL CAPITAL AND THE COMPONENTS INDUSTRY

As was pointed out above, by the 1970s the terminal motor industry in Latin America was virtually under total foreign control. On the other hand, there was a significant participation of local capital within the motor industry as a result of the importance of national firms in the parts and components industry. In the three main Latin American countries, substantial growth occurred in the parts industry prior to the transition to manufacturing in the 1950s and 1960s. In Argentina, the output of repair shops and parts factories almost tripled between 1943 and 1954 (CONADE, 1966, table 3), while in Brazil the number of firms producing parts increased from 30 in 1946 to 300 in 1953 (Guimaraes 1981, p. 5). In Mexico, the parts industry employed as many as 10 000 workers in 1960, two years before the promulgation of the decree to develop local manufacturing (Jenkins, 1977, p. 219). Because of the low local content of domestically produced vehicles in the assembly phase, most of the production of these firms went to supply the replacement market rather than for original equipment. The scale of production was reduced and the capital involved was local in most cases, apart from the tyre industry which has been mainly foreign controlled since its establishment in the region.

With the transition to vehicle manufacturing in these countries, many of the major component suppliers in the advanced capitalist countries like Eaton, Bendix, Borg Warner, Lucas and Bosch followed their customers overseas. Increased local content requirements led to a rapid growth of the components industry and the TNC part manufacturers were able to penetrate the industry extensively. In Argentina and Brazil, a number of established national firms were acquired by the TNCs during the 1960s (Jenkins, forthcoming, table 4; Galeano, 1969). Nevertheless, despite such denationalisation local firms still accounted for roughly half the production of the parts industry in Argentina, Brazil and Mexico in the 1970s.

Before examining the relationship between the TNCs in the terminal industry and local firms producing parts, it is necessary to emphasise several points concerning the position of local capital in the industry. First, it is disproportionately concentrated amongst the smaller firms in the sector. In Argentina and Mexico, he average sales of the foreign component producers were respectively 14 and 13 times those of local companies (Sourrouille, 1980, table 21; Lifschitz, 1979, table 27), while in Brazil foreign subsidiaries accounted for 52 of the largest 100 firms in the industry but only 55 of the remaining 352 (De Oliveira and Travolo Popoutchi, 1979, p. 197). This is particularly significant because differences in firm size are associated with differences in the distribution of sales between the original equipment and the replacement markets. In general in both Argentina and Brazil, the larger the firm the greater the proportion of its sales which are made directly to the assemblers as opposed to the replacement market (Sourrouille, 1980, table 25; De Oliveira and Travolo Popoutchi, 1979, table 61). The exception in the case of the largest group of firms in Argentina is probably because of the inclusion of the tyre producers amongst this group and the fact that the demand for tyres is primarily a replacement demand). It seems likely therefore that whereas TNCs in the auxiliary industry will tend to concentrate on the original equipment market, local firms will rely to a much greater extent on the production of spare parts.

Looking at the structure of the motor industry as a whole, the terminal sector clearly occupies a central position. It is the focal point of the industry to which much of the production of the parts industry is directed, and further downstream it has a system of dealers who, although not usually directly owned by the terminals, are subject to the control of the assemblers. This position gives the terminals considerable economic influence extending beyond their direct operations, enabling them to appropriate surplus value from other parts of the industry, and to pass on the brunt of fluctuations to other producers. One manifestation of this is the tendency for the terminals to pay much lower prices for parts which they buy as original equipment than the prices which are charged for the same parts on the replacement market. This is an almost universal feature of the motor industry in the advanced capitalist countries and there is evidence to suggest that the pattern is reproduced in Latin America. Tyres, for instance, are sold as original equipment to the terminals at a lower price than on the replacement market.

Two factors contribute to the unequal relationship between terminals and suppliers. First, in a number of sub-sectors there is considerably more competition in the parts industry than in the terminal industry, and as a result the more concentrated sector enjoys greater bargaining strength. For instance, out of 49 different groups of parts produced in Brazil, there were ten or more firms producing them in 26 cases (De Oliveira and Travolo Popoutchi, 1979, table 68).

Second and more important, the terminal firms are generally much larger than their suppliers. In Brazil, the four largest terminal firms were five times as large as the four largest component firms in terms of capital invested, and almost ten times as large in terms of sales (De Oliveira and Travolo Popoutchi, 1979, tables 32, 33 and 34). In Mexico, the corresponding ratios were more than four times for total assets and almost six times for sales (AMIA, 1976, pp. 182–3).

Such differences in size are particularly important because there is usually a possibility of the terminal firm entering the production of any one particular component, whereas part manufacturers cannot develop their own captive markets by embarking on vehicle production. The bargaining power of suppliers is constantly weakened by the threat of production by the terminals or a threat to import competing parts from abroad. That the threat is real is clear from the extent to which the terminals have in fact integrated backwards into parts production in these countries. In the mid 1970s, there was considerable concern in Brazil over the increased entry of the terminals into parts production, which was particularly marked in those products produced by a large number of small and medium firms (De Oliveira and Travolo Popoutchi, 1979, ch. 5). In Argentina in the early 1970s, over 12 per cent of the parts purchased by the terminals were supplied by their own subsidiaries (Sourrouille, 1980, table 23).

Often the terminals enjoy additional sources of leverage over their suppliers. The position of the parts manufacturer is frequently that of a sub-contractor who is required to produce according to blueprints provided by the terminal, subject to strict quality and cost control. The pattern of activity of these firms is totally determined by the actions of the terminals (Sourrouille, 1980, p. 166). Most of the larger local firms in the parts industry work with licenses from foreign companies. These factors further weaken their negotiating capacity *vis-à-vis* the TNCs.

While producers of original equipment are at a disadvantage in their relationships with the terminals, with the possible exception of large part manufacturers owned by the major component TNCs, the situation of those local firms which produce only for the replacement market is even more marginal. In Latin America, as elsewhere, the dealers of the major terminals are an important outlet for sales of spare parts. The terminals impose quotas on their dealers for sales of replacement parts which act as a disincentive to the acquisition of parts from other sources. As a result firms which do not produce original equipment are put at a competitive disadvantage by not having access to this network.

The ability of small and medium local parts producers to survive, and also the attraction of using outside suppliers for the terminals, derive from substantially lower levels of wages which they pay. On average, wages in the parts industry are around 40 per cent lower than in the terminals in Argentina, Brazil and Mexico (Sourrouille,

1980, p. 148; De oliveira and Travolo Popoutchi, 1979, p. 80 and table 58; Lifschitz, 1979, table 29), although there is considerable variation within the parts industry between firms of different size (De Oliveira and Travolo Popoutchi, 1979, table 60). Sourrouille states that there are no appreciable differences between wages paid by the terminals and those of large parts producers in Argentina (Sourrouille, 1980, p. 152). If the terminals undertook production of these parts themselves then they would probably have to pay the higher wages which they pay to their other workers.

For the most part therefore, the operations of the locally owned parts manufacturers are severely circumscribed by the operations of the terminals. As suppliers of original equipment many of the key production decisions are not under their control and the prices which they receive are much lower than those on the replacement market. (In Brazil it is reported that the terminals profit from selling parts, which they buy at low prices from the auxiliary industry to their own dealers who are required to stock original parts (De Oliveira and Travolo Popoutchi, 1979, pp. 256–7). As direct suppliers of the replacement market, they are marginalised by a lack of access to crucial channels of distribution. There are important areas of conflict between these suppliers and the terminals over such issues as the level of vertical integration permitted to the terminals and the access of the terminals to imports. Nevertheless, in more general terms the existence and accumulation of these firms depends to a large measure on the continuation of the TNC-led industrialisation which has characterised the industry. In other words, the overall pattern of accumulation is not questioned by this section of local capital.

## 7 THE MOTOR INDUSTRY AND THE 'STYLE OF DEVELOPMENT'

In the advanced capitalist countries, the growth of the motor industry has brought about a major transformation in patterns of work and living. By becoming a mass consumption good, the car has totally altered much of everyday life. In Latin America, the lower levels of per capita income and the higher price of cars has meant that they are still luxury goods, access to which is restricted to a minority of the population. Nevertheless, despite this fact the

allocation of resources to support private transport has led to very
similar patterns emerging in Latin America to those found in the
advanced capital countries.

Data from the early days of the development of the motor
industry in Latin America indicates that the market for cars was
made up of only the top 10 per cent or 20 per cent of the population.
In Argentina in 1963, it was estimated that the top 18 per cent of
families accounted for more than 70 per cent of total expenditure on
cars, while in Brazil in the early 1960s, the top 11 per cent accounted
for over 80 per cent of expenditure on transport equipment
(Jenkins, 1977, table 6.1; Morley and Smith, 1973, tables 4.1. and
4.3). In Mexico in the late 1960s, the top 14 per cent of families in
metropolitan areas (Mexico City, Guadalajara and Monterrey)
and the top 8 per cent in other urban areas accounted for more than
85 per cent of expenditure on cars in those areas (Lustig, 1979,
tables 3 and 9).

Although the expansion of the car industry in these countries since
the 1960s must have led to some diffusion of car ownership (as is
indicated by the increase in the ratio of cars in circulation to the
number of families) the effective market is still composed of only the
highest income groups. In Brazil in the early 1970s for instance, the
top two deciles accounted for 80 per cent of all the cars owned in the
country (Wells, 1977, table 1). Moreover, since the higher income
groups buy the larger, more expensive models and are also more
likely to buy them new, expenditure on cars was probably even
more concentrated than ownership.

Diffusion of ownership, in so far as it has taken place, is a result
mainly of the middle class and in some cases the better-off sectors of
the working class acquiring second-hand cars. This has been
facilitated by a substantial fall in the price of second-hand cars
compared with the situation during the earliest days of the
industry's implantation. The market for new cars remains highly
restricted. As indicated above, in order to maintain the level of
demand for new cars the manufacturers have emphasised the
introduction of new models, which encourages the replacement of
existing cars and increases the availability of second-hand cars.
Thus, for the companies it makes more sense to exploit the top
income market intensively than to try and provide cheap basic
transport for the lower income groups. The second way in which this
market is exploited is through the encouragement of multiple car
ownership. In Brazil, more cars are owned as second cars by the top

3 per cent of households than the total number of cars owned by the bottom 60 per cent (Guimaraes, 1981, p. 46).

It is clear that the TNCs in the motor industry benefit from the regressive distribution of income which characterises the Latin American economies. Since the market for new cars is confined to the top 20 per cent of the population, it is increases in the incomes of this group that is of interest to the car manufacturers. Consequently, a more regressive income distribution which increases the incomes of this group more rapidly than the average, tends to increase the rate of growth of car sales, while conversely a more equitable distribution of income will reduce the growth of demand. Simulations of the effects of redistribution on the demand for cars in Brazil and Mexico confirm this picture (Morley and Smith, 1973; Lustig, 1979). Moreover both Brazil and Mexico, which are the Latin American countries in which the industry has expanded most, were characterised by increased income inequality during the period of the industry's most substantial growth.[1]

The relationship between the type of development strategy, income distribution and the growth of the motor industry was also brought out in the debate over the plans for car production in Chile during the Popular Unity Government (1970–3). The socialist government was committed to a substantial measure of income redistribution, and at the same time attempted to develop the Chilean motor industry, through rationalising the number of producers and increasing local content to include local production of the engine, gear-box and differential. According to the plan for the motor industry, car production was due to increase to 35 000 units in 1973 and 85 000 units by 1980. Moreover in 1969, less than 5 per cent of all Chilean families accounted for more than three-quarters of total expenditure on transport equipment and fewer than 20 per cent accounted for more than 90 per cent of all such expenditure (Bitar and Moyano, 1972, pp. 25–44). (Since transport equipment included items other than cars, such as bicycles, the concentration of expenditure on cars would have been even higher). Critics of the motor industry policy argued that given a substantial redistribution of income, the Chilean market would be incapable of absorbing the numbers of cars which the government planned to produce. Furthermore, such a policy would require the government to devote a large proportion of public funds to building new roads, remodelling urban centres and creating parking facilities. A socialist transport policy should, on the contrary, give much greater emphasis to the development of collective transport rather than continuing to increase private car ownership (Barkin, 1973).

### *The 'private affluence/public poverty' dichotomy*

The Chilean example raises major issues concerning the relationship between the growth of the motor industry in Latin America and the pattern of capitalist development which has characterised the region over the past two decades. In the advanced capitalist countries, the development of the motor industry has been based primarily on the growth of private transport. In the United States the 'private affluence/public poverty' dichotomy (Galbraith, 1962, especially ch. 18) is nowhere more marked than in the field of transport, with urban motorways jammed with cars and run-down inadequate public transport. While the United States is undoubtedly an extreme case, the trend away from public transport towards increased reliance on private transport characterises the advanced capitalist countries generally (Bhaskar, 1980, figure 3.2). Moreover, in the United States the Big Three car companies helped deliberately to accelerate this trend by acquiring and running down public transport companies (NACLA, 1979, p. 9).

The TNC-led model of development being applied in the Latin American motor industry is tending in the same direction. With the establishment of manufacturing operations in the region in the 1950s and 1960s, the vested interests in favour of expanding the road network and developing the necessary ancilliary facilities for car ownership were greatly strengthened. Large numbers of firms and workers became dependent on the industry and constituted a significant pressure group. In this situation, a shift away from public transport is more than likely. In Mexico, the proportion of total expenditure on transport and communications accounted for by public transport declined from around 85 per cent in the late 1950s to less than 70 per cent in the early 1970s (Bhaskar, 1980, figure 3.2). Another indicator of the same trend is the sharp increase in the ratio of cars to buses in the vehicle park of the major producing countries in the 1960s and 1970s. This rose from 28:1 to 51:1 in Argentina (1958–76), from 13:1 to 34:1 in Brazil (1957–74) and from 19:1 to 47:1 in Mexico (1960–75).

The extension of car ownership creates an important demand for greater expenditure on road improvements and new roads, which in turn further fuel the demand for cars. In Argentina for instance, public expenditure on road building in the five years after the beginning of manufacturing operations (1960–4) was double the level in the preceding five years, and there was a similar sharp increase in the length of road built (CIFARA, 1970, p. 163). Thus, the development of a local motor industry implies not only the allocation of resources to producing cars for a high income market, but also requires the commitment of substantial resources by the state to developing the necessary conditions for the use of these vehicles. Moreover, as an increasing proportion of the rich and influential acquire cars, there is less and less pressure on the state to maintain an adequate system of public transport, with the likely result that services deteriorate. This phenomenon acquires particular significance in Latin America where the bulk of the population does not own cars and are forced to rely on the inadequate public transport system.

Another important cost of the growth of car ownership is the increased consumption of oil which is required to maintain the vehicles on the road. For oil importing countries which gave the motor industry a central role in their development strategy, the increase in oil prices in the 1970s created a major problem as the Brazilian experience indicates all too clearly. The past growth of the industry thus becomes a major constraint on the continued accumulation of capital because of the resulting balance of payments crisis. In the Brazilian case, the state attempted to resolve this contradiction through the development of alternative fuels (the alcohol programme) and promoting vehicle exports, rather than through a major reorientation of the industry which would be required if the role of the private car in the country was to be altered. The Brazilian alcohol programme represents a further diversion of resources to satisfy the needs of the motor industry. It has been estimated that total substitution of alcohol fuel for petrol would require at least 2.5 to 4.0 million *hectares* of land producing sugar cane and an investment of US$ 15 billion (Buarque, 1981). Thus, major decisions on agricultural production are governed by the requirements of the motor industry.

In the major oil producing countries of Latin America, Mexico and Venezuela, the influence of the industry presents itself in a different fashion. The extremely low price of petrol at the pump in these countries subsidises the private car user in a major way. In addition to its direct inequitable effects on the distribution of income, such a policy contributes to further rapid motorisation in

Latin America. Perhaps to an even greater extent than in the advanced capitalist countries, the costs of ownership to individual car users are substantially below the social costs, taking into account the increasing pollution and congestion of many Latin American cities. Moreover, these costs and benefits are unevenly distributed between those few who benefit from car production and car ownership and the majority, who bear a considerable part of the costs in the form of pollution, congestion and inadequate public transport services.

NOTE

1. The role of income concentration in Brazil after 1964 in the growth of demand for cars is a matter of debate. It is stressed by Serra (1973) and Mericle (forthcoming). J. Wells (1977) believes that other factors, particularly consumer credit and rising real incomes, were more important.

# 4 The Pharmaceutical Fix

## 1 THE INTERNATIONAL PHARMACEUTICAL INDUSTRY

The pharmaceutical industry, although far less important in terms of its size than the motor industry, is of particular interest because it is one of the most international industries in the world today. The leading pharmaceutical TNCs have more overseas manufacturing subsidiaries than any other branch of industry (Vaupel and Curhan, 1973 tables 2.61 and 2.62). In terms of reliance on profits from abroad, pharmaceuticals is the second most internationalised manufacturing industry in the United States (Bergsten, Horst and Moran, 1978, table 3.2). The leading TNCs are heavily dependent on foreign sales, which make up between a third and a half of the total sales of the leading US companies, and well over half (often more than 90 %) in the case of European firms (UNCTC, 1979, table 6). Moreover, the importance of foreign sales has been on the increase (UNCTC, 1979, table 22).

The origins of the pharmaceutical industry as it is known today date from the discovery of the 'sulfa drugs' in the mid-1930s, which sparked off a 'therapeutic revolution' in medicine. Up to this time, the pharmaceutical industry was composed of full-line drug firms which manufactured and sold all the ingredients required by the pharmacist to make up the preparations prescribed by doctors (UNCTC, 1979, p. 14). Pharmaceutical companies were not engaged in extensive research or the kind of intensive promotional activities directed at the medical profession which have subsequently become their hallmark. Subsequently, there emerged an industry which controlled all stages of drug production from discovery through production and marketing as far as the final outlets.

Until the 1940s, the pharmaceutical industry could be characterised as being technologically fairly static (at least in comparison to what it was to become) and highly cartelised, with a division of the

world market amongst the major producers (Gereffi, forthcoming).
The Second World War altered the position in three important
respects. First, the development of new drugs was given a tremendous boost. The US government gave substantial financial support to
research aimed at developing mass production techniques for
manufacturing penicillin (Davies, 1967, p. 4). This gave a major
boost to the 'therapautic revolution' in the industry, which led to a
surge in new drug discoveries in the 1940s and 1950s. Rapid
technical change in the industry undermined the basis for cartel
agreements in the post-war period. Second, the break up of I.G.
Farben by the allies after the war removed the lynch-pin of many of
the pre-war agreements. Finally, the fact that the United States
became the main centre of technological advance in the pharmaceutical industry in this period made it more difficult to
implement such agreements because of US anti-trust legislation.

The new technological breakthroughs led to a rapid expansion of
the pharmaceutical industry. Although there was some extension of
foreign operations, mainly by US firms, until the 1950s the main
emphasis was on the domestic market. In the 1950s, however, there
was an acceleration in the rate of formation of foreign subsidiaries by
US pharmaceutical TNCs (Vaupel and Curhan, 1969, table 3.4.11)
and a much faster rate of growth of overseas sales than of domestic
sales.[1] In the lead in this expansion were the market leaders in the
US industry which were riding the crest of the 'therapeutic
revolution'.

In the 1960s, the rate of innovation in the US pharmaceutical
industry slowed down considerably.[2] The decline in innovation
enabled a number of medium-sized firms to increase their market
share at the expense of the leaders, by initating them. Thus, a sort of
catching up took place amongst firms which had not been involved
in the major breakthroughs of the 'therapeutic revolution'. A
number of firms which had been leaders in particular therapeutic
fields in 1960, saw their position decline considerably by the early
1970s, for example Lederle in antibiotics, Smith Kline and French
in oral ataractics and Merck in oral diuretics (Schwartzman, 1976,
p. 178). At the same time, the growing importance of some new
therapeutic fields such as tranquilisers enabled firms such as
Hoffman La Roche to grow rapidly. This catching up also occurred
at the international level, with a number of the medium-sized
pharmaceutical companies from the United States and from Europe
setting up overseas operations. In the late 1960s, employment

overseas by the smaller US TNCs grew much more rapidly than for the largest firms (Ginsberg, 1973, p. 168). Thus, increasing competition characterised the pharmaceutical industry both within the advanced capitalist countries and at the international level from the 1960s.

*Reasons for internationalisation of production*

The high degree of internationalisation of production in the pharmaceutical industry is a consequence of a number of specific characteristics of this branch. The major cause is the high cost of R & D expenditure in the industry. As was noted above, the emergence of the research-intensive pharmaceutical industry in the aftermath of the Second World War was accompanied by an acceleration in the rate at which foreign subsidiaries were established. To justify R & D expenditure requires production for the widest market possible and overseas expansion is a major way in which the drug companies can spread the fixed costs of innovation over the largest possible number of units produced. Indeed, it may only be through the contribution of overseas earnings that many companies are able to reach the critical minimum level of R & D expenditure which they must have in order to maintain their competitive position (Cooper and Clark, 1972, p. 13).

The objective of obtaining a wider market could, in theory at least, also be met by the international circulation of commodities and does not necessarily imply direct foreign investment by pharmaceutical firms. In practice, however, foreign investment has been a major form of internationalisation in the industry. Total overseas sales by the US pharmaceutical industry in 1974 were 38 per cent of global sales, and over 80 per cent of such sales came from overseas production (UNCTC, 1979, p. 79).

There are two further factors which have contributed to the industry expanding internationally primarily through foreign investment, rather than exports or licensing of local producers. Pharmaceutical manufacturing technology, particularly dosage form fabrication as opposed to the production of active ingredients, is technologically relatively unsophisticated, labour intensive, and not subject to substantial economies of scale. Governments, particularly in the third world, have therefore been able to force TNCs to undertake such operations locally, either through subsidiaries, licensees or contract manufacturers (Wortzel, 1971, pp. 17–27).

This may be done either through tariffs, import controls or sanitary regulations which have the effect of prohibiting imports. In some countries, the TNCs have a further incentive to undertake some local manufacturing activities because local patent legislation may not protect imported products if local production is not undertaken. As a result, only the very least industrialised countries did not have any local pharmaceutical industry by the late 1970s, while very poor countries such as Tanzania, Haiti and Nepal had already started to repack formulated drugs and process bulk drugs into dosage forms (UNIDO, 1978, p. 3).

There is also some evidence to suggest that the major pharmaceutical TNCs prefer to invest in majority or wholly owned subsidiaries rather than have licensing agreements or joint ventures. One indication of this is the much higher proportion of subsidiaries that are majority owned in pharmaceuticals than in other branches. US TNCs had majority ownership in 93 per cent of their subsidiaries in pharmaceuticals, compared to 78 per cent for manufacturing as a whole, while the comparable figures for non-US TNCs were 85 per cent and 71 per cent (Vaupel and Curhan, 1973, tables 10.1, 10.6.1 and 10.6.2). In Latin America, it has been argued that drug firms faced with the choice between direct investment and entering a licensing agreement with a local firm have tended to prefer the former (Cooper, and Clark, 1972, pp. 17–21). A major reason for this preference has been the greater control which the TNC can exercise over a majority owned subsidiary and the low cost which has to be paid because of the relatively small capital investment required. Control is particularly important in the industry because of the crucial significance of innovation – the application of new knowledge in production – and the need for capital to appropriate the fruits of that knowledge for private gain and not to diffuse it to other capitals. The fear of 'patent thieves' is a constant factor in the pharmaceutical industry and the danger of a licensee becoming a competitive threat cannot be dismissed. That these fears are real in Latin America is illustrated by the reported practices of some Brazilian firms which 'rely on several "industrial guerrilla" tactics. They may bribe officials of a competent governmental agency to get a xerox copy of an application for a new product filed by a competitor in order to obtain an approval' (Bertrero, 1972, p. 209). Control is also particularly important in this industry, since it gives maximum flexibility which can be used to shift funds between different subsidiaries. The extent of transfer pricing of intermediate inputs in the industry is well known and this is facilitated by having wholly owned subsidiaries (see below for a fuller discussion of transfer pricing in Latin America).

A final element which has contributed to the internationalisation of production has been the competitive strategies of capital in the industry. As in the motor industry, although not with such disastrous effects in terms of industrial efficiency, oligopolistic reaction has contributed to the proliferation of foreign subsidiaries, as firms match each others' movements into new markets. As will be seen below, this has resulted in the fragmentation of the local market in each Latin American country between a large number of foreign subsidiaries, so that no one firm has a share of more than 3 per cent or 4 per cent.

## 2 THE DEVELOPMENT OF THE LATIN AMERICAN PHARMACEUTICAL INDUSTRY

A useful classification of the stages in the development of the pharmaceutical industry in third world countries has been developed by the United Nations Industrial Development Organization. The five stages which they identify and the level of development in a number of Latin American countries in the late 1970s is as follows:

*Phase 1*  No local manufacturing – Honduras.
*Phase 2*  Repacking formulated drugs and processing bulk drugs into dosage form – Bolivia, El Salvador, Guatemala, Haiti.
*Phase 3*  Manufacturing a broad range of bulk drugs into dosage forms and some simple drugs from intermediates – Colombia, Ecuador, Peru.
*Phase 4*  Manufacturing a broad range of bulk drugs from intermediates, and some intermediates using locally produced chemicals – Chile, Venezuela.
*Phase 5*  Manufacturing most of the intermediates required and undertaking local R & D on products and manufacturing processes – Argentina, Brazil and Mexico. (Gereffi, forthcoming, table 9)

The development of the industry in Latin America during the twentieth century can be described with reference to these stages, particularly in the case of Argentina, Brazil and Mexico which have reached the most advanced phase of development of the pharmaceutical industry.[3] These phases are affected both by developments in the international pharmaceutical industry and the evolution of the Latin American economies, and the progress of import-substituting industrialisation in the various countries of the region.

Until the 1930s, the pharmaceutical industry in Latin America was mainly in *Phase 1*, relying almost entirely on imports of pharmaceutical products. (although of course there was local small-scale production of patent medicines). In some cases, however, especially the larger countries, some move into *Phase 2* was underway. Particularly after 1925, a number of US pharmaceutical companies began to set up subsidiaries in the region, and by the early 1930s, US investment in the industry was estimated at US $1.7 million (Phelps, 1936, table 3). The local plants that were set up in this period were mainly engaged in packaging imported commodities, although often some mixing operations were also involved. This phase preceded the 'therapeutic revolution' in the industry, and production continued to be characterised by an important production of patent medicines both in the developed countries and in Latin America.

In Argentina, Brazil and Mexico particularly, the Great Depression sparked off a significant process of import-substituting industrialisation, especially in consumer goods. In the pharmaceutical industry in the three countries, this took the form of import substitution in finished drugs and a definitive move into *Phase 2* of the industry's development. There was a marked acceleration of foreign investment in the region, with the leading US drug TNCs setting up seven new subsidiaries in 1935–9, twelve in 1940–5 and thirteen in 1946–50. These included firms such as Merck, Abbott, American Home Products, Sterling, Warner-Lambert, and Upjohn. The leading European pharmaceutical TNCs such as Hoffman-La-Roche, Ciba, Sandoz and Bayer also began manufacturing in Latin America in the 1930s and 1940s. Despite the influx of foreign firms in the industry, there was also a significant expansion of locally owned drug companies in this period. The 1940s have been described as the 'Golden Age' of locally owned firms in the Brazilian pharmaceutical industry (Evans, 1977, pp. 123–4). In Mexico, a number of important locally owned pharmaceutical companies (some of which were sub-

equently acquired by TNCs) were set up in the 1940s, including
Syntex, Diosynth, Laboratorios Grossman, Laboratorios Carnot
Productos Cientificos, and Chinoin Productos Farmaceuticos
(Gereffi, 1978; Campos 1981, table 1).

After the Second World War, particularly from around 1950, the
pharmaceutical industry in Argentina and Brazil moved into *Phase
3* of the industry's development, characterised by the initiation of
production of active ingredients, first with local manufacture of
antibiotics and subsequently a number of other products. At the
same time, some of the medium-sized Latin American countries,
such as Colombia, moved into *Phase 2*. These developments
involved further foreign investment, both through the entry of new
firms and the expansion of those already established. As indicated
above, there was substantial internationalisation of the major drug
TNCs during the 1950s. This was reflected in the denationalisation
of the industry in most Latin American countries in this period,
involving both the displacement of existing local firms by TNC
competition and direct acquisition. The Brazilian pharmaceutical
industry is often cited as a classic example of denationalisation in
Latin America (Bertrero, 1972; Evans, 1979, pp. 121–31). As late as
1957 there were still eleven locally owned firms amongst the largest
thirty-five in the industry, but by the late 1960s, their number had
been reduced to only three (Evans, 1979, table 3.6). In Mexico, the
late 1950s and early 1960s saw the denationalisation of the steroid
hormone industry (Gereffi, 1978). A similar pattern of increasing
foreign penetration also characterised the Colombian pharmaceutical industry from the mid-1950s (Matter, 1976, pp. 117–8).

In the 1960s and 1970s, the same pattern occurred as in the 1950s.
Argentina and Brazil extended local production of active ingredients to move into *Phase 4* by the late 1960s and *Phase 5* by the late
1970s. Mexico embarked on *Phase 3* production in the early 1960s
and was also considered to have reached *Phase 4* by the late 1960s
and *Phase 5* by the late 1970s. The intermediate level countries
moved into *Phase 3* or *4* in this period, embarking on some
production of active ingredients, while some of the smaller countries, such as those of Central America, moved into *Phase 2*
production. By the early 1960s, the domination of the Latin
American pharmaceutical industry by TNCs was well established.
It was completed in the next decade or so in all the major countries
with the exception of Argentina. Further penetration by foreign
capital took place as many second-rank pharmaceutical TNCs

established subsidiaries in the region.[4] These included companies such as Syntex, Revlon, Lepetit, A. H. Robbins, Smith-Kline-French, ICI, Glaxo, Rhone Poulenc and Akzo. These companies, which had not dominated the wave of pharmaceutical innovations in the 1950s, were able to expand rapidly both at home and abroad once the initial technological advantage of the market leaders had been overcome. The expansion of these companies into Latin America during the 1960s and 1970s gave rise to intensified competition within the industry.

   The extent of foreign ownership by the mid-1970s is illustrated in Table 4.1. In all countries except Argentina, at least 70 per cent of sales are in the hands of foreign subsidiaries. When the structure of foreign ownership in the industry is analysed in more detail, the leadership of TNC subsidiaries is even more apparent. By the mid-1970s there was only one locally owned company amongst the thirty-five largest pharmaceutical firms in Brazil (Evans, 1979, table 3.6), none amongst the largest thirty-five in Mexico (Campos, 1981, table 1) and one in Central America (Alfaro lara *et al.*, 1977, table 9). Only in Argentina and Chile do local firms ranks amongst the industry leaders. The position of TNCs is also particularly strong in the manufacture of active ingredients as opposed to finished drugs. In Argentina, despite the strong position of national firms in the drug market, production of active ingredients is entirely in the hands of TNCs. Furthermore, when production for export rather than just for the domestic market is considered, the dominance of the TNCs is also accentuated. In Argentina, 98 per cent of drug exports under license were by TNCs in the early 1970s

TABLE 4.1    *Market share of foreign firms in the pharmaceutical industry in selected Latin American countries*

| Country | Year | % of output by foreign subsidiaries |
|---------|------|-------------------------------------|
| Argentina | 1978 | 59 |
| Brazil | 1979 | 88 |
| Colombia | 1978 | 90 |
| Costa Rica | 1977 | 82 |
| Guatemala | c. 1975 | 90 |
| Mexico | 1980 | 85 |
| Peru | 1977 | 79 |
| Venezuela | 1977 | 70 |

SOURCES    Rosales (1977, p. 16); UNCTAD (1981, table 9).

(Chudnovsky, 1979, p. 47). In Brazil, over 75 per cent of pharmaceutical exports were by foreign firms in the late 1960s (Evans, 1976, p. 130) while in Mexico, foreign subsidiaries accounted for 94 per cent of exports of finished products and 99 per cent of active ingredients (Jenkins, 1979b, table 6.7).

## 3 CONCENTRATION IN THE LATIN AMERICAN PHARMACEUTICAL INDUSTRY

In analysing concentration in the pharmaceutical industry, it is important to distinguish between concentration in the industry as a whole and concentration within a particular sub-market. Compared to many other highly internationalised branches, overall concentration is relatively low both at a world level and within individual countries (Table 4.2). Within each therapeutic category (the closest one can get to data on sub-markets) much higher levels of concentration prevail.

In Latin America it has been noted that, as in the case of the motor industry, foreign control of the industry has been associated with a more fragmented market structure than that which prevails in the advanced capitalist countries. Whereas in the countries of origin of the major drug TNCs, the market share of the four largest firms in the industry is usually in excess of 20 per cent, in Argentina, Brazil and Mexico their share was only around 12 per cent to 14 per cent (see Table 4.2). Similarly, in the developed countries the share

TABLE 4.2  *Concentration in the pharmaceutical industry worldwide and in selected countries*

|  | Four-firm | Eight-firm | Twenty-firm |
|---|---|---|---|
| Capitalist world (1970) | 13 | 22 | 40 |
| US (1969) | 22 | 39 | 70 |
| UK (1973) | 27[1] | 43[2] | 66 |
| Japan (1969) | 24 | 37 | 59 |
| Argentina (1972) | 14 | 23 | 44 |
| Brazil (1969) | 14 | 26 | 50 |
| Mexico (1974) | 12 | 22 | 45 |

[1] 5 largest firms
[2] 10 largest firms.
SOURCES UNCTAD, (1975, table A.4); Evans, (1977, Table 3); EEC, (1975); Chudnovsky, (1979, table 1); Campos, (1981, table 2).

of the largest twenty companies is often over 60 per cent, while in
Latin America it is 50 per cent or less. This lower level of
concentration in Latin America also characterises the major
therapeutic groups of the industry. Whereas in the United States
the four-firm concentration ratio in the thirteen major therapeutic
groups is in the range 60 per cent to 80 per cent (UNCTAD, 1975,
p. 15), and in the United Kingdom it is over 60 per cent in all but two
of the thirty major therapeutic groups (Slatter, 1977, table 3.3), in
Latin America the corresponding figures are much lower. In
Argentina, only six out of the twenty-four top therapeutic categories
had a four-firm share of over 50 per cent (or eight firms with more
than 70 per cent; Chudnovsky, 1979, p. 47). In Mexico, four firms
accounted for 30 per cent of sales of antibiotics, 40 per cent of
antihistamines, 54 per cent of sulphonamides and 63 per cent of
bronchodilators (Bernal Sahagun, 1979, table 12). A comparison of
concentration in antibiotics, the most important therapeutic group,
is particularly interesting. The four leading firms accounted for 30
per cent of sales in Mexico, less than 50 per cent in Argentina, 69 per
cent in the United States and 80 per cent in the United Kingdom
(Chudnovsky, 1979, p. 47; Schwartzman, 1976, table 6.14; Slatter,
1977, table 3.3).

There seems little doubt therefore, that the market structure of
the pharmaceutical industry in Latin America, in terms both of
concentration amongst the largest firms and the overall distribution
of firm size, is radically different from that found in the home
countries of the TNCs, particularly those which have relatively little
foreign investment such as the United States and Japan (Evans,
1977). The presence of most of the world's drug TNCs in each
country explains the more fragmented structure of the market in
Latin America. Oligopolistic reaction in a highly differentiated
industry, in which economies of scale in production are relatively
unimportant, has led to a rush of foreign firms anxious to locate in
the region. This has caused a 'miniature replica' effect (Evans,
1977) where the structure of the pharmaceutical industry in each
Latin American country reproduces the structure of the international pharmaceutical industry, which is less concentrated than
the industry in any single major advanced capitalist country. This
can be seen by comparing concentration in Argentina, Brazil and
Mexico with that in the global pharmaceutical industry. The share
of both the top four and top eight firms are virtually identical to
those found at the international level and it is only amongst the top

twenty firms that there is a slightly higher level of concentration in the Latin American countries.

Not only is the drug industry in Argentina, Brazil and Mexico significantly less concentrated than in the major centres of world production, but there also appears to be little tendency for the level of concentration to increase. In Argentina, the shares of both the largest five and the largest fifteen firms were unchanged between 1962 and 1972 (Katz, 1973, table 13; Chudnovsky, 1979, table 1). In Brazil, there was little change in concentration amongst the top four and eight firms although there was a tendency for the share of the top twenty firms to increase in the 1960s (Evans, 1977, tables 2 and 3). In Mexico, the tendency between the mid-1960s and the mid-1970s appears to have been towards deconcentration amongst the leading firms, while the top twenty firms maintained their share constant (Wionczek *et al.*, 1971, ch. 3, table 4; Campos, 1981, table 2). This also bears out the 'miniature replica' hypothesis, in that it is unlikely that a largely foreign dominated industry will be rationalised through mergers and the elimination of firms because subsidiaries are backed by parent companies whose financial resources are vast in relation to the size of the industry.

## 4 COMPETITIVE STRATEGIES

In the advanced capitalist countries, the competitive strategies of the pharmaceutical TNCs in the post-war period have been largely two fold – product differentiation created through innovation and protected by patents, and marketing to promote the company's trademark. The emphasis on R & D to produce a stream of new drugs has led to a short market life for new products. The bulk of new products introduced are not new chemical entities and it appears that the competitive strategies of the TNCs lead to unnecessary product differentiation and the duplication of research simply to get around the patent protection on existing drugs.[5]

Price competition in the pharmaceutical industry has not been a major competitive weapon. In addition to the association between oligopoly and non-price forms of competition there is a further important peculiarity of the drug trade which makes price competition unlikely. This arises from the separation between the person who makes the decision about the choice of medicine (generally the prescribing doctor) and the final consumer. Since the doctor is not likely to be very sensitive to price differentials because he does not have to pay, the elasticity of demand for pharmaceutical products tends to be low. In these circumstances, the potential for increasing an individual firm's profits through price cuts is minimal.

There is considerable evidence in the pharmaceutical industry of large differences in prices charged for the same generic product. In the United States, a study of antibiotics found that in every case the market was dominated by a higher priced, branded product and in several cases, the highest priced product has the largest market share (Brooke, 1975, quoted in Lall, 1980, p. 204). In this, and in other cases, it appears that the first producer on the market with a branded product can command a higher price and a larger market share than its competitors (UNCTC, 1979, pp. 48–50). What this illustrates is the importance of competition to introduce new products, compared to price competition in the industry. Moreover, although the antibiotics market provides some evidence to support the claim of those defenders of the industry who argue that the expiry of patents leads to falling price levels, in other products firms have been able to increase prices on the expiry of a patent with no adverse effects on market shares (Slatter, 1977, pp. 111–7).

## Product differentiation

The pharmaceutical TNCs have adopted the same type of competitive strategies in Latin America as in their domestic markets in the advanced capitalist countries. In other words, considerable effort has been devoted to product differentiation and introduction of new products on the one hand, and sales promotion on the other. The major difference, compared to their home countries is that the introduction of new products is not based on local R & D but on the diffusion of products developed in the advanced countries.

An indication of the extent of product differentiation in the industry is given by the number of pharmaceutical products on the market in the various Latin American countries. In the early 1970s, these came to 17 000 in Argentina, 14 000 in Brazil, 15 000 in Colombia and over 12 000 in Mexico (Paredes, Lopez, 1977, tables 10; Chudnovsky, 1974, table 13). These figures were considerably higher than those found in a number of advanced capitalist countries such as France and the United Kingdom, and particularly Norway and Sweden which have state-run distribution systems for drugs (UNCTAD, 1975, p. 30). The extent of this differentiation is indicated, for example, by the existence of almost 1 600 different makes of antibiotics in Mexico. Such degrees of product differentiation are indicative both of the more fragmented structure of the industry in the Latin American countries and the ease with which firms are able to introduce imitative products to ensure a foothold in a particular market segment.

The introduction of new products plays a major role in competition within the industry. Indeed, both the share of new products in the value of sales and the number of new products introduced suggest that it may be a more important competitive weapon in Latin America than in the advanced capitalist countries.[6] It has been shown in the case of Argentina that the rate of introduction of new products has been a major element in determining the growth of sales of individual firms, and that this strategy has been adopted, by locally owned firms in particular (Katz, 1973, ch. 3). Apart from the fragmented markets of the Latin American countries, a second important factor leading to a high rate of introduction of new products, most of which involve no substantial improvement on exisitng products, is the prevalence of price control on finished products. The introduction of new products thus becomes an important means of increasing turnover for the drug companies (Katz, 1973, ch. 3, on Argentina; Bernal, Sahagun, 1979, p. 38, on Mexico).

*Sales promotion*

The second element in the competitive strategy of capital in the pharmaceutical industry is sales promotion. In Latin America, these expenses account for at least as high a proportion of the value of sales as in the advanced capitalist countries and probably even higher shares (see Slatter, 1977, table 5.2. for data on a number of countries). In Argentina, sales promotion was estimated at 26 per cent of the value of sales (Katz, 1973, table 1) while in Brazil, commercial expenses have been put as high as 40 per cent of the value of drugs sold by foreign companies (Ledogar, 1975, p. 13). An estimate of 27 per cent has been made for Mexico on the basis of a sample of fourteen firms (Campos, 1981, p. 623). In Colombia, it was calculated that for a sample of eighteen pharmaceutical companies, advertising came to 6.8 per cent of sales, and commis-

sions to a further 5 per cent (Chudnovsky, 1974, p. 136), and it is
likely that this figure underestimates the total amount spent on sales
promotion.

The main technique used to promote sales are visits to doctors,
and sales representatives (detailmen) account for about a quarter of
the industry's labour force in both Argentina and Mexico (Katz,
1973, table 2; Bernal Sahagun, 1979, p. 40). The extent of product
differentiation in the Latin American pharmaceutical industry
serves to increase the importance of sales promotion techniques in
order to make doctors aware of a particular company's brand of
drug amongst a host of competing products. Indeed, the ratio of
detailmen to doctors in Brazil, Guatemala and Mexico is more than
three times higher than in the United States (Silverman, 1976, p.
122). Moreover, the extent to which drugs, which are normally sold
only on prescription in the advanced countries, are available 'over
the counter' in Latin America increases the importance of promotion activities other than those directed at the medical profession, particularly those directed at pharmacists and the general
public. One significant feature of sales promotion in the Latin
American industry is the importance of free samples within the
overall sales promotion budget, which is greater than is normal in
the United States or the United Kingdom, with correspondingly
less being spent on the distribution of literature and advertising in
medical journals. In Argentina, over a third of the industry's total
expenditure on sales promotion was accounted for by samples and
less than 10 per cent went on literature distribution and journal
advertising (Katz, 1973, table 8). In Brazil, free samples are 8 per
cent of the value of pharmaceutical sales (Ledogar, 1975, p. 23). It
seems, therefore, that sales promotion in Latin America is likely to
be more biased towards promoting a particular brand name and less
towards diffusion of medical information.

Furthermore, the pharmaceutical companies in Latin America
have come in for considerable criticism for their failure to provide
accurate information about the drugs which they market.
Comparisons of forty different prescription drugs sold in the United
States and Latin America by twenty-three TNCs revealed striking
differences in the way in which the same drug was described to
doctors. In general, the diseases for which a drug was recommended
were much fewer in the United States than in the Latin American
countries, while the contra-indications, warnings and potential
adverse reactions were given in much greater detail in the United

States (Silverman, 1976). In some cases, products which have been ordered to be taken off the US market by the Federal Drug Administration continue to be sold in Latin America, and it has been claimed that some TNCs produce certain drugs in a Latin American country for sale to other countries in the region, in order to ensure approval for marketing which would not be available if the drugs were produced in the United States.

In view of these findings, the claim of the pharmaceutical industry that heavy sales promotion is necessary in order to provide doctors with up to date medical information in a rapidly changing industry, is particularly difficult to swallow in Latin America. Instead, sales promotion appears to be an essential concomitant of a highly fragmented industry with a high level of product differentiation, in order to ensure that the company's product is well known by doctors, pharmacists and consumers alike.

*Price competition*

As in the advanced capitalist countries, price competition is limited in the Latin American pharmaceutical industry. Prices vary considerably between different brands of the same generic product. In Costa Rica for example, the highest priced brand was 360 per cent more expensive than the cheapest for chloramphenicol, and 160 per cent more expensive for ampicillin (Alfaro Lara *et al.*, 1977, tables 4 and 5). In Mexico, price differences of up to 100 per cent have been found between different brands of drugs based on ampicillin and metronidazol (Mohar, 1979, table 22; Moya, 1979, p. 82). In Peru, generic products were generally available at between 20 per cent and 40 per cent of the prices of equivalent branded products (Hushloff, 1979). Comparisons in Argentina revealed considerable variation in the price charged by different firms for transquillisers and antibiotics (Chudnovsky, 1979, table 3). There is little doubt that prices charged by major pharmaceutical firms for their branded products are far in excess of the costs of producing these drugs. In Brazil for instance, it is claimed that prices charged by TNCs are up to 2 500 per cent greater than for those produced in government-owned laboratories (Ledogar, 1975, p. 10).

The view that leading pharmaceutical TNCs normally charge high prices for their products is borne out by the experience of countries in which the state is a major purchaser of pharmaceutical products. In Costa Rica for example, the public sector medical insurance organisation, CCSS, was able to obtain drugs at a third of the price paid by the private sector to the same foreign manufaturer for the same drug, by importing drugs on the basis of tendering under generic names (UNCTAD, 1981a, p. 11). The Mexican social security institute, IMSS, also obtains drugs at a fraction of the price charged to the public in pharmacies (Mohar, 1979, p. 65; Moya, 1979, p. 83). These differences could not be explained purely in terms of the margin between wholesale and retail prices, or discounts on bulk purchases. What these two examples illustrate is that only when the usual forms of compatition through product differentiation were blocked did the pharmaceutical companies resort to price competition.

## 5 PROFITABILITY

In the advanced capitalist countries, the pharmaceutical industry has consistently shown profits that are well above the average for manufacturing as a whole, and it is frequently the most profitable branch of industry (UNCTAD, 1975; UNCTC, 1979, ch. 6). It might be expected that drug TNCs in Latin America would show similarly high rates of profit on their operations. Fragmentary evidence from various Latin American countries suggests that this is by no means the case (see Table 4.3). Indeed, the figures for Argentina and Colombia particularly suggest that in some countries the industry is making very low profits. This seems somewhat implausible in view of the relatively low production costs which

TABLE 4.3 *Profitability of TNCs in the pharmaceutical industry in selected Latin American countries*

| Country | Date | Declared profits/ Net worth | Declared profits and royalties/ Net worth | Data base |
|---------|------|------------------|--------------------|-----------|
| Argentina | 1972 | 5.2% | 12.3% | Foreign subsidiaries in a sample of 81 companies |
| Brazil | 1972 | 21.9% | 24.9% | 18 US TNCs |
| Colombia | 1968 | 6.7% | 23.7% | 15 foreign subsidiaries |
| Mexico | 1972 | 15.0% | 23.8% | 23 US TNCs |

SOURCES Chudnovsky (1979, p. 53); Connor (1977, table 5.1); Vaitsos (1974, p. 62).

characterize the industry and the fact that very little is spent on research and development locally. One reason for these low figures is that the declared profits of the local subsidiary do not include royalty payments to the parent company, which are an important part of the global earnings which the parent derives from its subsidiary.

The pharmaceutical industry in Latin America is one of the industries which shows the highest ratio of royalty payments to sales. In Argentina, the average royalty in the industry has been in the range of 5 per cent to 6 per cent (Katz, 1973, table 1; Chudnovsky, 1979, p. 50), in Colombia around 10 per cent (Chudnovsky, 1974, p. 586). [7] A royalty rate of 5 per cent or more on sales can lead to a substantial increase in the return on net worth, as the second column of Table 4.3 bears out. The figures for profits plus royalties which are given there are much closer (with the exception of Argentina) to the high profits earned by the industry in Europe and North America.

*The use of transfer pricing*

This is by no means the end of the story as far as the profitability of the pharmaceutical TNCs in Latin America is concerned. The industry has acquired world-wide notoriety as the 'locus classicus' of transfer princing, the practice whereby TNCs are able to shift funds between affiliates by manipulating the prices of their intra-firm imports and exports. The first major study of transfer pricing in a third world country was carried out by Vaitsos (1974) in Colombia and the most important branch covered by the study was pharmaceuticals. On the basis of imports of a large range of intermediate products by foreign subsidiaries in Colombia, an average level of overpricing of these imports of 155 per cent was calculated – in other words, the difference between the price at which the products were sold to Colombia and the international price was 155 per cent of the international price.

Subsequently similar calculations, albeit on a more modest scale, were made in a number of other Latin American countries. These revealed that overpricing of more than 30 per cent was common in Argentina, Chile, Mexico and Peru as well as Colombia, and that for a number of products the level of overpricing was in excess of 300 per cent (see Table 4.4). Contrary to the claims of some pro-TNC writers (for example Vernon, 1977, pp. 154–6), the prevalence of

TABLE 4.4   *Extent of overpricing of pharmaceutical imports in selected Latin American countries*

| Level of Overpricing | No. of products with overpricing in the indicated range | | | | |
|---|---|---|---|---|---|
| | Argentina | Colombia[1] | Chile[1] | Mexico | Peru[1] |
| 0–30 % | 3 | 6  (0) | 8  (19) | 1 | (7)[2] |
| 30–100 % | 3 | 17  (6) | 15  (8) | 3 | (9)[3] |
| 100–300 % | 2 | 22  (6) | 5  (12) | 3 | (5) |
| > 300 % | 3 | 42  (5) | 7 | 5 | (1) |
| Total: | 11 | 87  (17) | 35  (39) | 12 | (22) |

[1] Figures in brackets refer to the number of firms with weighted overpricing in this range.
[2] 0–20 %
[3] 20–100 %
SOURCES   Katz (1973, table 5); Vaitsos (1974, table 4.3, table 4.4, appendix 5); UNCTAD (1974, table 11); Wionczek *et al.* (1971, ch. 3.4, table 10).

transfer pricing on a large scale cannot be explained simply in terms of unusual conditions which prevailed in Colombia such as the existence of a ceiling on profit remittances and the way in which the ceiling was calculated. On the contrary, the practice is widespread in the Latin American pharmaceutical industry and was used even in countries where there were no such restrictions.

The view that transfer pricing is used primarily to disguise the true profitability of foreign subsidiaries is borne out by the fact that overpricing is much more frequent and on a much larger scale in transactions between parent companies and subsidiaries than when the importing firm is an independent locally owned company. In Colombia, the average level of overpricing on the imports of the seven largest locally owned firms was only 19 per cent, compared to 155 per cent for seventeen foreign subsidiaries (Vaitsos, 1974, table 4.3). The studies of Chile and Peru also indicated that high levels of overpricing were much more common amongst foreign subsidiaries than locally owned firms.

The fact that the pharmaceutical industry in Latin America, even in the most industrialized countries of the region, continue to rely on imports of raw materials to a significant extent, gives considerable scope for using transfer pricing in this way. In Brazil, Colombia and Mexico, the share of imports in total raw material inputs in the industry ranged between 55 per cent and 75 per cent in the mid-1970s (Paredes, Lopez, 1977, table 10). In Mexico in 1974, the total imports of the forty leading pharmaceutical companies were equal to 39 per cent of the value of their sales (Campos, 1981, tables 2 and 6). In Argentina, imports by foreign subsidiaries related to licensing agreements amounted to 41 per cent of the value of licensed sales (Chudnovsky, 1979, p. 50). In these circumstances, even relatively low levels of transfer pricing can multiply declared profits several fold, while levels in excess of 100 per cent can give rise to enormous profit rates.

This is illustrated by the calculations made by Vaitsos of the effective return on net worth of the foreign pharmaceutical companies in Colombia when transfer pricing was taken into account. This came to an average of 136 per cent, with individual firms showing returns in excess of 300 per cent (Vaitsos, 1974, p. 62). The breakdown of profits showed reported profits accounting for 3.4 per cent of the total, royalties 14 per cent and overpricing 82.6 per cent. Although comparable figures are not available for the other countries included in Table 4.3, there is little doubt that the rate of profit would be considerably higher if overpricing was included.

The use of transfer pricing is not confined to imports by pharmaceutical firms in Latin America, but may also arise when these firms export. As already indicated, a number of TNC subsidiaries in the region, particularly in the more industrialised countries have developed exports and the bulk of pharmaceutical exports from Argentina, Brazil and Mexico are made by foreign subsidiaries. In the case of exports, a TNC wishing to shift funds out of Latin America will underprice its exports to other countries. There is some evidence that exports of pharmaceuticals from Mexico have indeed been underpriced. The major part of Mexican exports of pharmaceuticals consist of hormones which are produced from the local root *barbasco* and production of which is controlled by six TNCs (Syntex, Schering Corp., G. D. Searle & Co., Akzo, Ciba-Geigy and Schering A. G.). These subsidiaries export mainly or entirely to their parent companies or to affiliates elsewhere, often in countries which are known as tax havens. There is a considerable incentive for these companies to underprice their exports and as Table 4.5 indicates, in a number of cases they have done just that. It has been estimated that the loss of income to Mexico from underpricing of hormone exports may have come to as much as US $80 million a year in the early 1970s. There is also some evidence to suggest that underpricing has occurred on exports of other pharmaceuticals from Mexico (Jenkins, 1979b, pp. 149-55).

TABLE 4.5    *Estimates of transfer pricing of steroid hormone exports from Mexico*

| Product | Firm | Export price | US price | Export price as % of US price |
|---|---|---|---|---|
| | | Mexican pesos | | |
| Mestranol | Syntex | 18 640 | 39 630 | 47.0 |
| Estinil-Estradiol[1] | Syntex | 11 250 (1974) | 31 250 | 36.0 |
| Fostao Diosódico de betametazone[2] | Beisa | 33 095 (1972) | 328 130[3] | 10.1 |
| Propionato de Testosterona | Searle | 1 800 | 10 630 | 16.9 |
| Progesterona | Searle | 3 000 | 6 250 | 48.0 |
| Progesterona[1] | Steromex | 1 375 (1973) | 6 250 | 22.0 |

[1] Exported to the parent company.

[2] Exported to an affiliate in a tax haven.

[3] Because this is a patented product it is considered that the price in 1972 was as or higher than in 1975.

Data refer to 1975 unless otherwise indicated.

SOURCE    Productos Químicos Vegetales Mexicanos, SA de CV, *Informe que presenta a la consideración del H. Consejo de Administracion, El Director General de la Empresa por el período comprendido de 29 de agosto de 1975 al 15 de enero de 1976.* Own elaboration.

## Motives for transfer pricing

There seems little doubt therefore that pharmaceutical TNCs in Latin America have used transfer pricing of both imports and exports in order to shift profits out of the region. The theoretical literature on transfer pricing suggests a number of reasons why this method might be used in preference to declaring profits locally, (Vaitsos, 1974, ch. 6; Chudnovsky, 1974, pp. 55–66; Lall, 1980, ch. 5). As already indicated, there is an advantage in using transfer pricing in countries where profit remittances are subject to a government-imposed ceiling. Another reason related to government policies arises where the tax rate on profits abroad is lower than the tax rate in the host country of the subsidiary, a factor which acquires particular importance when imports or exports can be routed through a tax haven. In the case of transfer pricing to reduce the overall tax burden of the TNC, the tariff paid on imported inputs (or in the case of exports any tax credit related to the value of exports) must also be taken into account. Often, however, the tariffs on intermediate inputs used by foreign subsidiaries in Latin America have been low, as part of the policies of promoting import substitution and attracting foreign capital.[8] Thus, the tendency for increased payments of customs duties to offset the savings in profit tax arising from transfer pricing is minimised.

There are also a number of further tactical reasons why a TNC may prefer high import costs to high local profits. Where the company is involved in negotiations with the host government over the level of tariff protection or the level of prices for its product, it is obviously easier to argue for high tariffs or prices on the basis of high costs, albeit for imported materials, than on the basis of a high local profit rate. Indeed, high profits by foreign subsidiaries are likely, if they are publicly known, to lead to charges of 'imperialist exploitation' by certain local groups. Foreign companies may therefore prefer to keep a low profile, which means keeping local profits within limits. In this respect pharmaceuticals are particularly sensitive because they are a 'matter of life or death'. Even in the advanced capitalist countries, the high rates of profit earned in the industry have been subject to criticism. Relatively low profits are useful not only in bargaining with host governments but also in wage negotiations with the company's workers who are more likely to settle for low increases if the company is not earning high profits. Another motive for transfer pricing arises in the case of joint ventures, where any declared profits have to be shared with a local partner, whereas profits realised through transfer pricing accrue entirely to the TNC. This does not necessarily mean that transfer pricing will be more prevalent in joint ventures, however, since the local partner clearly has an interest in minimising its extent and this may even result in a lower level of transfer pricing than in wholly owned subsidiaries.

A more complex motive for transfer pricing is what Vaitsos (1974) has termed the 'relative-expenditure-requirement'. This arises, even if tax rates are the same between two countries, if the total costs of the firm in the home country (including managerial expenses, R & D, and financial management costs, as well as direct operating costs) exceed the revenue from sales in the domestic market plus exports to non-affiliates abroad. In this case, it pays the firm to transfer untaxed income from its affiliates to cover these costs. Therefore, the greater the extent to which a firm depends on income earned from foreign subsidiaries and the more it concentrates certain fixed expenses in one country, the more likely it is that the 'relative-expenditure-requirement' will act as an incentive for transfer pricing. Finally, it has also been noted that transfer pricing is a more flexible method of transferring funds than profit remittances. Whereas transfer pricing can be used to generate a continuous flow of funds as imports and/or exports are made, profit remittances must usually await the end of the financial year. In countries characterised by high rates of inflation and periodic devaluations, there is an advantage in shifting profits sooner rather than later.

The analysis of transfer pricing suggests a number of reasons why it is so prevalent in the pharmaceutical industry.[9] First, the industry is one of the most profitable, if not the most profitable industry on a world scale. It is therefore more likely to have high profits in Latin America which it wishes to disguise. Second, it is an industry in which the 'relative-expenditure-effect' is likely to be particularly strong. It is one of the most internationalised of industries, in terms of the proportion of the income of the major companies which is derived from foreign subsidiaries. It is common for the home country to account for less than half of world-wide sales. It is also an industry with a substantial concentration of overheads in the home country. This is particularly evident in the case of R & D, which accounts for around 10 per cent of sales for the major TNCs and is heavily concentrated in the home country of the corporation. Thus, the degree of internationalisation and the concentration of fixed costs in one country are both high which would tend to contribute to an incentive to use transfer pricing as a result of the 'relative-expenditure-effect'.

In conclusion then, it can be said that despite the fragmented structure of the Latin American pharmaceutical industry compared to the industry in some advanced capitalist countries, it remains an extremely profitable industry for the major TNCs. These high profits are often hidden from public view by the use of transfer pricing, and there are even cases where TNC subsidiaries appear to be less profitable than local firms.[10] In practice however, when transfer pricing is taken into account the Latin American subsidiaries of the TNCs are even more profitable than their global operations. These high profits are obtained through the same competitive strategies as in the advanced countries with a heavy emphasis on product differentiation and sales promotion.

## 5 RESEARCH AND DEVELOPMENT

As noted above, R & D by the major drug TNCs is heavily concentrated in their home countries. In the case of US companies, 93 per cent of all R & D expenditure was in the United States in the early 1970s and most of the remaining 7 per cent was spent in Western Europe (US Senate, Committee of Finance, 1973, p. 582). There has recently been a tendency for the proportion of overseas R & D by US TNCs to increase as a result of a significant part of their clinical testing being shifted abroad, in the face of stricter regulatory control and rising costs in the United States (UNCTC, 1979, pp. 78–9). Expenditure on R & D in the underdeveloped countries is insignificant in terms of the companies' global operations. One survey of US pharmaceutical firms indicated that they employed 410 people in R & D in the Pacific and Far East, Latin America and Africa. This represented 2.2 per cent of total employment in R & D by the companies (Wortzel, 1971, table 6).

Even amongst the most advanced Latin American countries, local R & D is extremely limited in the industry. In Argentina and Mexico, the average level of R & D expenditure is around 1 per cent of sales, a tenth of the level observed in some industrialised countries (Katz, 1973, table 1; Hernandez, 1975, p. 34). Such low overall levels of R & D reflect the small proportion which TNCs spend on local research. In 1972, this was estimated at 1.1 per cent for foreign subsidiaries in Argentina (Chudnovsky, 1979, p. 53), 0.6 per cent for US TNCs in Brazil and 0.9 per cent for US TNCs in Mexico (Connor, 1977, table D1). Many TNCs perform no local R & D in their Latin American subsidiaries. Only just over half the companies sampled in Argentina claimed to do any local R & D. In Brazil a survey of twenty-four companies revealed that the only R & D carried out by most of them was clinical testing which was in most cases a formality, since the drugs concerned had already passed all the relevant stages of R & D in the home country of the parent. None of the companies carried out basic research, only one claimed to do applied research and only two carried out toxicological and pharmacological testing (Bertrero, 1972, pp. 197–200).

### Why is R & D so limited?

The lack of local R & D foreign subsidiaries in Latin America is usually explained by the firms themselves in terms of technological

imperatives. These usually fall under two headings – economies of
scale in R & D and the lack of an 'appropriate research environment' (Evans, 1979, p. 179). Plausible though these reasons may
seem, they are in fact highly controversial issues. The argument that
there are economies of scale in R & D can be broken down into two
parts. The first is that large firms are able to devote proportionately
more resources to research. The second is that innovative output
increases more than proportionately to R & D effort. On both these
points, different studies have come to opposite conclusions (Reekie,
1975, pp. 113–8). On balance, what these studies indicate is that the
largest firms are not the most research intensive. Moreover, the
earlier studies on innovative output seemed to indicate dis-
economies of scale in R & D. Later studies, however, seem to
indicate either constant returns to scale or even increasing returns to
scale in R & D. This difference is probably related to the slow down
in the rate of innovation since the 1960s, and the increased costs of R
& D which has been accompanied by an increase in the proportion
of new chemical entities in the United States accounted for by the
largest firms.[11].

All these studies are agreed that a minimum size of firm is
required to facilitate R & D. One study in Britain suggested that in
1970 a minimum research programme would cost $£\frac{1}{2}$ million and
that a budget of £2 million would be required in order to support a
full range of facilities and provide some insurance against failure
(NEDO quoted by Reekie, 1975, p. 113).[12] A firm spending 10 per
cent of sales on R & D would then require a turnover of around £20
million in order to support a minimum R & D programme. This fits
in well with a figure quoted by an executive in Brazil who estimated
that annual sales of $55 million would be required to support
applied research (Bertrero, 1972, p. 205). While it is true that these
figures are substantially above the turnover of the largest pharmaceutical enterprises in Latin America, a number of further points
need to be borne in mind. One reason why firms are not sufficiently
large is because the leading firm usually only accounts for 3 per cent
or 4 per cent of the market. In other words, it is the way in which the
international market structure is reproduced in each Latin
American market that partly accounts for the small size of firms.
Second, as was indicated above, the need for such a large R & D
programme is partly because of the inherent riskness of these
activities and the need to insure against failure. Since the foreign
subsidiary is part of a global organisation, the risks of research in the

subsidiary can be pooled with those of the parent company's other R & D activities. Third, the estimates of economies of scale in R & D are all based on comparisons of total company R & D effort and innovational output, which does not necessarily imply that there are economies of scale related to the size of research establishments, or that R & D has to be concentrated in one location. Finally, even if it were the case that economies of scale did exist in R & D this would not put it in a radically different situation from that which existed in other industries when they were established in Latin America and which led many critics to argue that the comparative advantage of the region lay in producing agricultural products and raw materials.

The problem with the inappropriate environment argument as Evans (1979, p. 181) has pointed out is that TNCs seem to find any environment outside their home country 'inappropriate', as the above figures on the regional distribution of US pharmaceutical companies' R & D bear out. In these terms, as far as US TNCs are concerned, Britain, France or Germany appear to be only marginally more appropriate for R & D than Argentina, Brazil or Mexico, although of course British, French or West German TNCs find their home country's environment perfectly appropriate.

This is not to suggest that economies of scale in R & D, or the level of development of the local scientific environment are irrelevant as factors in the concentration of R & D in the home country, but simply that they are not the only factors. The drug companies are not guided in these decisions purely by technological considerations but also by the need to maximise profits. Since the super-profits to be earned from introducing new products are a major source of profit in the pharmaceutical industry, control over the flow of innovation acquires a crucial importance in the industry. This, of course, explains the significance of patents in the industry. But patent protection is not perfect. Some countries do not recognise patents on pharmaceutical products at all, while others only grant patent protection on processes and not on products. Even where complete patent protection exists legally, proceedings against firms which breach a patent may be long drawn-out and costly. It is, therefore, in the interest of capital to ensure close control over the output of its research laboratories. Thus, the need for control is an important factor inhibiting the location of R & D facilities in Brazil or Argentina, thousands of miles away from the head office (Evans, 1979, pp. 182–4).

*Consequences of limited local R & D*

The geographical concentration of pharmaceutical R & D has a number of consequences. It tends to perpetuate the technological dependence of the Latin American countries in that they have to continually turn to the advanced capitalist countries for the new products on which competition in the local market is based. This leads to the reproduction of an international division of labour within the TNC, reflecting the division of mental and manual labour, in which the high paid, white collar jobs are concentrated in the advanced countries and the Latin American countries remain 'hewers of wood and drawers of water'.[13] As was seen above, it is also an important underlying factor causing TNCs to shift large sums out of Latin America through transfer pricing in order to cover the fixed costs in the advanced countries.

It is sometimes argued that the location of R & D in the advanced countries also leads to a bias in the type of research which is undertaken, towards those diseases which are most important in the advanced countries and to the neglect of tropical diseases. Indeed there is evidence to suggest that R & D by the pharmaceutical TNCs is concentrated in those areas of most interest in the developed countries such as cancer, heart disease, mental illness and neurological disorders (Gereffi, forthcoming). This is not, however, a result of the location of R & D but is rather a reflection of the relative importance of different markets. The share of third world countries in the total consumption of drugs outside the socialist countries is only around 13 per cent (UNCTC, 1979, p. 19). Moreover, within Latin America the incidence of different kinds of diseases varies considerably according to social class. As a recent study of Mexico points out:

> the most serious problems of the upper and middle classes in the urban areas of the country are similar to those of the same classes in other parts of the world; cancer, heart diseases and cerebrovascular diseases. On the other hand, the main causes of death in the countryside continue to include two contagious diseases which have been almost eliminated in the urban areas (measles and whooping cough), as well as anaemia, vitamin deficiency and bronchitis. (quoted in Campos, 1981, pp. 634–5).

Since the object of capital in the pharmaceutical industry as in other branches is accumulation and not the production of use values, the direction of R & D is determined by what is profitable. The ill health of the mass of the population in the third world is clearly not as profitable an area as the neurosis of the well-off, both in the advanced capitalist countries and in Latin America and elsewhere, because the poor do not have the income with which to express their preferences in the market place. It is the logic of capitalist accumulation rather than the location of R & D facilities which dictates the direction taken by research in the industry.[14] Having said this, it may also be the case that the lack of local R & D in Latin America makes it more difficult to bring pressure to bear on the companies to undertake less profitable lines of research which may have substantial social benefits.

## 7 LOCALLY OWNED FIRMS IN THE LATIN AMERICAN PHARMACEUTICAL INDUSTRY

Do the above arguments concerning the profitability of TNCs, their use of transfer pricing and the location and the direction of their research and development efforts imply that the performance of locally owned firms in the industry is better and that there are advantages to be gained from having an industry free from TNC control? Unfortunately the extent of denationalisation in the Latin American pharmaceutical industry make it rather difficult to evaluate such a proposition in most countries because of the marginal contribution of local firms. However, in the case of Argentina the existence of a significant and apparently thriving group of local firms does make it possible to consider the question.[15]

Contrary to the situation in other Latin American countries, the pharmaceutical industry in Argentina has not been subject to wholesale denationalisation. Although the share of TNCs increased from 50 per cent in 1962 to 57 per cent in 1972, the share of nationally owned firms continues to be high, even compared to some of the advanced capitalist countries. Perhaps even more significant is the increased participation of local firms amongst the largest fifteen firms in the industry. The number of local firms in this group doubled from three to six, and their market share increased even more from 6 per cent to 15 per cent of the total pharmaceutical market. By 1972, three of the five largest firms in the industry were Argentinian including the largest firm.

What factors made possible this apparently successful perform-

ance by local firms in Argentina, and what are its implications for
other Latin American countries? Chudnovsky attributes the success
of local firms to the declining rate of innovation by the major TNCs
from the early 1960s, and the reduced interest in the Argentinian
market by TNCs generally in the 1960s and early 1970s. In these
circumstances, the weak patent protection given to pharmaceuticals
in Argentina, where patents are only granted on processes and not
products, enabled local firms, through aggressive product differentiation and marketing, often on the basis of imports of active
ingredients from non-patented sources, to compete with the TNCs.

It is necessary to qualify this view by some further comments. Both
the decline in innovation by the major TNCs and the relative lack of
interest in the Argentine market compared to say Brazil or Mexico
are well established, although in other countries in Latin America,
as was argued above, the decline in innovation led to a wave of
investment by minor TNCs, so that it is not sufficient to explain the
success of local firms in Argentina. Moreover, the concept of a
successful performance by local firms needs to be looked at in more
detail. The figures given above imply that small and medium local
firms (those not ranked amongst the first fifteen firms in the
industry), have performed very badly. Their share of the local
market fell from 44 per cent in 1962 to only 28 per cent a decade later
(although of course three firms which would have been classed as
medium-sized in 1962 were large by 1972). Thus, what appears to
have happened is an increasing differentiation of local firms in the
industry between a small number of successful firms and a much
larger number who are doing badly. There is also some reason to
believe that the patent system in Argentina was not a major factor
contributing to the success of local firms. First, other countries such
as Colombia and Venezuela, which have totally foreign dominated
pharmaceutical industries have also only given patent protection to
processes and not products, while the abolition of all patent
protection on pharmaceutical products in Brazil in the late 1960s
appears to have done nothing to halt the trend towards denationalisation in that country. Secondly, the national firms which have been
involved in patent disputes with TNCs have been medium-sized
firms, and none of the six largest local firms have been involved in
such actions. It seems, therefore, that the large local firms have
chosen to stick to the TNC 'rules of the game'.

Indeed, the success of these firms is based on imitating the
strategies of the TNC subsidiaries, and locating market positions

behind the TNCs. Thus, the large local firms are much more active than the large foreign subsidiaries in launching new products and spend proportionately more on advertising (in relation to sales) than the foreign subsidiaries. Thus, in terms of the two classic competitive techniques which characterises the pharmaceutical industry, they outperform the TNCs. That they are able to adopt such a strategy is a reflection of the relatively low costs of launching new products.[16] A comparison of the number of sub-markets in which the leading local and foreign firms operate, indicated that the former were considerably more diversified, while the latter tended to have correspondingly higher market shares in the markets in which they operated. In other words, TNC subsidiaries were more likely to enjoy positions of leadership within the major sub-markets.

Although local firms spend a slightly higher proportion of their sales on R & D, the difference was not large (1.6 per cent compared to 1.1 per cent) and certainly not sufficient to indicate that local firms were engaged in a major research effort. The slightly higher level of R & D is probably related to the larger number of new products being launched by local firms. The amount of real technological innovation being undertaken locally is extremely limited, and these firms depend heavily on sales of products acquired under license which accounted for 42 per cent of the total sales of the six large local firms.

Some of the consequences of the existence of a group of successful national firms in the industry have already been implicit in the discussion of the strategies which they have adopted. One further consequence noted by Chudnovsky is the tendency for the prices charged by local firms to be higher than the prices charged by foreign firms within the group of fifteen largest firms.[17] Thus, it appears that the higher advertising, royalty and research and development costs of local firms are passed on to consumers in the form of higher prices.

In conclusion, therefore, it appears that there are no advantages to the mass of the population from the relative success of large Argentine firms in the industry. The result has been exactly the same pattern of product differentiation and high sales promotion expenditures as in the denationalised pharmaceutical industries of other Latin American countries. Indeed if anything, the result has been to accentuate these patterns because of the imitative strategies of local firms. Moreover, there is no reason to believe that the limited amount of R & D undertaken by local firms is any more directed towards the needs of the Argentinian people than that of the TNCs. All the evidence suggests that it is an adjunct to the strategy of product differentiation. Finally, prices remain high in order to support a local bourgeoisie in this industry. What evidence there is on local firms in other Latin American countries tends to corroborate this view. As Evans (1979, pp. 127–31) emphasises, those local firms which have been able to survive in the Brazilian pharmaceutical industry have done so on the basis of producing imitative products and emphasising their commercial and marketing capabilities.

## 8 THE STATE AND THE PHARMACEUTICAL INDUSTRY

The state plays a particularly important role in relation to the pharmaceutical industry in Latin America, over and above the role which it plays in other branches and in relation to the TNCs in general. The industry is peculiar since an important element in its operations is the legal monopoly granted to individual firms through the patent system. It is also subject to government health and safety regulations to a greater extend than other branches. Moreover, the government is also an important customer of the pharmaceutical industry.

### The role of the patent system

The costs and benefits of the patent system has long been a source of controversy amongst economists, and in recent years the role of the patent system in third world countries has come in for considerable criticism (Vaitsos, 1972; Katz, 1973; Patel, 1974; O'Brien, 1974). The general arguments in favour of granting patents usually fall under one of three headings. First, it is argued that the inventor has a natural right to some return for his efforts and that the patent system is the best way of providing such a return. Second, it is claimed that the patent system is necessary for innovation to take place. Without patent protection it would not be worthwhile undertaking the costs of R & D and technological progress would be slowed down. Finally, it is argued that in the absence of patents innovations would tend to spread more slowly, since without legal protection firms would seek to protect their technical advances through secrecy.

In the case of the pharmaceutical industry in Latin America (in common with many other branches), it has been noted that the bulk of patents have been taken out by TNCs who revalidate their patents locally. In Chile for instance, 98.4 per cent of all pharmaceutical patents were taken out by foreigners (Vaitsos, 1972), while in Mexico the corresponding figure has been estimated at between 85 per cent and 90 per cent (Campos, 1981, p. 614) and in Peru at around 75 per cent (Hulshoff, 1979, p. 181). The fact that in the Latin American countries most patents are totally unrelated to local inventive activity, raises fundamental questions about the justification of the patent system that is usually given. In fact, it is unlikely that the existence or non-existence of the patent system in a third world country can be an important factor determining the flow of innovation which is mainly concentrated in the advanced capitalist countries. Moreover, far from serving to diffuse innovations, there is evidence that the patent system in Latin America is used to restrict the diffusion of technology and to preserve the monopoly rents of the TNCs. In Argentina for instance, it was estimated that fewer than a quarter of the patents held by drug TNCs were exploited, in the sense that the firm concerned undertook local production. Over a third of the patents registered covered processes to produce drugs which were being imported by the local subsidiary from the parent company or from another affiliate (Katz, 1973, pp. 130–1).

In these circumstances, it appears that the benefits from the patent system accrue entirely to the foreign corporations and the costs are borne in the host county. These costs include not only the higher prices of drugs arising from the monopoly position which the patent gives, but also the barriers to increasing local production arising from firms continuing to supply the local market with imported goods which are protected by patents. Indeed, there is a clear conflict here between the global profit-maximising strategies of the TNCs on the one hand, and the interests of local capital and local accumulation on the other. Since the late 1960s a number of Latin American governments have taken steps to reduce the monopoly privileges granted to TNCs through the patent system (UNCTAD, 1981).[18] In Brazil, in 1969, the government abolished patents on both products and processes in the pharmaceutical industry. In the 1960s, the national firms had expressed their opposition to the patent system which they saw as an obstacle to their own technological development, while the TNCs were in favour of the system and opposed its abolition (Bertrero, 1972, p. 85). A year later in Argentina, the Supreme Court ruled that a process patent does not give the holder the right to prevent the import of pharmaceutical products manufactured using the patented process (Chudnovsky, 1979, p. 52). Again, the majority of locally owned firms were opposed to patent protection while the TNCs were the major defenders of the system. In Mexico a new Law of Inventions and Trademarks introduced in 1976 removed patent protection on pharmaceutical products replacing it with a certificate of invention which guarantees a payment to the firm when a competitor uses its patent (Campos, 1981, p. 614). In the Andean Pact countries Decision 85, on patents and trademarks aroused strong opposition from the pharmaceutical TNCs (especially Swiss and German ones). The companies particularly objected to the clause that limited the monopoly privileges of patents to local production, and excluded them from the area of imports (Vaitsos, 1978, pp. 134–5). It is clear from these examples whose interests the patent system has served in the pharmaceutical industry.

## The public sector

In addition to its role in promoting local accumulation, the state has a particular interest in the pharmaceutical industry in a number of Latin American countries because it is an important customer of the industry. In Mexico for instance, almost a quarter of the total consumption of drugs is accounted for by the public sector (Mohar, 1979, table 18). As a consumer therefore, it has a direct interest in the price of pharmaceutical products. In some cases, the state has attempted to intervene more directly in the pharmaceutical industry. In Brazil, the Central de Medicamentos (CEME) was created in 1971 with the declared objective of making basic drugs available to those who could not afford to buy them at commercial prices. Although this did not apparently run contrary to the interests of the pharmaceutical TNCs, since CEME would not compete directly in their market and indeed offered them an apportunity to increase their sales since it only supplied two-thirds of the drugs which it distributed from its own laboratories, nevertheless the TNCs looked with some suspicion on CEME, especially when it began to do some research into local production of pharmaceutical raw materials. Moreover, the entire concept of CEME was a threat to the model of profit-oriented supply of medicine which the TNCs represented. Within four years of its creation, CEME was dismembered with the task of distributing drugs being allocated to the Welfare Ministry and research activities to the Ministry of Industry and Commerce (Evans, 1979, pp. 255–62). In Peru, an attempt to draw up a list of 180 generic products which would be distributed through the Ministry of Health at prices well below those of equivalent branded products met with a brief period of success in the early 1970s, but ran into problems within a short time in the face of opposition from the TNCs and an unsympathetic response from the medical profession (Hulshoff, 1979, pp. 181–4).

One Latin American country which has achieved unequivocal success in the introduction of a 'generic' policy in Cuba. Here, of course, the entire industry is state owned and the implementation of a generic policy did not give rise to any difficulties (UNCTAD, 1981a, pp. 10–11).

The various experiences of state intervention in the Latin American pharmaceutical industry have not fundamentally altered the structure of the industry or the behaviour of the leading firms. Despite their strong support for patent protection in the region, the TNCs have not had their operations adversely affected when the patent system has been weakened. Moreover, as innovation becomes less important in the international industry, the competitive advantage of TNCs is likely to be based increasingly on their marketing techniques and brand names, and the role of patents may decline. Where state intervention appears to be undermining the profit-oriented system of health care on which the transnational pharmaceutical operation is based, it has been possible for TNCs to mobilise in opposition to the new organisation and maintain their dominant position.

## 9 THE PHARMACEUTICAL INDUSTRY AND THE 'STYLE OF DEVELOPMENT'

Although, unlike cars, pharmaceutical products can be considered necessities not luxuries, the implications of the type of development brought about by the internationalisation of capital in the pharmaceutical industry can be questioned in much the same as was done in the last chapter. Here, it is necessary to step outside the narrow confines of the specific branch and locate it within a broader socio-economic context. One aspect of this which has already been mentioned is the possible divergence between the types of drug produced by TNCs and the objective needs of the Latin American countries in terms of the incidence of disease and the causes of death. Whereas in countries with a relatively equitable distribution of income and a high overall level of income per capita, the divergence between objective health needs and those expressed through the market are likely to be reduced (particularly if there is a socialised medical system), in the Latin American countries, with highly inequitable income distribution and low per capita income levels this divergence is large.

Because drugs are not luxuries, high prices for pharmaceutical products bear particularly heavily on the lower income groups. These groups spend proportionately more of their incomes on pharmaceuticals than higher income groups and are also more likely to have to pay for their own remedies.[19] As was indicated above, high prices are directly related to the competitive practices of the TNCs in this industry. The lack of price competition keeps prices high, often enabling the highest priced products to obtain dominant market positions. The emphasis on product differentiation and sales promotion substantially increases costs above those which would be required to produce non-branded generic equivalents, while at the same time enabling firms to obtain high profit margins. The implications of this in a Latin American context has been pointed out by Ledogar:

> Free samples, detailmen, unnecessary duplications and combinations, and massive publicity efforts are standard techniques of the pharmaceutical industry the world over. But in the context of Brazil . . . these sales practices help keep the cost of drugs generally out of reach of the majority, while encouraging irrational overconsumption among the well to do. (Ledogar, 1975, p. 24)

A further feature of pharmaceutical company behaviour which is likely to have particularly adverse effects for the poorest sections of the population when they are able to obtain drugs, is the practice of providing inadequate directions and counter-indications concerning the use of their products in Latin America. The poor are more likely to acquire drugs 'over the counter' without qualified medical advice, and because most drugs are available in this way the lack of adequate directions is potentially extremely dangerous.[20]

The penetration of the international pharmaceutical industry in Latin America has also led to the displacement of traditional herbal remedies by drugs developed in the advanced capitalist countries. This has led some commentators to argue that this has adverse effects because a cheap, locally available medicinal source is replaced in the rural areas by much more expensive, modern drugs which have to be brought into the area from the outside (Hushloff, 1979a). The publicity campaigns of the TNCs lead to a loss of confidence in the traditional remedies and the increased cost of drugs is not matched by any improvement in the health of the population. Certainly, in countries such as Peru and Mexico the potentialities of the vast wealth of traditional herbal medications remain largely unexplored.

The most important way in which the pharmaceutical industry affects the pattern of development in Latin America is its bias towards curative rather than preventive medicine. It has been estimated that 80 per cent or more of the significant diseases in the third world fall into two main groups: nutritional deficiencies and communicable diseases such as intestinal infections and infestations, acute chest infections and other specific communicable diseases (malaria, bilharzia, tuberculosis, leprosy) (Segall, 1975, p. 5). Most of these diseases are preventable by means which are technically fairly simple, and which are generally much cheaper than curative services. These include measures to improve agricultural and nutritional practices, improved sanitation and water supply, personal hygiene, control of mosquitoes, and so on and immunisation. The returns to such preventive measures in terms of improvements in health, particularly in rural areas, are likely to be much greater than in the introduction of the latest patented drugs.[21] However, the major interest of the pharmaceutical companies is in a curative approach, and the vast expenditure of TNCs on sales promotion ensures that the model of health care in which they are allocated pride of place is never seriously challenged. As a result, a far higher proportion of current expenditure on health goes on drugs in Latin America than in the advanced capitalist countries.[22] A very rough estimate suggests that the total expenditure of the Brazilian government on public health in 1970 was only some 50 per cent more than the amount which the local pharmaceutical industry would have spend on sales promotion in the same year.[23] The relative importance of the accumulation of a handful of phar-

maceutical TNCs and the health of the mass of the Brazilian people
are vividly illustrated by these figures.


NOTES

1. Between 1955 and 1960, domestic sales by US pharmaceutical companies grew
   by 4.8 per cent per annum while foreign sales increased by more than 20 per
   cent per annum (calculated from Silverman, 1976, p. 119).
2. This is usually attributed to one of two factors, the introduction of tougher
   regulatory controls on the industry and the 'exhaustion' of the wave of
   innovations based on antibiotics which made further innovation more difficult
   and costly. The relative importance of these two factors is a matter of
   controversy and will not be discussed here (see UNCTC, 1979, pp. 61–5).
3. It is possible that the classification in fact exaggerates the level of development
   of the pharmaceutical industry in these countries but it does provide a broadly
   correct stratification of the Latin American countries in terms of the
   development of the industry.
4. This refers to firms which were not amongst the fifteen top pharmaceutical
   companies in terms of world-wide sales.
5. Silverman and Lee (1974) quote a former research director of Squibb who
   estimates that only a quarter of the research carried out by the firm was related
   to 'worth while' projects while the remainder was on 'me too' drugs and
   unimportant combinations, a situation which he believed to be typical of the
   industry as a whole (quoted in UNCTC, 1979, p. 46).
6. In Argentina, the market share of new products in total sales was 13 per cent
   for nationally owned firms and 6.4 per cent for foreign owned firms, amongst
   the leading fifteen firms in the industry in 1972 (Chudnovsky, 1979, table 2).
   This was much higher than the corresponding figures in the US (Slatter, 1977,
   table 3.20). In 1972, 275 new drugs were launched in Argentina (Chudnovsky,
   1979, p. 49). This was more than the number launched in any West European
   market except Spain in 1969 (Reekie, 1975, table 4.3).
7. The situation is different in Brazil because royalty payments by majority
   foreign-owned subsidiaries are not permitted.
8. In Colombia, the tariff on imported intermediate products for the pharmaceutical industry was only 1 per cent (Vaitsos, 1974, p. 91).
9. Although evidence of transfer pricing has also been found in other industries in
   Latin America, the levels of overpricing which have been estimated are less
   spectacular than in the pharmaceutical industry. It has been suggested by
   some critics that the extent of transfer pricing in the pharmaceutical industry
   has been exaggerated by the use of prices charged by Italian firms, which did
   not have to bear the R & D costs of developing new drugs, as the basis of the
   international price. However as the following discussion indicates there are
   strong theoretical reasons for expecting the industry to be characterised by
   relatively high levels of over pricing.
10. For example in Argentina, the declared profit of local firms was 17.9 per cent
    on net worth in 1972 compared to 5.2 per cent for TNC subsidiaries
    (Chudnovsky, 1979, p. 53). In Brazil, the average profit rate of three large

local firms in the industry was 37.4 per cent in 1970–73 compared to 20.8 per cent for fourteen foreign subsidiaries (von Doellinger and Cavalcanti 1975, table 4.13).

11. See Gereffi, forthcoming, table 6. The average pre-tax cost of a successful new drug in the United States increased from an average of US $1.3 million in 1960 to US $24 million in 1973.

12. An earlier figure of £1 million is quoted by Davies, 1967, p. 35.

13. This is a point particularly emphasised by Hymer in a number of his works, (see Hymer, 1979, especially chs 2 and 6).

14. It is interesting to note in this context that the Labour Party in Britain expressed concern that 'at present commercial criteria set the main direction' in pharmaceutical R & D. This is clearly not because R & D is not located in Britain, which is the home country of a number of pharmaceutical TNCs, but because of the profit motive in the industry (Reekie, 1975, p. 57).

15. Chudnovsky (1979) has studied 'The Challenge by Domestic Enterprises to the Transnational Corporations' Domination' in the Argentinian pharmaceutical industry. Unless otherwise indicated, the information in the following paragraphs is derived from this study or an earlier one by Katz (1973).

16. In the 1960s, it was estimated that it cost US $10 000–15 000 to launch a new product on the Argentinian market (Katz, 1973, p. 168).

17. The basis of the comparison appears to be rather crude but it is at least suggestive. (See Chudnovksy, 1979, table 3.)

18. This should be seen in the context of a general trend in the direction of more restrictive policies towards TNCs in this period. See below Chapter 7.

19. See Laurell *et al.* (1979), for an analysis of the patterns of consumption and ways of acquiring medicines for different social groups in Mexico City.

20. In Mexico for instance, virtually all pharmaceutical products are freely available through pharmacies. The only exceptions are psychotropic drugs, amphetamines and some tranquillisers (Mohar, 1979, p. 48).

21. This is illustrated by the experience of Cuba since the Revolution where, as a result of much greater emphasis on a preventive service, infectious and parasitic diseases have been virtually eliminated (UNCTAD, 1980a, p. 6).

22. 26.4 per cent in Venezuela as opposed to 8.7 per cent in the UK in the early 1960s (Heller, 1977, table 2).

23. Federal expenditures on public health in 1970 were US $144 million (Dos Santos, 1974, p. 488). The value of pharmaceutical production was US $471 million (UNCTAD, 1975, table A1) and on the basis of figures for other Latin American countries, sales promotion may have accounted for 20 to 25 per cent of the value of output.

# 5 A New International Division of Labour? TNCs and Industrial Exports

## 1 INTRODUCTION

As the previous chapters have shown, the great surge in direct foreign investment by TNCs in Latin America in the post-war period was closely linked to the strategy of import-substituting industrialisation. Industrial production as a whole was geared primarily to the domestic market, and most TNC investment was undertaken to meet local demand. Since the mid-1960s, the contradictions of this strategy of import substitution have become increasingly evident. Capital accumulation generated imports of equipment, raw materials and intermediate inputs on a major scale, as well as increasing outflows of profits, royalties and interest payments. These led to increasing foreign indebtedness and frequent balance of payments crises which forced the state (often at the behest of the International Monetary Fund) to intervene to interrupt the accumulation process. At the same time, the high costs and heavy protection given to the new industries led to high prices, which, combined with the low income of the mass of the population (particularly in the rural areas), restricted the internal market for consumer goods. Finally, the limited employment generated by industry created social problems with the rapid expansion of marginality in the urban areas. This became a major concern in the 1960s when it came to be seen as a threat to political stability and continued capital accumulation in the region.

Faced with these internal contradictions, the state in most Latin American countries attempted to give accumulation a new impetus through a strategy of export diversification and international expansion.[1] This strategy, referred to as sub-imperialism by some critics (Marini, 1972) would, its advocates claimed, lead to a restructuring of Latin American industry, with consequent benefits in terms of productive efficiency, the balance of payments and employment (Balassa, 1973; Schydlowsky, 1972).

The strategy was pursued in two distinct ways. First, an attempt was made to re-orient existing industry towards foreign markets, both within Latin America and internationally. Second, in a number of countries steps were taken to attract entirely new firms specifically to produce for the world market. The re-orientation of industry towards exports was promoted through a variety of measures – tax exemptions, duty drawbacks and subsidies for export of manufactured goods, frequent adjustment of the exchange rate to offset domestic inflation (particularly in Brazil and Colombia) and the provision of special credit facilities to exporters.[2] Steps were also taken to force increased exports by certain industries and firms, particularly the subsidiaries of TNCs. This approach has been used most extensively in the motor industry, particularly in Brazil, Mexico and Argentina, and since it is specifically directed at increasing the exports of foreign firms deserves particular attention here. In all three countries in the 1970s, subsidiaries of motor industry TNCs have ranked amongst the largest exporters of manufactures and have accounted for a significant share of manufactured exports.

The pioneer in this field was Mexico where in the late 1960s, the government began to require vehicle assemblers to cover an increasing proportion of the foreign exchange needed to import parts and components, with exports. Thus, each firm's production quotas for the expanding domestic market was tied to an improved export performance (Jenkins, 1979b, ch. 5; Bennett and Sharpe, 1979). In 1973, the Argentinian government introduced a similar but even more ambitious programme whereby the companies had to export vehicles equal to an increasing proportion of domestic sales (Jenkins, forthcoming). In 1972, the Brazilian government negotiated the first of the special Fiscal Benefits for Exports (BEFIEX) programmes with Ford and between then and 1978, all the TNCs in the Brazilian terminal industry with the exception of Toyota signed such agreements. In return for a commitment to export a certain amount over a ten year period the firms were granted tax concessions and the necessary investment authorisations by the Brazilian government. In contrast to the legislation in

Argentina and Mexico which applied across the board, the Brazilians approached each case individually, taking into account the particular national and international situation of each firm (Muller and Moore, 1978). Such arrangements have also been extended to other industries with a significant TNC participation, such as photo-copying machines and tractors in Mexico (ECLA, 1976, p. 175).

The development of entirely new industries to supply world markets was promoted by the establishment of free production zones. By the mid-1970s, such zones were reported in eight Latin American countries, Brazil, Colombia, the Dominican Republic, El Salvador, Guatemala, Haiti, Mexico and Panama, while five more countries had free production zones under construction (Fröbel *et al.*, 1980, table 3.3). These zones are characterised by the complete freedom of capital to bring in machinery, inputs and manpower and to take out profits without any of the restrictions normally imposed by the local state. Equally, they are often free to exploit local labour without having to put up with unions, social security benefits etc. In addition to offering tax incentives and subsidies, the state may also provide subsidised inputs (for example, water and electricity) or buildings at low rents.

Latin American exports of manufactures have indeed expanded rapidly since the mid-1960s. Between 1965 and 1975, they grew at over 17 per cent per annum in real terms and increased their share of total exports from 8 per cent to 22 per cent over the decade (ECLA, 1976a, table 2). This had led some commentators to speak of the 'post import substitution era' in Latin America (Baer and Samuelson, 1977), while others refer to a new international division of labour in which Latin America (along with other third world countries) is becoming a supplier of industrial goods for world markets (Vuskovic, 1979; Fröbel et al., 1980).

## The growth of exports – the role of the TNC

To what extent have TNCs participated in this growth of exports, and how have they responded to this new pattern of accumulation in Latin America? There are strong '*a priori*' grounds for expecting TNCs to play a leading role within an export expansion strategy. Many of the obstacles to exporting manufactured products which are often noted such as the lack of knowledge of foreign markets, difficulties of access to distribution channels or lack of adequate finance, do not apply to subsidiaries which are part of the world-wide operations of large corporations. Equally, foreign subsidiaries produce products with brand names and trade marks which are well known in international markets.

There is little doubt that TNCs do account for a significant share of the region's industrial exports, with between 40 per cent and 50 per cent of the total in each of the four major exporting countries in the mid-1970s (Table 5.1). Indeed their share of manufactured exports was, if anything, slightly higher than their share in industrial output, although not nearly as great as suggested by some of their supporters.[3] Unfortunately, there is little data available over a period of several years, which would make it possible to compare the share of foreign and local firms in the growth of exports. Data on the Latin American exports of US majority owned affiliates indicates that their share has been on the decline since the mid-1960s, falling from a peak of 40 per cent in 1967 to under 20 per cent in 1974 (Nayyar, 1978, table 4). It is not clear, however, whether this has been the result of growing exports by local firms or other foreign subsidiaries. Data on Mexico, however, suggests a slight increase in the share of all foreign firms from 38.5 per cent in 1970 to 42.4 per cent in 1977 (Jenkins, 1979b, table 11.2; Ramirez de la O., 1981, table 2).

More detailed analysis of the export performance of TNCs suggests that they have not played a major role in re-orienting Latin American manufacturing towards international markets. The bulk of sales by TNCs in the major Latin American countries are to the domestic market, and exports account for a small fraction of total output. In the early and mid-1970s, this ratio was well below 10 per cent in all the countries which accounted for the greater part of the region's manufactured exports (see Table 5.2). The same was true of

TABLE 5.1    *Share of foreign firms in manufactured exports from selected Latin American countries*

|  | Year | Share of exports |
|---|---|---|
| Argentina | 1973 | 42% |
| Brazil | 1974 | 40% |
| Colombia | 1974 | 50% |
| Mexico | 1974 | 50% |

SOURCES    UNCTAD, (1981b); New farmer (1980); ECLA/UNCTC (1979); Jenkins (1979b).

TABLE 5.2     *Exports as a proportion of total sales of foreign subsidiaries in selected Latin American countries*

| Country | Year | % Exports | Universe |
|---------|------|-----------|----------|
| Argentina | 1972 | 5.7% | 130 firms with > 80% foreign ownership |
| Brazil | 1973 | 7.9% | 133 firms with > 25% foreign ownership |
| Colombia | 1974 | 6.5% | 374 firms with > 0% foreign ownership |
| Mexico | 1970 | 2.8% | All firms with > 15% foreign ownership |

SOURCES  INTI (1974, table 11); Van Doellinger and Cavalcanti (1975, table IV 9); ECLA/UNCTC (1979, table 19); Fajnzylber and Tarrago (1975, table 12).

US subsidiaries in the region as a whole. Indeed, despite the rapid growth of manufactured exports generally since the 1960s, the share of exports in sales by US subsidiaries in fact declined from 6.2 per cent in 1966 to 6.0 per cent a decade later.

Even when compared to locally owned firms, the export performance of TNCs is unremarkable. A detailed analysis of 500 firms in Brazil found no statistically significant difference between the proportion of sales exported by local firms and foreign subsidiaries (Newfarmer and Marsh, 1981, ch. 4). A study of over 600 Mexican firms found that, far from TNCs performing better than local firms, the reverse was true in both those industries usually classified as traditional (food, drink, textiles, clothing and footwear, wood furniture and leather) and intermediate industries (pulp and paper, rubber, chemicals, petroleum and coal derivatives, non-metallic minerals and basic metals) (Jenkins, 1979a). Even in the engineering industries where the advantage of TNCs in terms of brand names and distribution channels is marked, there was no significant difference in export performance. Clearly, TNCs are far from spearheading a transition from import substitution to a new international division of labour in Latin America. In order to understand why this is the case, it is necessary to look more closely at the strategies of international production pursued by TNCs in the region.

## 2 FROM IMPORT SUBSTITUTION TO EXPORT EXPANSION

*TNC strategies and exports of manufactures*

Although the search for cheap labour has been the strategy most commented upon in discussion of TNC exports from underdeveloped countries, this is by no means the only one involved, and as will be seen in the next part of this chapter it is of relatively limited importance in Latin America. This is not to deny that TNCs exporting from the region benefit from the lower wages there, but simply that this is not the primary motive for export in many cases, and that in the absence of other factors, such exports would not be undertaken. Before analysing the consequences of TNC exports from Latin America then, it is necessary to consider in some detail the different strategies of TNCs in the region.

In analysing exports of manufactures by TNCs from their Latin American subsidiaries, one is looking at internal decisions of the parent company about the allocation of its global production and sales. It is not simply a question of market forces determining the international division of labour. TNCs *are* affected by these forces, but their decisions are influenced by a constellation of other factors and subject to different constraints from those of the one-country firms of orthodox trade theory. In international trade, as in other areas, TNCs aim to utilise their global network of affiliates to maximum advantage with a view to the profitability and accumulation of the total system. It is in this context that the growth of TNC exports from Latin America since the mid-1960s must be analysed.

Two features of TNC exports of manufactures from Latin America stand out. First, they are concentrated in a small number of branches of industry (see Table 5.3). In both Brazil and Mexico, around three-quarters of exports by TNCs were in chemicals, non-electrical and electrical machinery and transport equipment. In Colombia, there was a slightly different pattern with chemicals, metal products, paper and cement accounting for over 60 per cent of total exports by foreign firms, rising to three-quarters if food products are included. For US majority owned affiliates in Latin America, 55 per cent of exports were accounted for by chemicals, the two machinery industry and transport equipment, with a further 24 per cent coming from the food industry (US Department of Commerce, *Survey of Current Business*, March, 1977). In general, foreign firms have below average shares of exports in the traditional industries and concentrate on the more technologically advanced sector which are the same branches in which the bulk of direct foreign investment to serve the domestic market has been located.

Second, TNC exports are directed primarily towards other Latin American countries. Data for a number of countries in the early 1970s suggests that at least half of manufactured exports by foreign subsidiaries go to other countries within the region, except in the

TABLE 5.3    *Distribution of exports by foreign firms by sector of origin, 1974 ( %)*

|  | Brazil[1] | Colombia | Mexico |
|---|---|---|---|
| Food | } 12.7 | 14.8 | 1.9 |
| Drink |  | – | 1.4 |
| Tobacco |  | 2.0 | – |
| Textiles | } 6.9 | –[2] | 0.6 |
| Clothing and footwear |  | 3.2 | 3.3 |
| Leather |  | 1.5 | 0.1 |
| Wood | – | 1.3 | 0.1 |
| Furniture | – | 0.1 | – |
| Pulp and Paper | 0.3 | 9.0 | 0.4 |
| Printing and Publishing |  | 0.2 | 4.3 |
| Rubber | } 13.0 | 2.6 | 0.5 |
| Chemicals |  | 28.8 | 25.7 |
| Petroleum and Coal derivatives |  | – | 0.2 |
| Non-metallic minerals | 0.3 | 13.4 | 1.6 |
| Basic metals | 5.4 | 2.6 | 3.9 |
| Metal products | 0.4 | 11.1 | 1.9 |
| Non-electrical machinery | 12.8 | 3.1 | 7.0 |
| Electrical machinery | 10.8 | 3.8 | 11.1 |
| Transport equipment | 37.4 | 1.7 | 33.2 |
| Other manufacturing | – | 1.2 | 2.6 |
| TOTAL | 100.0 | 100.0 | 100.0 |

[1] Refers to the exports of 79 largest exporters amongst the country's largest TNCs.
[2] Exports of textiles excluded because other sources indicate that the leading firms in this sector have a minimal foreign shareholding but have been included because the data covers all firms with any foreign capital.
SOURCES   Garcia (1978, table F.1); ECLA/UNCTC (1979, table 19); Jenkins, (1979b, Table 3.4).

case of Mexico where the proportion is only about a third (Table 5.4). In all cases, the proportion of intra-regional exports by TNCs is significantly higher than their share in the exports of locally owned firms.

*Regional export strategies.* These two characteristics of TNC exports reflect the strategies which have been implemented by such firms in the region. A number of companies have developed regional strategies, integrating the operations of their affiliates in different Latin American countries. This has been carried out largely under the auspices of complementarity agreements negotiated within the framework of the Latin American Free Trade Association

TABLE 5.4 *Share of manufactured exports going to other Latin American countries ( %)*

|  | Year | Exports by TNCs | Total manufactured exports |
|---|---|---|---|
| Argentina | 1972 | 82 | 39 |
| Brazil | 1971 | 72 | 31 |
| Colombia | 1973 | 54[1] | 25 |
| Mexico | 1974 | 32 | 19 |
| Peru | 1973 | 71 | 42 |

\* Data for TNC exports from Brazil, Colombia and Peru refer to samples of firms.
[1] Unweighted average share of exports going to other Latin American countries for sample firms.
SOURCES INTI (1974, p. 39); Newfarmer (1977, p. 380); Vaitsos (1978, table 16); Jenkins (1979a, table 6); ECLA (1976a); ECLA (1976, table 8).

(LAFTA). These agreements provided for preferential trade in particular branches of industry amongst the participating countries, and were intended to promote regional specialisation within each branch. The TNCs themselves played a major role in the development of these agreements and the first to be signed, covering machines for statistical processing and perforated cards, was directly promoted by IBM. Moreover, the most active participants in the negotiations on sectoral concessions were TNC subsidiaries (Vaitsos, 1978, table 58). It has also been widely argued that the TNCs are in a better position than local firms to take advantage of the partial measures of trade liberalisation which such regional schemes have involved.

Such exports fall into two main groups. Some firms allocate particular product lines (or models) to their subsidiaries in different Latin American countries, which then exchange products between themselves, often under the aegis of a LAFTA complementarity agreement. Olivetti, with subsidiaries in Argentina, Brazil and Mexico is a classic example of this strategy. It produces calculators in Argentina, electric and standard typewriters in Brazil and portable and semi-portable typewriters in Mexico. Similarly, Cyanamid specialises in the production of medical products for veterinary use in Argentina and antibiotics for human use in Brazil, exchanging these products between the two countries.

A somewhat different strategy occurs when firms specialise in the production of different parts and components, rather than finished products, in different countries of the region. This is only possible in those industries in which the labour process is of a discontinuous nature, and where it is therefore possible for the finished product to be assembled in each country with parts and components of different origin. The strategy has been used by firms in the electrical industry and in the motor industry. It was particularly important in the 1960s and early 1970s in trade in vehicle parts between Argentina and Chile.

Of course not all exports to regional markets are of the bilateral kind. The major Latin American countries each try to establish a sphere of influence in its smaller neighbour, Mexico in Cental America, and Brazil and Argentina in Bolivia, Paraguay and Uruguay. This is sometimes reflected in the strategies of the TNCs which use a major Latin American country as a base from which to supply its local neighbours. Such a strategy usually involves exports of finished products since the recipient countries have a relatively low level of industrialisation. Ford, for instance, exports to Central America from Mexico, to Bolivia from Brazil and to Uruguay from Argentina. Pharmaceutical TNCs with subsidiaries in Mexico have tended to regard the Central American countries as an extension of the Mexican market and to supply them with finished products from Mexico.

*International export strategies.* Some TNCs have gone beyond regional specialisation to integrate Latin America into their global operations. Again, two major variants of this strategy exist. Latin American countries may either be allocated the production of particular product lines or models for international markets, or produce certain parts and components. In the early 1970s, Volkswagen sourced its Safari model in Mexico for world-wide distribution, and since stopping production of the Beetle in West Germany, it has also been sourced from Brazil and Mexico. IBM follows a similar strategy, exporting electric typewriters from Mexico and printers, card sorters and copiers from Argentina. A number of car firms have sourced parts and components from Latin America. General Motors in Mexico for instance, exports engines not only to the United States but also to its affiliates in Canada, Australia, South Africa and the United Kingdom. Fiat exports engines from Brazil to Italy, and Mercedez Benz exports parts from its Brazilian subsidiary to the United States.

A further strategy which had led TNCs to export from Latin America in some branches is a desire to utilise excess capacity. It has been observed that TNCs often 'build ahead of demand' in setting up new plants in developing countries (Fajnzylber, 1970) and thus tend to suffer from excess capacity. This is particularly likely in continuous process industries where there are significant plant indivisibilities.[4] As a result, it may be profitable to utilise excess capacity for export even though the prices received may not cover average costs. It is not surprising, then, to find that in a number of econometric studies of manufactured exports from Latin American countries the level of capacity utilisation has been found to be a significant explanatory variable (see Felix, 1974, on Argentia; Tyler, 1973 on Brazil and Wogart, 1978 on Colombia).

The existence of an international system made up of different national states with contradictory economic policies gives rise to another export strategy by TNCs in some cases. This is aimed not at increasing revenues or reducing production costs, but at reducing the tax burden which the TNC has to bear in its global operations. This involves utilising tax havens to declare profits, and taking advantage of the various tax rebates and subsidies offered by governments. Squibb in Argentina has been cited as an example of the exploitation of tax conditions in international trade. The bulk of the Argentine subsidiary's exports go to Ireland (a tax haven) which acts as an intermediate point *en route* to the final destination, the United States (Katz and Albin, 1978, pp. 42–3). Two Mexican TNC subsidiaries in the steroid hormone industry routed a significant share of their total exports, one via the Bahamas and the other Puerto Rico. These are also tax havens and there is concrete evidence of underpricing of these exports (see above Table 4.8).

Where transport costs and tariff barriers are low relative to the export incentives and tax rebates offered by government, this may also provide a stimulus to trade even where there are no savings in production costs. For example, as a result of export incentives, Mexican transistors have been found to be cheaper than the local equivalent in Brazil, while in Mexico, Brazilian transistors are cheaper than the Mexican (Tomasini, 1977, p. 135). The general point is that with export incentives estimated at a fifth or more of the value of the product, if cost differentials amongst Latin American countries are small, an increase in the value of bilateral trade increases the subsidy received by the TNC and hence its post-tax profits.

*Some implications of export expansion and the role of TNCs*

The implications of TNC exports from Latin America depend in part on the type of export strategy pursued. As has already been

indicated, a substantial proportion of TNCs exports of manufactures occur within Latin America, indicating a strategy of
regional specialisation. A major motive of such a strategy for firms is
to enable their subsidiaries to achieve greater scales of production,
while at the same time being able to sell on the protected market of
each country. However, this does not necessarily lead to the
achievement of any of the three objectives of export promotion
policies mentioned above – lower prices, an improvement in the
balance of payments or greater employment.

Intra-regional exports tend to be concentrated in the more
capital-intensive branches of industry. Studies in a number of Latin
American countries have indicated that exports to other LAFTA
countries or to underdeveloped countries generally (the bulk of
which are to Latin America) generate less employment than exports
to the advanced capitalist countries (see the Latin American case
studies in Krueger *et al.*, 1981). Perhaps not surprisingly, since such
exports are an extension of the import-substitution strategy on a
regional scale, exports to Latin America often appear to be as
capital intensive as import substitution.

The balance of payments effects of regional exports (except
possibly where these are directed to small neighbouring markets
where they may permit further import substitution at the regional
level) are also likely to be insignificant. It is often the case that intra-
regional exports are directly compensated for by corresponding
imports. The LAFTA complementarity schemes provide a clear
example of this, in which a company exports some products from
one Latin American country while at the same time importing
another product of roughly similar value. Moreover, even when this
is not taken into account there is reason to suspect that intra-
regional exports may have a higher import content on average than
exports to the rest of the world.[5]

The main rationale of such schemes, however, is not primarily
their impact on employment or the balance of payments (except
indirectly in the case of small national markets where they may
permit further import substitution at the regional level) but rather
to permit a rationalisation of production, eliminating costly
duplication of activities and permitting economies of scale to be
realised. The tendency for the LAFTA complementarity agreements to be concentrated on a relatively small number of branches,
primarily in electrical products and electronics and in the chemical
industry, which are generally highly oligopolistic and dominated by

TNCs, raises further questions. Far from leading to increased competition, tariff reductions under such circumstances may simply serve to consolidate the dominant position of a small group of TNCs.

A detailed study of six of the twenty-one LAFTA complementarity agreements revealed that TNCs accounted for 97 per cent of trade in office equipment (agreements nos. 10 and 11), 100 per cent in electronic valves (agreement no. 2) and over 87 per cent in electronics and electrical communications (agreements nos. 4, 12 and 19) (Tomasini, 1977, p. 139). The same study concluded that the principal beneficiaries of these agreements were the participating firms themselves, which were able to specialise in particular production lines, thus achieving longer production runs, increasing capacity utilisation and reducing fixed costs. Nevertheless, the oligopolistic structures of the markets in which these firms operated inhibited any reduction in prices. In some cases, such oligopolistic positions were reinforced with one firm accounting for more than 60 per cent of trade under the relevant agreements in both office equipment and electronic valves (Tomasini, 1977, p. 140). Indeed, there is reason to believe that the mechanisms of the complementarity agreements were used by firms to restrict competition. In pharmaceuticals certain products were excluded from the agreements to avoid competition. Another way in which competition was restricted was to reserve the widest possible area for an agreement including products not necessarily included subsequently in the agreement. This effectively prevented trade in these products being liberalised except under a sectoral agreement. Moreover, the inclusion of products in an agreement was no guarantee that trade would take place and indeed there was trade in only a minority of the products included (Vaitsos, 1978, pp. 176–7).

The strategy of international integration has been pursued most actively in the motor industry. This has, of course, been brought about primarily by the particular policies which have been applied to TNCs in this industry to force them to export. However as was indicated in Chapter 3 it has also been made possible by developments in the international motor industry which have led to increased integration of their international operations by the major TNCs. The growth of such exports are unlikely to have a substantial effect on employment because, again, the major sectors involved are capital intensive. Indeed, the industries usually considered as labour intensive (textiles, clothing, wood products, furniture and fixtures, and leather products) accounted for only 6.9 per cent of all

TNC exports of manufactures from Brazil, 6.0 per cent in Colombia
and 4.1 per cent in Mexico in 1974 (Table 5.3).

In considering the impact of such exports on the balance of payments
one must remember the substantial imported content of many of the
products exported. Not only have a number of studies found that
TNCs tend to make greater use of imported inputs than local firms
in Latin America (see below Chapter 8), but it is also the case that
TNC exports tend to be concentrated in those industrial branches
which have the highest direct and indirect import requirements.
Moreover, there is evidence to suggest that exports tend to have a
higher import content than production for the domestic market, not
surprisingly in view of the facilities which are usually offered to
exporters such as 'drawbacks' on import duties or permission for
temporary duty-free imports. In fact there is good reason to believe
from the scanty evidence that exists, that in those Latin American
countries where import substitution has led to a relatively low level
of import content in production for the domestic market, export
production continues to be highly import intensive. In Brazil in the
late 1960s, the estimated average import content of manufactured
exports was 28 per cent while for certain products it was much
higher – for example condensers 47 per cent, electric typewriters 44
per cent, punching machines 42 per cent and electronic valves 36
per cent (Fajnzylber, 1970, appendix 6). In the early 1970s, the
same situation persisted with an average import content which
ranged from a fifth to a third of the value of exports (Garcia, 1978,
table 1.2). In Colombia, most manufactured exports were under the
Plan Vallejo, which permitted duty-free imports. In the early 1970s,
the average import content was around 40 per cent (Wogart, 1978,
table 40). In Mexico, evidence on a number of products typically
exported by TNCs showed low levels of local content, 26–42 per
cent for photocopiers, 24–44 per cent for electronic calculators, 58
per cent for electromechanical cash registers, 55 per cent for telex
equipment and 60 per cent for electric typewriters. In some cases,
exported products have a lower local content than the minimum
which is legally required for sales to the domestic market (Jenkins,
1979, pp. 200–2).

A further point is suggested by the experience of the Latin
America motor industry, where increased exports by the TNCs
have been accompanied by pressures to reduce or keep constant the
level of local content required in the industry. It is necessary to take
account of this lower local content of production for the domestic

market, to calculate the net effect of the increase in exports, if, as seems to be the case, the two are linked.

*Drawbacks for the exporting country*

International integration along these lines has wider implications, however. The gearing of production to world markets contributes to the process of standardisation which the internationalisation of capital is bringing about. It makes necessary both the latest products and the latest production techniques in order to be able to supply world markets. Thus, in the Mexican motor industry, for example, it has been pointed out that the strategy of export promotion requires that parts and components correspond to the models and makes produced in the major international markets, and that this is a constraint both on the rationalisation of the structure of the indstry and on the possibility of freezing models for a number of years to reduce costs of cars sold on the local market (Bennett and Sharpe, 1979). Similarly, the most modern means of production are required irrespective of costs. In Brazil for instance, during the 1950s when the major emphasis of government policy was on import substitution, there was widespread use of second-hand machinery. In the late 1960s and early 1970s, when the expansion and diversification of exports became a priority, accumulation was based primarily on new equipment (Baer quoted in Mathias, 1978, pp. 43–4).

In the case of international integration based on the specialisation in certain parts or components, further problems arise. Such parts are usually highly specific in nature and often the only outlet for them is the parent TNC and its other affiliates. In other words, there is no international market for these parts on which they can be sold. Thus continued exports are entirely dependent on internal decisions of the TNCs about the location of international production. All these factors represent an extension of the internationalisation of capital, which binds the Latin American economy much more closely to the world economy than was the case in the import-substitution period.

Exports to small neighbouring markets and exports to utilise excess capacity are both extremely limited as far as the long term growth of exports is concerned. The former strategy can only be maintained as long as the recipient country does not pursue an import-substitution policy of its own for the product concerned.

Thus, for example, pharmaceutical TNCs in Mexico have seen the Central American export market for finished products contract as the countries of the region begin to develop their own pharmaceutical industries. In any case, the fact that these markets are small means that they will always remain marginal from the point of view of the exporting subsidiaries.

The use of excess capacity for export is also only a short-term expedient. If, as was suggested above, excess capacity comes about from TNCs when they enter a particular market building ahead of demand, then as demand grows in the local market, the margin of capacity available for export is reduced. Thus, only with import substitution in new products creating excess capacity in new areas can the level of exports be maintained. This is confirmed by evidence from Brazil which indicates that by the mid-1970s capacity utilisation had lost its significance as a variable explaining the growth of exports, suggesting that it is only an important factor at an early stage in the development of manufactured exports (Tyler, 1976).

The drawbacks of the strategies of minimisation of global tax liabilities and maximisation of subsidies are obvious. Where TNCs underprice exports from Latin America in order to transfer (undeclared) profits to a tax haven, the exporting country is adversely affected in two main ways. There is a corresponding reduction in the foreign exchange generated by these exports and there is also a reduction in the revenue which the government receives from taxes on profits. If, on the other hand, exports are motivated by a desire to obtain tax credits or government subsidies, there is also a drain on the government's finances. The widespread adoption of export incentives has meant that substantial sums are either foregone by the government, or paid out in subsidies. The total cost of such incentives was estimated at 13 per cent of government revenues in Brazil in 1975 (De Oliveira and Travolo Popoutchi, 1979, table 52), while in Colombia the major tax incentive (CAT) represented 7 per cent of government income in 1974 (Ffrench-Davis and Pinera Echenique, 1976, table 13). Clearly, not all the financial costs of the export-promotion policies go to support TNCs, but there is some evidence from Mexico to suggest that their share of such incentives is at least as great and probably greater than their share in the value of manufactured exports (Jenkins, 1979b, pp. 171–2).

The use of transfer pricing to undervalue exports and shift profits from Latin America is possible because the bulk of TNC exports of manufactured exports from the region involves intra-firm trade. In other words, exports do not involve the circulation of commodities between different national markets, but are part of the inter-nationalisation of the productive process itself, established when the TNC allocated different products or processes to different countries. The prevalence of intra-firm trade is found whether the strategy of the TNC concerned is regional or international, although it is probably more likely to be at 'arm's length' when exports are to smell neighbouring markets or to utilise excess capacity. In Brazil, 64 per cent of US subsidiaries' manufactured exports to Latin America were intra-firm, and 73 per cent of such exports to all destinations in 1972, while the corresponding figures to Mexico were 70 per cent and 83 per cent (Newfarmer and Mueller, 1975, tables 4–11 and 6–11). Moreover in both Brazil and Mexico the share of intra-firm trade had increased since 1960. In 1977 intra-firm trade accounted for 38 per cent of all (not just US TNCs) manufactured exports from Brazil to the United States and 71 per cent of Mexican exports (Helleiner, 1978, table 4). Information on individual TNCs confirms that a large proportion of their exports go to the parent or to other affiliates. This is certainly the pattern in both the motor industry and the pharmaceutical industry in the region.

## 3 WORLD-WIDE SOURCING AND LATIN AMERICAN EXPORT PRODUCTION

The second type of manufactured exports arise where TNC investment in Latin America is directed primarily to serve external markets. In this type of activity the firms are oriented to export from the outset, rather than being initially concerned with supplying the local market. Usually this form of investment involves the relocation of a particular production process to Latin America. It is difficult to estimate the extent of such exports from the region because of the problems of identifying the relocation of processes from trade data which refer to products. The closest proxy to such a figure can be derived from US imports under Tariff Items 806.30 and 807.00, which are specifically designed to promote this type of activity.[6] In 1977, total imports from Latin America under these two items came to over US $1.5 billion (Balli, n.d., table 2), roughly 17 per cent of

the region's total manufactured exports of almost US $9 million in
that year. Given that it is US and Japanese firms which have been
most extensively involved in this type of world-wide sourcing and
that the Japanese have relocated operations primarily in East Asia,
the figure for US imports probably does not substantially under-
estimate the extent of this kind of activity.

As can be seen from Table 5.5, by far the most important country
in the region in this field is Mexico, followed a long way behind by
Brazil, El Salvador, Haiti and the Dominican Republic. Such
production is often undertaken in free trade zones and it is not
surprising to find therefore, that these same countries, together with
Colombia, are the most important in Latin America in terms of
employment in such zones, again with Mexico in a pre-eminent
position (Fröbel *et al.*, 1980, table 3.8). While in Mexico, and the
Central American and Caribbean countries, such exports account
for a significant share of all manufactured exports, they are of minor
importance in Brazil and Colombia and totally insignificant in
Argentina, the other major Latin American exporter of
manufactures.

TABLE 5.5  *Exports from Latin America to the United States under Tariff Items 806.30
and 807.00, 1977*

|  | Total (mn US$) | Dutiable Value (mn US$) | Dutiable Value/ Total Value % |
|---|---|---|---|
| Mexico | 1 155.6 | 524.4 | 45 |
| Brazil | 120.9 | 103.5 | 86 |
| El Salvador | 74.3 | 34.5 | 46 |
| Haiti | 84.3 | 23.0 | 27 |
| Dominican Republic | 45.7 | 14.0 | 31 |
| Costa Rica | 26.2 | 9.2 | 35 |
| Colombia | 14.7 | 5.5 | 38 |
| Nicaragua | 6.3 | 1.9 | 30 |
| Honduras | 2.6 | 0.9 | 33 |
| Argentina | 0.4 | 0.3 | 80 |

SOURCE  Balli (n.d., table 2).

The bulk of Latin American exports to the United States under
these special tariff regimes come from two industries, textile products
and electrical and electronic products which between them accounted for three-quarters of the total value added of such exports in

1978 (Balli, n.d., table 3). Such exports are therefore considerably more concentrated in terms of sectors of origin than manufactured exports as a whole or even other exports of manufactures by TNCs. (Other branches which are represented on a much more limited scale in this type of trade include toys, sporting goods, food products and some engineering components).

## The internationalisation of the production process

The growth of this form of internationalisation dates from the 1960s, and in Latin America it emerges with the introduction of the Mexican Border Industrialization Programme in the mid-1960s. In order to understand the emergence and growth of this phenomenon, it is necessary to locate it within the dynamic of accumulation of specific branches of production at an international level.[7] As already indicated, the major branches involved have been clothing and electrical and electronic products and components.

In general terms, the dynamic of accumulation in capitalist economies is governed by both the contradiction between capital and labour and the competition between individual capitals. In considering the internationalisation of the production process, both elements are significant. The long boom of the post-war period, with high levels of employment, was accompanied by a increase in the level of real wages. Capital, if it was to maintain the rate of profit, needed to increase labour productivity through increased mechanisation and new technology. Both in the clothing industry and the electrical and electronic industries, however, there were particular difficulties in reducing labour costs in this way, which made access to low-cost labour of crucial significance in these branches. In the case of clothing the variety of designs to be manufactured, and the frequent changes imposed by fashion, generally prevent the product standardisation which would be necessary in order for mechanisation to take place at the existing level of technology (Chavez, n.d.). In the case of the electronics industry, rapid technological change in the industry's products has made it uneconomical to invest heavily in fixed capital for assembly operations because of the short time period within which such equipment would be rendered obsolete (Minian, 1981). It is, therefore, the lack of malleability of fixed capital, and the peculiar need for such malleability, in these branches, which has led to their leading role in the internationalisation of the production process.

At the same time, the intensity and nature of competition in these branches gave a particular impetus to the relocation of production from the 1960s. In the case of the clothing industry, US producers faced increasing competition from imports, first of all from Japan and then from Hong Kong, South Korea and Taiwan. In several products, the level of import penetration was such that one garment of every three sold in the United States was being produced abroad (Rubin, 1977, p. 29). The clothing industry in the advanced capitalist countries is characterised by a larger number of medium and small firms, with a considerable emphasis on price competition. Price is of particular significance where sales are made to the large chains and specialty stores. In order to meet competition from imports based on lower labour costs in the Far East, many US clothing firms moved the most labour-intensive part of the production process, the sewing operations necessary to make cut fabrics into garments, abroad.

The electronic industry is also characterised by intense competition, often through price cutting. Although the industry is highly concentrated internationally, with twenty firms estimated to account for almost 95 per cent of world production of semi-conductors in the mid-1970s (Minian, 1981, table 16), this has not led to the avoidance of price competition seen in other concentrated international industries, such as cars and pharmaceuticals. The main reason for this is the rapid rate of technological progress in the industry and the speed with which companies have been able to follow the leading firms in introducing more sophisticated products (NACLA, 1977, p. 6).

The relative ease of entry into many parts of the industry, often by personnel from an existing firm setting up a new firm, is an important contributory factor to the intensity of competition. In the case of electronic components such as semi-conductors, offshore assembly operations began in the early 1960s in Hong Kong, the mid 1960s in Taiwan and South Korea and the late 1960s in Mexico and Singapore (Chang, 1971, table 10). The major cause of this relocation was intensified domestic competition within the United States' industry. This was brought about by the increased importance of industrial and consumer markets, and the relative decline of military demand for electronic components in the 1960s (Ocampo, 1980, pp. 25–7). In the case of a number of consumer products such as television sets, radios and casette tapes, foreign competition from countries with lower labour costs, particularly Japan, led US

manufacturers to relocate their labour-intensive assembly operations overseas. In all these cases, the ability to relocate part of the
productive process abroad was regarded as vital to competitive
survival by the manufacturers involved (USTC, 1970, pp. 99–119).

Although in two important respects the clothing and electronic
and electrical industries are similar (that is, in the problems faced in
mechanising assembly activities, and in the intensity of price
competition), the pattern of internationalisation differs somewhat
between the two branches. Whereas overseas assembly in the
electrical and electronic industry is virtually always in the hands of
subsidiaries of TNCs, and the exports of the Latin American
countries take place within the same company, sub-contracting to
independent local producers is more common in the clothing
industry. Only two out of every five firms involved in making up
garments for the United States market were owned in whole or in
part by the contracting firm and the remainder were independent
sub-contractors (USTC, 1970, p. 94). This is not entirely surprising
given that the clothing industry in the advanced capitalist countries

TABLE 5.6   *Hourly earnings in Latin American countries of workers processing and
assembling US materials and earnings for comparable work in US, 1969*

|  | Foreign ($ per hour) | U.S. ($ per hour) | (Foreign/ U.S. (%)) |
|---|---|---|---|
| *Mexico* | | | |
| Consumer electronic products | 0.53 | 2.31 | 22.9 |
| Office machines and parts | 0.48 | 2.97 | 16.1 |
| Semi-conductors | 0.61 | 2.56 | 23.8 |
| Wearing apparel | 0.53 | 2.29 | 23.1 |
| Toys, dolls and models | 0.65 | 2.59 | 25.1 |
| Scientific instruments | 0.85 | 3.01 | 28.2 |
| *Brazil* | | | |
| Office machines and parts | 0.38 | 2.75 | 13.8 |
| *Costa Rica* | | | |
| Wearing apparel | 0.34 | 2.28 | 14.9 |
| *Honduras* | | | |
| Wearing apparel | 0.45 | 2.27 | 19.8 |
| *Caribbean* | | | |
| Other | 0.16–0.39 | 1.93–2.10 | 7.3–18.6 |

SOURCE   USTC (1970, table 24).

is usually composed of a large number of medium and small firms and that there is often considerable sub-contracting within the advanced countries.

While the problems of mechanisation and intense competition led to the relocation of certain industrial processes from the 1960s, it was of course substantial differences in wages and unit labour costs which made such moves so attractive for capital. By the late 1960s, wage rates in various Latin American countries, although higher than in Asia, ranged from about a third to one-fourteenth of comparable hourly earnings in the United States (see Table 5.6). Moreover, productivity levels in this type of industry are often as high, or even higher, in Latin America than in the United States so that the difference in labour costs per unit of output is even more marked. This situation was often guaranteed through a ban on trade unions or very weak union organisations in the exporting countries.

## *The impact of world-wide sourcing on the local economy*

As has already been indicated, the Mexican border industries known locally as *maquiladoras* are far and away the most important group of export-oriented industries of this kind in Latin America. Therefore, in discussing some of the implications of this type of activity, attention will be concentrated primarily on this area. The declared objective of the Mexican Border Industrialization programme, which was embarked upon in 1965, was to create an alternative source of employment in the north of Mexico following the cancellation (by the US Government in 1964) of the *bracero* programme, which had provided jobs in the United States for 200 000 Mexicans. Further objectives of the industrialisation programme were to earn foreign exchange, train workers and increasingly integrate the border regions with the rest of the Mexican economy (Newton and Balli, 1979, pp. 17–8). To this end, firms setting up plants to produce exclusively for export along the northern frontier were allowed to import machinery and raw materials duty free, were exempt from general Mexican requirements concerning local participation in share ownership, and from immigration controls on US citizens working in the plants. In addition industrial parks were constructed in a number of northern cities in order to attract foreign companies. In the 1970s the legislation was changed to permit *maquiladoras* to be established in

:he interior of the country, and to permit them to sell part of their
)utput on the domestic market.

At first sight, the programme has been a considerable success in
generating new jobs in the frontier regions. By the late 1970s the
number employed in the *maquiladoras*, primarily in the frontier
zones, had reached over 90 000 (Table 5.7) despite a slight set-back
.n the mid-1970s (To put this figure in context however, it is less
:han 1 per cent of the number of Mexicans who are believed to be
working illegally in the United States). It cannot, however, be
assumed that this increase in the number of jobs in the *maquiladoras*
necessarily corresponds to an equivalent reduction in the level of
unemployment, either in the frontier regions or in the country as a
whole. A prime reason for this is that the greater part of the labour
force employed in the *maquiladoras* is female, particularly in the two
principal branches, electrical and electronics and garments. On
average more than three-quarters of the total labour force are
women (Balli, n.d. table 8) while in the main branches the proportion of women workers is over 80 per cent (Pearson, 1979, p. 12).
Moreover, the bulk of these workers enter the *maquiladoras* with
no previous work experience. A survey of a sample of almost 300
women operators in the border zones revealed that three-quarters

TABLE 5.7  *Principal characteristics of the Mexican* maquiladora *industry*

| | Average no. employed | Net exports[1] (mn US$) | Net exports[2] (mn US$) | Net exports (2) ÷ (net exports plus imports) |
|---|---|---|---|---|
| 1970 | *n.a.* | 80.9 | 54.6 | *n.a.* |
| 1971 | 26 967 | 101.3 | 84.9 | *n.a.* |
| 1972 | *n.a.* | 164.7 | *n.a.* | *n.a.* |
| 1973 | 64 300 | 277.6 | 197.0 | 36% |
| 1974 | 75 977 | 443.4 | 315.6 | 31% |
| 1975 | 67 214 | 454.4 | 321.2 | 32% |
| 1976 | 74 496 | 535.7 | 351.7 | 32% |
| 1977 | 78 433 | 524.7 | 315.3 | 29% |
| 1978 | 90 704 | 713.4 | 439.2 | 29% |

[1] Refers to the figure used by the Banco de Mexico in calculating the country's balance of
payments accounts.
[2] Refers to the figures collected by the Secretaria de Industria y Comercio and subsequently
the Secretaria de Programacion y Presupuesto, converted to dollars at the current exchange
rate.
SOURCES  Pearson (1976, table 1); Balli, (n.d., tables 5 and 6); Newton and Balli (1979,
table 4).

either had no previous work experience or had only previously
worked in another *maquiladora* (Konig, 1975, table 5). Of a sample
of 205 operators and supervisors with no previous work experience,
only 3 per cent had previously searched for work without success,
while 44 per cent had not done so and the remainder were either at
school or below working age (Konig, 1975, table 7). Clearly a large
proportion of those who are employed in the *maquiladoras* were not
previously classified as unemployed (because they were not seeking
work) or even as belonging to the economically active population.
Indeed it is possible that the recorded level of unemployment could
be increased because ex-*maquiladora* workers 'will not simply go
back to their families, but rather join the ranks of those looking for
work' (Konig, 1975, p. 74).

Unfortunately there is no data available which enables the
structure of the economically active population of the frontier zone
to be analysed. The latest data is for 1970 when the *maquiladora*
programme was only five years old and the total employment
created was only 20 000. At that time, open unemployment in the
northern frontier was almost 90 000, while disguised unemployment was estimated at between 200 000 and 340 000 (SIC, n.d., p.
45, 47). The above analysis suggests, however that little inroad will
have been made into these totals by the expansion of the
*maquiladoras* in the 1970s, and the growth in the number of women
looking for work and immigration from other areas is likely to have
increased these totals.

It is questionable how far the *maquiladoras* are contributing to the
training of the local labour force in Mexico. The bulk of the labour
force employed in these industries, particularly the women, are
classified as unskilled – 87 per cent in a sample of *maquiladora*
workers in Tijuana (Gambrill, n.d., table 7). This is not surprising,
since the process of de-skilling accompanies the decomposition of
the labour process which characterises the type of production
undertaken. The types of skills which are required either involve
little training because, like sewing, they are learnt as part of the
socialisation process which women undergo outside the work-place
(Elson and Pearson, 1980, pp. 13–16), or where some training is
given, they are highly specific to the particular plant and process in
which they are used and hence of little applicability elsewhere
(König, 1975, p. 91).

The other major claim for the *maquiladoras* is of course, that they
can earn considerable foreign exchange. In the late 1970s, the

amounts earned, in excess of US $500 million a year, accounted for more than 10 per cent of Mexico's total export earnings and a quarter of its earnings from exports of manufactures (Balli, n.d., table 5). There is reason to believe, however, that the official balance of payments data which is usually used in estimating the impact of the *maquiladoras* gives a considerable overestimate of their true contribution (for a detailed analysis of the reasons for this overestimation, see Pearson, 1976). Clearly the nature of *maquiladora* operations, which consists primarily of assembly of imported components, means that the balance of payments effect must be calculated net of such imports. The use of US data on the dutiable value of imports from Mexico under USTS items 806.30 and 807.00 is misleading as a starting point for the calculation of the foreign exchange earned in Mexico, however, since the US concept of dutiable value includes a number of items, such as a hypothetical profit margin and a contribution to costs which arise in the US, which are not generated in Mexico.

A lower estimate, based on direct cost data provided by the firms operating in Mexico gives a more accurate indicator of the total foreign exchange earned of only around US $440 million in 1978 compared to more than US $700 million (see table 5.7), equivalent to only 6.5 per cent of total exports and 15 per cent of exports of manufactures (Balli, n.d., tables 5). Even this is a considerable overestimate of the total balance of payments impact of these firms. The main local cost item is of course labour costs, accounting for around 60 per cent of the total (Balli, n.d., table 6). There is undoubtedly a substantial leakage from wages as a result of workers spending a large part of their income in the United States. Rough estimates indicate that as much as 60 per cent of wages are spent in the United States (ECLA, 1976, p. 72), which would reduce the total foreign exchange contribution by over a third. It is not known what proportion of the remaining 40 per cent of local costs also consists of indirect imports, but it is reasonable to suppose that it may be significant, while in addition, the provision of industrial facilities particularly the construction of industrial parks in order to attract foreign capital may also have generated additional imports. It seems therefore that the contribution of the *maquiladoras* to foreign exchange earnings is much less than official Mexican sources indicate.

The very nature of *maquiladora* operations makes it even less likely that they will contribute to the integration of the regions in which

they operate with the rest of the Mexican economy. Indeed the
attraction of the border industrialisation programme is that it
minimises the impact of the border between Mexico and the United
States (through duty free imports, freedom of movement for US
personnel, and so an) and hence promotes the integration of the
area with the US economy. This is illustrated by the relatively low
local value added within Mexico of such exports, which in the 1970s
varied from 29 per cent to 36 per cent, tending to fall over time (see
table 5.7). It is brought out even more graphically by the proportion
of local materials, which accounted for between 1.5 per cent and 3
per cent of total material inputs in the late 1970s (Balli, n.d., table
9). In the electrical and electronics industries, where exports are
almost exclusively from foreign subsidiaries, these tendencies are
even more marked, with local materials accounting for only 0.3 per
cent of all inputs (ECLA, 1976, table 20).

Thus, of the principal declared objectives of the *maquiladora*
programme, the only one where it appears to have met with some
success is in generating additional foreign exchange, and even here
the impact is considerably less than is often claimed. There are,
however, a number of further aspects of this type of industry which
need to be analysed. The 'footloose' or 'runaway' character of many
of these industries implies that the benefits which they offer in terms
of foreign exchange earnings or employment are highly unstable.
(The term 'runaway industry' seems particularly apposite for a
number of cases where firms have closed down and shipped out their
machinery overnight without paying the required indemnisation to
the workers (NACLA, 1975, p. 17).) In the recession of the mid-
1970s a large number of *maquiladoras* closed down and the labour
force dropped by 11.5 per cent in one year, with the electrical and
electronics industry, where employment dropped by 21 per cent,
being worst hit (ECLA, 1976 table 19). Not only is the industry at
the mercy of developments in the advanced capitalist countries, but
it is also always subject to the threat that the firms will relocate to
other underdeveloped countries. While Mexico has a peculiarly
favoured position as a result of its 2000 mile border with the United
States ('so far from God and so close to the United States' as the
Mexican dictator, Porfirio Diaz once said), it still competes for
labour-intensive assembly industries not only with the Caribbean
and Central America but also with the countries of East Asia. The
Haitian Assembly Industry Association sent a letter to US firms
operating on the Mexican border trying to persuade them to

relocate to Haiti, pointing out the advantages in terms of lower wage rates and no union problems (NACLA, 1975, p. 22).

A further element which casts a shadow over the long-run viability of *maquiladora* industries is the possibility that the conditions which created them could in future be radically altered. Two particular factors stand out. First, as was seen above a major cause of such internationalisation of production was the block to mechanisation which was particularly marked in two industries, electronics and garments. Technological change in these industries may already be on the point of undermining this pattern. In general terms, it is to be expected that the microelectronic revolution will substantially increase the flexibility of fixed capital and make mechanisation a possibility. There is already evidence of the way in which technical change is making it possible to save labour in the garment industry through the introduction of electronically controlled laser cutters, programmable sewing machines and so forth (Chavez, n.d. p. 64). Similarly in the electronics industry, automated bonding machines have been developed which enable one worker to produce ten times as much as one working with a microscope could do (Elson and Pearson, 1980, p. 35).

Second, the possibility of international sourcing depends in part on the continuation of the US tariff concessions under which the bulk of such trade takes place. This is particularly true for the garments industry, where tariffs on imported products are high and the saving of duty on imports of products initially exported from the United States for assembly abroad is considerable. The US Tariff Commission estimated in the early 1970s that in the absence of Tariff Item 807.00, the cost of imports of wearing apparel from Mexico would be increased by 24 per cent which would clearly be a major blow to the industry's competitiveness (USTC, 1970, figure 22).

While it is claimed by advocates of this type of industrialisation that it serves to improve the quality of the labour force through the training provided, it often has quite the opposite effect of exhausting the labour force and rendering it less able to work. One of the most vivid examples of this is the effect of long hours of meticulous work on the womens' eyesight in the electronics industry. As one worker put it 'the only disadvantage of this work is that we all start with perfect eyesight and come out wearing spectacles' (Pearson, 1979, n. 22. See also the cases reported in NACLA, 1975, p. 18). This contributes to a continuous turnover of workers who are no longer able to maintain the required levels of productivity.

In broad outline, the situation in the other Lating American countries which have developed *maquiladora* type industries is similar to that discussed in Mexico. Indeed, conditions elsewhere are generally worse than Mexico. Wages are substantially below Mexican levels in the Caribbean and Central America (see table V. 6). Whereas in Mexico, there is a significant degree of unionisation, repressive regimes in other Latin American countries ensure that unions are either non-existent or strictly controlled. This is often regarded as one of the selling points of these countries in trying to attract assembly industries (NACLA, 1975, p. 22). The local value added is often even lower in these countries than those levels found in Mexico, not surprisingly since as was seen above, wages are the major local cost (see Table 5.5). (As was indicated in the discussion of Mexico, these figures which correspond to the dutiable value of US imports under Tariff Item 806.30 and 807.00 considerably overestimate the true level of local value added contained in such exports.) As in Mexico, a large proportion of such exports are controlled by foreign subsidiaries. In the mid-1970s, there were more than 150 US firms producing for export in Haiti (Morrison, 1975). In the Dominican Republic, the La Romana Export Processing Zone is actually owned by a US corporation, Gulf and Western.

The primary beneficiaries of this type of export-oriented industrialisation are very clearly the US firms, which establish foreign subsidiaries or develop sub-contracting arrangements with local firms in the exporting zones. The cost savings which they can obtain from such operations are substantial. In the case of Mexico, they have been estimated at US $8000 a year for each person employed (Konig, 1975, p. 44). Motorola saved US $4 million a year by shifting its assembly plant 200 miles south from Phoenix, Arizona to Nogales, Sonora (NACLA, 1975, p. 7). For the Latin American countries, the most significant consequences are a few million dollars of additional foreign exchange and the incorporation of a considerable number of young women into industrial work for the first time.

## 4 TNCs AND A NEW INTERNATIONAL DIVISION OF LABOUR

It is clear that industiral exports from Latin America have grown rapidly over the past two decades. It also appears that TNCs have played an important role in this export expansion, although no more so than would be expected given their position within the manufacturing sectors of the major Latin American countries. Does this recent trend constitute the much heralded new international division of labour in which the under-developed countries become major producers of industrial goods for the advanced capitalist countries, organised by the TNCs?

To put this in perspective, it is necessary to recall that despite the rapid rise in industrial exports from the region, Latin America still accounted for only 1.6 per cent of world exports of manufactures in the mid-1970s (UNIDO, 1979, table 9.7). Moreover, although the composition of the exports of a number of Latin American countries has shifted significantly away from primary products towards manufactures, industrial production as a whole remains over-whelmingly directed towards the domestic market and exports account for a relatively small part of industrial growth. In 1974, the share of exports in the gross value of manufacturing output was 5.2 per cent in Argentina, 3.2 per cent in Brazil, 4.4 per cent in Mexico and 3.6 per cent in the Andean sub-region (ECLA, 1980, table 458). The same is true of production by TNCs in the region (see table 5.2). Moreover, the analysis of this chapter suggests that no major change is likely in the forseeable future. The situation in Latin America contrasts sharply with that found in a small number of countries in the Far East, where exports account for more than 40 per cent of manufacturing production (Hong Kong, Singapore, South Korea and Taiwan) (Balassa, 1978, table 2).

It is also important to stress that Latin American exports of manufactures are not predominantly or even primarily of labour-intensive goods, except in the case of exports of the *maquiladora* type, which do not account for more than a fifth of the total (see Felix, 1974 on Argentina; Tyler, 1976, pp. 176–7 on Brazil; Diaz Alejandro, 1976, pp. 45–6 on Colombia; Boatler, 1973 and Jenkins, 1979b, ch. 2 on Mexico). There is a wide diversity of patterns of manufactured exports from the region, both in terms of sectors of origin – traditional industries, intermediate industries and engineering industries are all represented – and in terms of destination. In the case of exports by TNCs by far the greater part is made up of products which are not labour intensive.

This has two major implications for the analysis of the 'new international division of labour'. First, the employment which is created is likely to be limited, and nowhere near meets the need for

new jobs in the larger countries of the region. This is particularly
true in the case of exports by foreign subsidiaries. Second, again
with the exception of the assembly industries, the major motive for
exporting from Latin America is not to take advantage of cheap
local labour. Outside the *maquiladoras*, low wage rates are often
more than offset by low levels of labour productivity, due to a lack of
scale economies, and by high input costs. In all but the most labour-
intensive industries, the reduction in costs from government
subsidies are greater than those which can be expected from lower
wage rates. To take a hypothetical example, a US firm with a wage
cost equivalent to 20 per cent of sales, could reduce this to 4 per cent,
with a total saving of 16 per cent of the value of sales, if wages in
Latin America were one-fifth of US levels and productivity and
other costs were the same. But as was seen above, the subsidies
offered by Latin American governments in the 1970s were considerably more than this. Even if wages were only a tenth of US
levels the saving would only be 18 per cent of the value of sales.

The expansion of industrial exports is a consequence of certain
international tendencies, such as the competitive struggle for the
world market and the development of the labour process in certain
branches on the one hand, and state intervention intended to
overcome some of the contradictions of capitalist accumulation
within Latin America on the other. It is possible that by integrating
the Latin American economies more closely with the advanced
capitalist economies some of the problems associated with balance
of payments crises can be overcome. (After all a region within a
country does not have a balance of payments problem.) In other
respects, however, the new export-oriented strategies do little to
resolve the contradictions which gave rise to them. In particular,
the problem of marginality remains untouched. The TNCs,
however, are in a position to take advantage of and influence the
formulation of these strategies. They are in privileged position to
exploit international differences in taxation, wages, tariffs and
working conditions to maximise world-wide profitability.

Some radical commentators have perceived a gleam of light at
the end of the tunnel of export-oriented industrialisation. It is that
this alleged new international division of labour is creating an
industrial working class in the underdeveloped countries which will
become a base for an anti-capitalist struggle (Fröbel *et al.*, 1980, pp.
405–6; Landsberg, 1979, p. 62). Their optimism is however
misplaced as far as Latin America is concerned. The gradual

opening of import-substituting industries towards export markets is unlikely to have a major influence in forming a more militant working class, while the predominantly female labour force of the *maquiladora*-type industries poses new questions about gender relations and cannot be subsumed into generalisations about the expansion of an undifferentiated proletariat. The incorporation of female labour into export production does not necessarily herald the liberation of women from male oppression (see the discussion of the intensification, decomposition and recomposition of gender subordination in these types of industry in Elson and Pearson, 1980). In the circumstances it is unlikely that this new industrial force will lead an anti-capitalist struggle.

## NOTES

1. This was of course not the only response to these contradictions. Others included the growing role of the state in the accumulation process, land reform, regional integration in the Andean Pact countries and restrictions on foreign capital.
2. It is difficult to quantify the exact value to the exporter of all the various incentives available, but there is little doubt that in aggregate it was substantial. A rough estimate suggests that export incentives for manufactured goods were about a fifth of export values in Mexico, between a fifth and a third in Colombia, between a third and two-fifths in Brazil and even higher in Argentina in the early 1970s.
3. The Council for Latin America, for instance, estimated that US subsidiaries accounted for more than 40 per cent of Latin American exports of manufactured goods in 1966, although their share of gross manufacturing value added was less than 10 per cent (Vernon, 1973, p. 107).
4. The importance of balancing exports to achieve fuller capacity utilisation has been noted, for example, in the petrochemical industry (Stobaugh, 1971).
5. For evidence of this in the case of Brazil see Fajnzylber (1970, appendix 6).
6. These items introduced into the US Tariff Schedule in the 1960s permit certain products manufactured abroad, which incorporate materials initially exported from the United States, to be imported without paying duty on the value which is of US origin. They are sometimes referred to as 'value added tariffs' since duty is not charged on the gross value of the imported item.
7. There are of course also general conditions associated with the development of capitalism which have been pre-requisites for this form of internationalisation. Of paticular importance are the decomposition of the labour process into a number of discrete units as a result of the development of the technical division of labour, and the developments in transport and communications which enable products to be shipped quickly and safely between different production sites and managerial decisions to be transmitted and coordinated as easily as possible.

# Part III
# Class, State and Capital

# 6 The Internationalisation of Capital and Class Structure

## 1 INTRODUCTION

One of the major areas of debate which was not touched upon in the case studies of the previous part was the implications of the internationalisation of capital for the class structure of the Latin American countries. Indeed, as was suggested in Chapter 1, one of the limitations of the study of individual branches of industry is the difficulty of dealing with issues whose full significance can only be grasped at the level of the economy as a whole. The two chapters in this part of the book attempt to deal with some of these issues.

Two central debates concerning Latin American class structure are considered in this chapter. The first focusses on the nature of the Latin American bourgeoisie; the second on the implications of the internationalisation of capital for the growth and structure of the working class in the region. Until fairly recently, class analysis of Latin America had mainly focussed on the former. This arose from the dependency critique of the position held by the Latin American Communist Parties that the region was still feudal and that revolutionaries should support the 'progressive national bourgeoisie' in its struggle to remove the vestiges of feudalism. The nature of the bourgeoisie was therefore a central question in determining the class alliances which should be forged in order to promote development on the continent.

While the debate on the bourgeoisie raged during the 1960s, the working class was relatively neglected. The predominant view in the early 1960s was of a weak proletariat with little class consciousness or class solidarity. This was usually explained in terms of the recent formation of the working class and the rural origins of many of its members. In the late 1960s, however, a new emphasis

appeared stressing the nature of the industrialisation process which
was creating new, capital-intensive, high productivity branches
alongside the traditional industries. The heterogeneous production
structure which resulted, it was argued, had led to a differentiation
of the working class and the creation of a labour aristocracy.
Clearly, the emergence of these new branches was part and parcel of
the internationalisation of capital in Latin America since the mid-
1950s, discussed in Chapter 2.

## 2 THE LOCAL BOURGEOISIE[1]

*Introduction*

In their critique of the Communist Party view of the national
bourgeoisie in Latin America as a progressive force, dependency
theorists placed particular emphasis on the ideological orientation
of local industrialists. Studies in Argentina, Brazil and Chile showed
that the views held by industrialists did not correspond to
theoretical expectations. In order to understand these findings,
however, it is necessary first to consider the structural position of the
industrial bourgeoisie in Latin America in terms of its internal
organisation and differentiation and its relationship to other social
classes and groups.

In their efforts to combat the Communist Party position many
dependency writers went to the opposite extreme, arguing that the
industrial bourgeoisie in Latin America was extremely weak, had
been co-opted by the traditional agrarian oligarchy and was
subservient to foreign capital (Chilcote and Edelstein, 1974, pp. 51–
7). Indeed, in the United States a simplistic version of dependency
theory was diffused which saw international capital and imperialism as all powerful, denying all autonomy to the local bourgeoisie in
Latin America. This interpretation, by assuming that the behaviour
of the bourgeoisie was totally externally derermined (seeing them as
'agents of imperialism') ended up by eliminating them completely
as a social force requiring analysis (O'Donnell, 1978, p. 5). This
view has the unfortunate consequence of also denying the possibility
of any conflict between local and foreign capital.

More recent writings on 'dependent development' have, in
contrast emphasised the symbiotic relationship between the local
bourgeoisie in Latin America (and particularly Brazil) and inter-

national capital. Far from the local bourgeoisie being entirely dependent on, and subservient to foreign capital, there is a recognition of mutual interdependence between sections of the local bourgeoisie and the TNCs. While local capital may depend on foreign capital for technology, trademarks, access to export markets, and so on, the TNCs may depend on the local bourgeoisie to play an integrative role because of their greater involvement in local networks through personal and family ties (Evans, 1979, pp. 158–62). In some cases, where well-established local oligopolies exist, the TNCs may even depend on them to gain access to the domestic market.

## The Structure of the Local Bourgeoisie

Before examining in more detail the links between the local bourgeoisie and international capital in Latin America, it is necessary to consider several key aspects of its internal organisation. Here, we shall focus on the importance of large, often diversified, economic groups, and the corresponding differentiation of the industrial bourgeoisie, as well as the extent of ties between industrial capital and other fractions of capital, particularly agrarian capital.

Studies of the largest, nationally owned enterprises in a number of Latin American countries have indicated that such firms often form part of highly diversified economic groups. These groups are not, moreover, simply industrial conglomerates but also often include banks, financial institutions, construction companies, real estate firms and enterprises in the service sector. The importance of such groups in Latin America and other third world countries can be attributed to a number of factors (Leff, 1978, pp. 666–9; Cordero and Santin, 1977, pp. 3–6). They are a way of overcoming the limitations of specialisation in one industry within relatively small markets, where industrial growth has been characterised by the diversification of consumption and production rather than the expansion of production of basic goods. They have also expanded through vertical integration, in order to avoid finding themselves at the mercy of monopoly supplies or buyers in small markets. However, the significance of groups in countries of such different size as Brazil and Nicaragua suggests that factors other than market size may be more important cause of their development. In the absence of well-developed local capital markets in Latin America, the role of the groups in channeling financial resources between

different activities is very important, and seems to be a major reason
for their existence and growth.

An economic group is usually defined as any group in which firms
are linked through share-holdings and inter-locking directorships.
Such groups are a major force in Latin American industry
accounting for the bulk of the largest firms and a significant
proportion of total manufacturing output. In Mexico, it was found
that in a sample of 168 of the largest Mexican-owned industrial
firms, 136 could be classified as belonging to an economic group and
only 32 were independent firms (Cordero and Santin, 1977, p. 10).
The 131 groups identified in the study, controlled 757 industrial
companies which between them accounted for 14 per cent of total
industrial production in 1971 (Cordero and Santin, tables 5 and 6).
A similar pattern emerges in other Latin American countries. In
Brazil, of the 18 majority Brazilian-owned industrial companies
amongst the country's largest 100 non-financial corporations, at
least thirteen could be identified as belonging to large economic
groups.[2] In Argentina, Bunge y Born alone has five firms amongst
the hundred largest in the country, and other powerful economic
groups include Tornquist, Siam di Tella and Techint-Dalmine,
(Vilas, 1974; Imaz, 1964, and Tokman, 1973). In Chile too, groups
such as Edwards, Cruzat-Larrain, Vial Angelini, and Matte control
industrial firms in a number of different branches as well as firms in
other sectors, including banking. Of the 250 largest private firms in
Chile, 178 are controlled by such groups, and over a hundred of
them by seven groups (Dahse, 1979).[3]

While these economic groups form the élite of national capital in
Latin America, with substantial economic and political influence,
they are by no means the entire local industrial bourgeoisie. It is
important to bear in mind the differentiation between these groups
on the one hand, and independent industrial firms on the other
which tend to be much smaller, and which have managed to find
themselves spaces in the industrial structure in which neither
foreign capital nor local economic groups have taken much interest.
Smaller local capitals have also been able to find positions as
suppliers to TNCs as in the case of the motor components industry,
or as customers – for example, local textile firms which buy
synthetic fibres from TNCs.

Far from the industrial bourgeoisie in Latin America being a class
opposed to the landed oligarchy, in most countries there are close
ties between agrarian and industrial capital, particularly the major

economic groups. These often have agricultural origins, as in the case of the Bungey Born conglomerate. In other cases, groups which were originally based in industry have bought agricultural estates. Similarly, there are family ties between the groups controlling large industrial firms and large landowners (Roxborough, 1979, pp. 76–7; Tokman, 1973).

The élite section of the industrial bourgeoisie represented by the economic groups is also integrated with financial capital. In Mexico, in the early 1970s fourteen of the largest fifty industrial groups controlled between them 47 banks, finance houses and insurance companies (Cordero and Santin, 1977, p. 18). The integration of industrial and financial capital in Mexico has taken two forms. First, industrial groups have created banking and financial institutions to serve their own credit requirements, and second, they have participated in the boards of directors of banks in order to obtain preferential credit lines. A similar integration is evident in other countries. In Argentina groups such as Di Tella, Braun-Menendez Behety, Drysdale, Tornquist and Shaw control a variety of banks, insurance and finance companies (Tokman, 1973), while in Chile, nearly all the major groups are involved in banking (Dahse, 1979, p. 56).

Finally, it should be noted that a number of the major economic groups in Latin America are theselves becoming internationalised (L. Wells, 1977; Diaz Alejandro, 1977). Some, such as Bunge y Born and Siam di Tella invested abroad before the Second World War II, but more recently the internationalisation of Latin American firms has become much more widespread. This again reflects the size and diversity of the major groups in the larger Latin American countries.

## Links to foreign capital

The ties between local and foreign capital in Latin America can be examined at a number of different levels. The most direct and immediate ties are those of ownership, where TNCs and local firms participate in joint ventures. A second type of link is established when a TNC supplies a local firm with technology through a contractual relationship. Third, links through exchange will be considered, particularly those which involve TNCs as major suppliers to, or customers of local firms.

Despite the often-declared preference of TNCs for complete

TABLE 6.1    *Distribution of foreign subsidiaries by type of outside owner ( %)*

|  | Local private | Local state | Foreign private | Dispersed | No. of subsidiaries |
|---|---|---|---|---|---|
| Argentina | 53 | 0 | 32 | 15 | 53 |
| Brazil | 35 | 8 | 39 | 19 | 80 |
| Chile | 60 | 10 | 15 | 15 | 20 |
| Colombia | 42 | 6 | 21 | 30 | 33 |
| Mexico | 52 | 1 | 13 | 35 | 112 |
| Peru | 31 | 0 | 46 | 23 | 13 |
| Venezuela | 39 | 4 | 20 | 37 | 46 |

SOURCE    Vaupel and Curhan (1973).

ownership of their subsidiaries, local participation in such firms in Latin America is very common. A study of 990 manufacturing subsidiaries of US TNCs in the region indicated that the parent company's shareholding was less than 95 per cent in as many as 41 per cent of the subsidiaries, and 50 per cent or less in almost a quarter of the cases. The same study showed even higher proportions for subsidiaries of non-US TNCs, with 56 per cent having a shareholding of less than 95 per cent and almost a third owning 50 per cent or less (Vaupel and Curhan, 1973, table 1). Table 6.1 shows that the most important category of outside owners for those subsidiaries in which the parent company owns less than 95 per cent of the shares, is a local private firm, both for US and non-US TNCs. There is clearly significant scope for an integration of the interests of TNCs and local capital in Latin America as a result of common ownership, and of course in some countries, particularly Mexico and those of the Andean Pact, the promotion of joint ventures has been an explicit policy of the State.

Turning to major economic groups in the Latin American countries, it is apparent that different groups have followed different strategies in terms of their relationship with foreign capital. In Brazil, an examination of seven major industrial groups revealed that two had kept their links with foreign capital to a minimum, two were moderately linked with foreign capital, and three epitomised a strategy of integrating local capital with international capital (Evans, 1979). A similar situation can be discerned elsewhere. In Mexico, of the ten most important groups (eleven if the Grupo Industrial Alfa is treated separately from the Cerveceria Cuauhtemoc Group from which it separated in 1974), four had ninimal links with TNCs, three moderate links, and a further three were closely integrated with foreign capital. In Argentina, groups such as Tornquist, Bungey Born and Techint-Dalmine are identified as having close links with foreign capital, while others such as Siam di Tella and Braun-Menendez are relatively independent (Vilas, 1974, chart 1). In Chile, the Edwards Group is notorious for its links with international capital, its head Augustin Edwards having spent the period of the Popular Unity in the United States as an international vice-president of Pepsi Cola.

In Mexico, the major economic groups have tended to concentrate their activities in the traditional industries in which local capital always tends to be strongest, particularly in non-durable consumer goods and some intermediate industries such as iron and steel and cement. Where new products are introduced this tends to be in conjunction with foreign capital, either through joint ventures or licensing. Association with foreign capital is more common among the larger groups than the small groups. Six of the largest ten groups had links with foreign firms, over a quarter of the other forty large groups and only 17 per cent of the 81 smaller groups (Cordero and Santin, 1977, p. 17). As well as the size of group, the extent to which a group is related to foreign capital also depends on the industries in which it operates, with groups in the traditional industries having few, if any, ties while those producing chemicals, metal products or motor components are more likely to establish such links. The pattern is not so clear in Brazil, however, where groups such as Villares and Votorantim compete with TNCs in industries such as electrical machinery, chemicals and aluminium, without establishing direct links with foreign capital.

The existence of links between many of the major economic groups and foreign capital does not mean that the former are totally subservient to international capital as some of the dependency literature implies. The fact that it is the largest local groups which tend to establish the closest links with foreign capital, and that they form joint ventures with a number of different foreign firms (often in different industries) gives them considerable bargaining power in their relations with foreign capital. Although the formation of joint ventures tends to integrate the interests of local and foreign capital, it also creates new areas of conflict, since such integration is never complete.

Despite the significance of joint ventures in Latin American industry, many more local firms are related to foreign capital through importing technology than through joint ventures. The creation of registries of technology-transfer contracts in a number of Latin American countries in the 1970s has indicated the extent of such arrangements. In Argentina, by the end of 1972 over 1 600 contacts had been registered by over 800 firms (INTI, 1974, p. 7, 41). In Mexico in 1974, a little over a year after the setting up of the Registro Nacional de la Transferencia de Tecnologia, more than 5 000 contracts had been presented for registration (Campos, 1974, p. 472), while in Brazil in the mid-1970s, there were over 4 000 contracts registered (Fung and Cassiolato, 1976, table 3.18). These figures of course include contracts between TNCs and their local subsidiaries and therefore exaggerate the extent of technology transfer to local firms, but at least a half of the Argentinian firms and two-thirds of those in Brazil were locally owned.

Large local firms are particularly likely to have technology contracts with TNCs. The most detailed evidence of this is in Mexico where a study of 99 large locally owned manufacturing companies showed that more than half used imported technology, and that the firms with technology contracts accounted for more than three-quarters of the total sales and employment of the group (Jenkins, 1979). Similarly in Brazil, it was found that in eight branches which accounted for the bulk of the country's imports of technology, at least a half of the largest twenty firms in each sector received technology from abroad (Almeida Biato *et al*, 1973, table 4.3). There is also ample evidence from various Latin American countries that firms which import technology tend to be significantly larger than the firms which do not.

It is an obvious, but frequently neglected point, that local capital acquires foreign technology in order to improve its own competitive position. In other words, the acquisition of foreign technology is part of the competitive strategy of local capital. Moreover, the fact that firms which buy foreign technology are predominantly large local firms operating in oligopolistic markets, suggests that its acquisition will be closely related to strategies of product differentiation and non-price competition. This is borne out by studies in Argentina and Brazil, which show that factors related to product differentiation such as the introduction of new products, trade marks and improving quality are seen as much more important motives for acquiring foreign technology than those aimed at reducing costs (Sercovich, 1974; Fung and Cassiolato, 1976, pp. 75–86).

Much of the literature on technology transfer to Latin America has emphasised the weak bargaining position of local firms and the consequent high cost of imported technology, both in terms of direct costs – royalties, technical assistance payments and so on – and the indirect costs, especially the restrictive clauses, included in such agreements. However, the picture often drawn of a weak and, crucially in terms of the argument, ignorant local firm (ignorant particularly in terms of knowledge of alternative sources of technology), at the mercy of the TNCs, is not consistent with the highly sophisticated economic groups which are such an important element of the local industrial structure, particularly in the more industrialised Latin American countries. In this context, it is worth mentioning that the spectacular instances of over-pricing which are often cited as evidence of "exploitation" of the Latin American countries by TNCs, have occurred between parent companies and subsidiaries and not when TNCs supply technology to local firms.[4] Cases *do* occur when, in the bargaining between a foreign technology supplier and a local firm the cards are stacked against the latter, but the need to differentiate between sections of local capital is crucial, rather than seeing it as uniformly weak and dependent.[5]

Another aspect of this situation is the mutual dependence between technology supplier and buyer in many industries. While the emphasis is usually placed on the local firm's reliance on foreign technology, on the other hand, the technology supplier needs markets in which to valorise its technology. Government protectionist policies in Latin America ensure that this must be done through local production rather than exports, and other factors may dictate that this should be done by licensing rather than direct investment. The capacity of the foreign firm to undertake direct investment may be limited for some reasons or there may be high barriers to entry to the local industry imposed by existing firms. In the extreme case where there is a local monopoly, the foreign firm may be faced with the choice of either licensing that monopolist, or incurring high costs in an attempt to enter the market through a subsidiary, or not being involved in that country at all. A more realistic situation would be one of oligopoly in the local industry so that the technology supplier is faced with a choice of licensees, but there is also likely to be some degree of competition in the supply of technology, so that local firms are also faced with alternative sources. Thus, the relationship between TNCs and large local oligopolies which often belong to wider economic groupings is not necessarily totally one-sided.[6]

While the extensive utilisation of foreign technology by large local firms in Latin America is not necessarily indicative of their subordination to foreign capital, it is, however, an indication of the development of the internationalisation of capital. The export of technology from the advanced countries is an important means by which the international standardisation of production techniques and product specifications occurs over and above those implied by direct foreign investment. In some industries, the imitative strategy of local capital which permits them to survive in competition with TNC subsidiaries, requires the use of imported technology and the competitive advantages which it brings (Sercovich, 1974, p. 57). The domestically owned firms in the Argentinian pharmaceutical industry are an excellent illustration of this. Thus the, transfer of technology is an important vehicle for the integration of local capital into the international circuits of capital.

In discussing links established in exchange between local and foreign capital, it is neither necessary nor practicable to look at all the transactions of this kind which may arise within the industrial system. What is of particular interest is the situation in which a local firm finds itself dependent on one or a small number of TNC suppliers for its crucial inputs, or where it sells the bulk of its output to one or a few TNCs. The relationship between motor manufacturers and the parts and components industry discussed in Chapter 3 is a classic illustration of the latter, while the former may be exemplified by a TNC manufacturing synthetic fibres which supplies local capital in the textile industry, as in the case of Rhodia in Brazil (Evans, 1979, pp. 140–3).

One methodological approach which highlights these types of relationships is that based on 'sectoral complexes' (Trajtenberg, 1977). By focussing on the major inter-industry linkages, this seeks to subdivide the economy into a number of complexes which involve not only manufacturing activities linked vertically but also the production of non-manufacturing inputs and distribution at the other end. Combining inter-industry analysis with a study of industrial concentration and the presence of TNCs, it is possible to identify dominant *nuclei* within each complex. These dominant *nuclei* are centres of economic power which can determine the direction of development of the entire complex and to which other parts of the complex are subordinated. Given that the bulk of industrial production can be classified into a relatively small number of complexes, a few key power centres can influence the entire structure and development pattern of the economy.

A similar approach, which emphasises relations of domination and subordination between firms rather than different industrial sub-sectors, is used by Friedman (1977, ch. 8). He applies the centre-periphery metaphor to analyse the unequal relationship between large and small firms. For instance, peripheral firms are often used by centre firms as a source of increased flexibility so that fluctuations in demand usually affect the peripheral firms to a disproportionate extent. Peripheral firms also tend to pay lower wages and generally have less favourable work conditions.

In Latin America, the tendency for TNCs to be located in concentrated sectors while local firms are more prominent in competitive sectors, and the tendency for TNC subsidiaries to be much larger than local firms, implies that most TNCs are central firms located in the dominent *nuclei* of economic power, while many local firms are peripheral and subordinated. (This is not of course to deny that some locally owned firms, particularly those which are state-owned or form part of large economic groups, are also central firms). Indeed, it is not unknown for TNCs entering Latin America to deliberately create a number of local suppliers in order to ensure their own hegemonic position within the network of inter-industry relationships.[7]

Such relationships establish a contradictory position for the local bourgeoisie. Often, the very existence of their enterprises is dependent on the presence of TNCs and the type of development model favoured by the TNCs. On the other hand their position of subordination, which may be reflected in lower profit rates and limited scope for accumulation, implies a conflict with the TNCs over the distribution of surplus value within the complex.

*Denationalisation and differentiation*

So far, we have concentrated on the predominantly symbiotic relationship between local and foreign capital through ownership, technology and exchange links, while at the same time seeking to emphasise the existence of areas of possible conflict or bargaining within these relationships, and to counter the view of local capital as a homogenous group subservient to international capital. It is now time to turn to a more detailed analysis of the most pervasive image put forward by nationalist critics of the TNCs, 'denationalisation'. It was shown in Chapter 2 that there has been a rapid denationalisation of both individual industries and the manufacturing sector as a whole since the 1950s. One of the most controversial aspects of denationalisation has been the take-over of locally owned firms by TNCs in a number of Latin American countries. At the same time, it was also seen that a local industrial bourgeoisie has been able to survive in a number of sectors where there is either minimal foreign penetration, or where foreign and local capital co-exist. In this section, two related issues will be addressed. The first, denationalisation, raises the question of where and why the local bourgeoisie is displaced. The second, the differentiation of roles in the accumulation process, raises the question of where the local bourgeoisie survives and thrives, and where it goes when it is displaced through denationalisation.

It was seen in Chapter 2 that a growing proportion of TNCs entering Latin American manufacturing in the post-war period tended to do so through the acquisition of existing firms, rather than through 'green field' ventures (see Table 2.1) and that this tendency was particularly marked in the most industrialised Latin American countries, Argentina, Brazil and Mexico. There is also a corollorary to this, namely that an increasing number of Latin American capitalists are selling off their enterprises to foreign companies. Evidence from both Brazil and Mexico indicates that the bulk of the firms acquired by US TNCs were going concerns. Only a quarter of the firms taken over in both countries made a loss in the year immediately preceding the take-over, and most were earning reasonable profits.[8] This raises the question of why local owners sell out as well as the one which is more commonly asked; why do TNCs acquire existing firms?

It is possible to point to a number of reasons why TNCs may place a higher valuation on a firm than its Latin American owners. Some of these merely reflect the general advantages enjoyed by large TNCs over their much smaller local competitors, such as preferential access to technology or capital, which enables the foreign subsidiary to obtain a higher rate of profit than is being earned by the existing local owner. Another possible reason is in order to acquire a monopoly position, which is more likely to come about through an existing foreign subsidiary acquiring a competing local firm than through the local firm acquiring a subsidiary. Alternatively, the threat of entry by a TNC may depress the Latin

American capitalists' valuation of his own enterprise. Newfarmer quotes a director and part-owner of one of Brazil's leading electronics firms in this vein, 'Today we are tops in our field, and expanding fast. But 15 years from now there will be no Brazilian electronics firms. The Japanese are starting to move into Brazil with force. They will lose money for some years, but they will win.' (Newfarmer, 1978, p.15).

All the factors mentioned so far contain an element of threat from the superior competitive position of the TNCs. From the standpoint of local capital, however, there are also positive reasons why they may wish to sell out to foreign capital. The continued prevalence of family firms in Latin America poses certain problems for local capital (Derossi, 1971, part I, ch. 3). These may arise as a result of difficulties in maintaining a family business when the founder dies or retires, or the need for additional capital for expansion which cannot be obtained on the local stock market. In these circumstances, the family may choose to sell all or part of the firm to a foreign investor. Alternatively, the sale of a company to a TNC may be a means of moving into new areas of investment, where higher profits can be made by local capital, or it may be a way of obtaining a position within the TNC structure.

Unfortunately, systematic evidence which would enable one to evaluate the importance of these different factors in foreign acquisitions of Latin American firms is not available. Some light is thrown on the issue by a study of sixteen TNC take-overs in Central America (Rosenthal, 1975). In eleven cases, the initiative in selling the local firms was found to come from its owners, and in two further cases although the foreign company made the initial approach, the owners were also interested in selling. Only in two cases were the owners initially not interested in selling out, but were persuaded to do so either because of the attractiveness of the offer, or because of the fear of future competition. In the one remaining case, some partners in the local firm were interested in selling while others were not. Admittedly, the main reason for the widespread interest in selling out in these cases was peculiar to the particular context in which the take-overs occurred. Specifically, the formation of the Central American Common Market led many firms to feel that they would not be able to adapt to the new conditions imposed by the expanded regional market, and the easiest solution was either to sell out or to seek a foreign partner. Looked at from the point of view of the foreign firms, the formation of the Common Market was also a factor making the region a more interesting area for accumulation. Moreover, acquisition of existing firms was doubly attractive as a means of entry both because of the speed with which operations could be started compared to a 'green field' venture, and the fact that the buyer was assured of all the fiscal incentives which the seller had obtained under national or regional industrial development laws.

Although this case study is based on a very small number of take-overs, which took place under very specific historical circumstances, it is possible to draw some points which may be of more general applicability from it. The most important is that denationalisation by TNC acquisition of local firms is not a one-way process in which local capital is inexorably swept aside, but it is frequently a process sought and initiated by local capital in the process of valorisation. It is a reminder that all purchases are also sales, and that sales of local firms in Latin America are by no means always forced sales.

As was also illustrated in the discussion of joint-ventures and technology transfer, local capital is not homogeneous. There is a world of difference between a large well-established firm and the presumably much smaller firms of the kind acquired in Central America. A firm such as Consul in the Brazilian electrical industry, faced with a number of electrical TNCs anxious to enter or expand in the local market, when it wished to sell out was in a strong position to drive a hard bargain (Newfarmer, 1978, pp. 12–4). Had the foreign companies attempted to expand in the refrigerator market in competition with Consul, they would have faced a prolonged competitive struggle, involving considerable costs.

In view of the concern aroused by foreign take-overs of local firms, surprisingly little research has been done on what happens to the sector of the local bourgeoisie which is displaced by such take-overs. Indeed, one is often left with the impression that it disappears into thin air! It is worth remembering that in many cases these acquisitions involve extremely large sums. Between 1960 and 1972, US firms took-over thirteen Mexican and fifteen Brazilian-owned companies valued at $5 million or more. (Newfarmer and Mueller, 1975, tables 4–7 and 6–7). Unfortunately, the study from which the figures are taken gives no indication of the uses to which these funds were put.

It is possible to conceive of a number of alternative uses for the funds generated by selling out to a TNC. They may be invested in other branches of industry, or in other sectors of the economy outside manufacturing. Alternatively, they may be used to acquire financial assets locally or they may be invested overseas. (It is assumed here that even the Latin American bourgeoisie would be hard put to consume sums in excess of $5 million). Fragmentary evidence seems to indicate that investment in other branches of industry is not common. In Central America, it was found that of the thirteen owners who sold their firms and did not continue to participate in management, only two invested in another manufacturing activity. Although it was difficult to obtain data on the remainder, it appears that the most common forms of investment were real estate and livestock, while it was also believed that a part of the proceeds found its way abroad (Rosenthal, 1975, pp. 12–3). Similar conclusions were arrived at in considering the denationalisation of the Brazilian pharmaceutical industry. Although some capitalists displaced from the industry moved into other branches such as printing and publishing, food and building materials, most were transformed into *rentiers*, acquiring shares in other people's companies (Evans, 1979, pp. 129–31).

The evidence suggests, therefore, that the sector of the bourgeoisie that is displaced by TNC take-overs, either finds a differentiated role for itself in sectors or branches where there is less direct competition from foreign capital, or is converted into rentiers living off financial or property investments either at home or abroad. This brings us back to the position of local capital within the Latin American economies as a whole. The corollary of the concentration of foreign investment in manufacturing, and within manufacturing in a few selected branches such as rubber, chemicals, machinery and transport equipment, is that in a number of sectors local firms face little or no competition from foreign capital. Even in some sectors where there is foreign competition, such as cement or textiles, TNCs do not enjoy the same competitive advantages that they do in foreign dominated industries. In some countries of course this is reinforced by the state intervening to reserve certain sectors and industries for local capital.

There are also important areas in which local capital is able to operate profitably outside the manufacturing sector. In Brazil and Mexico, construction is largely dominated by local capital and some of the largest local firms are in this sector.[9] Commerce has also tended to be mainly in local hands, as has real estate and a number of other service sectors. It is not surprising, therefore, to find that these are often the sectors in which the local bourgeoisie, displaced from manufacturing, invests.

*The ideology of the local bourgeoisie*

The discussion so far has analysed the structural matrix of relations between the local bourgeoisie and international capital in Latin America. It is only within this context that the ideological orientations of the bourgeoisie can be understood. Two key points are apparent from this analysis, namely the internal differentiation of the local bourgeoisie, and the contradictory position of important sectors of the bourgeoisie in relation to foreign capital. (A third point which may be acquiring growing importance is the internationalisation of Latin American firms which may be reflected in a change of ideological orientation). In this section, there will be no attempt to discuss the overall ideological orientation of the Latin American bourgeoisie, which is outside the scope of the present study. The focus on ideology will be twofold. First, the attitudes of local industrialists towards foreign investment and state control of foreign capital will be considered, and then the effect of the existence – or not – of links with foreign capital on the ideology of different sectors of the local bourgeoisie will be discussed.

It has been a tenet of much (particularly North American) dependency writing on Latin America that the local bourgeoisie is strongly in favour of foreign investment and is generally pro-US in its attitudes. This is the conclusion of leading North American 'dependentistas' such as Johnson and Petras who have carried out surveys of the attitudes of Latin American industrialists. In Chile it was found that

> they are not at all opposed to foreign investment nor are they anti-American. Opinion is nearly unanimous that 'the nation needs more capital in order to develop industry and means should be adopted to encourage private foreign investment in Chilean manufacturing' (Johnson, 1972, pp. 182–3).

In Argentina, over 90 per cent of the executives of nationally owned firms interviewed were favourably disposed towards foreign capital in industry, and the majority also supported all the various aspects of US policy on which they were questioned (Petras and Cook, 1973, table 1a).

On closer inspection, it is rather difficult to accept that these findings unambiguously characterise the local bourgeoisie in Latin America as a 'dependent bourgeoisie'. It would not be entirely surprising to find that British or West German industrialists were also neither opposed to foreign investment nor anti-American. More detailed consideration indicates that while the Latin American bourgeoisie does not fundamentally question the idea that foreign capital has a role to play in industry, its attitude towards the terms on which it does so is much more ambiguous, at least in the 1970s, than the above quotation implies.[10] Surveys carried out in three Andean Pact countries, Colombia, Ecuador and Peru, in the mid-1970s, indicated that a significant majority of local industrialists in the chemical and metal working industries favoured some degree of government control over foreign investment and the transfer of technology. Amongst local firms, control of foreign investment was favoured by 94 per cent of respondants in Colombia, 77 per cent in Peru and 64 per cent in Ecuador, while control of technology transfer was favoured by 93 per cent in Colombia, 81 per cent in Peru and 60 per cent in Ecuador (Mytelka, 1979, tables 3.9 and 3.10). Generally speaking, a majority of those in favour of controls on foreign investment supported flexible controls, but particularly in Colombia and Peru, a significant proportion were in favour of stiff controls including limits on profit repatriation and regulating the use of bank credit by foreign firms. In the case of technology transfer, a majority favoured stiff controls to limit royalty payments and prevent tie-in clauses. In Argentina too, on the key issue of profit repatriation, 89 per cent of those interviewed in locally owned firms were in favour of some control, while when questioned about the form which foreign investment should take, only a third favoured the presence of foreign firms with few or no controls (Petras and Cook, 1973, tables 2a and 3).

What these studies point to is that while the local bourgeoisie in Latin America is not anxious to exclude foreign capital, a significant sector is in favour of state intervention in order to influence the terms on which foreign firms operate. The ambiguity of the attitudes of the bourgeoisie is illustrated by Mytelka's finding in the Andean Pact countries that there is little relationship between the attitudes adopted towards foreign investment and technology transfer. Contrary to expectations those who favoured stiff control of technology transfer did not necessarily support stiff regulation of foreign investment. Particularly in Peru, a fear that state control of foreign investment could be extended to local firms contributed to the rejection of controls over foreign investment by 23 per cent of the national private sector. In Colombia, in contrast, where the local bourgeoisie saw opportunities to expand through divestment by foreign firms there was much greater support for stiff controls on foreign investment (Mytelka, 1979, pp. 95–6). The position of the bourgeoisie in relation to other classes and the state at the particular time at which the surveys were undertaken is an important underlying element in this ambiguity.

In what ways is the internal differentiation of the Latin American bourgeoisie, discussed in previous sections, reflected in their ideological orientations, and more specifically how are the structural links to foreign capital related to ideology? Cardoso has concluded, on the basis of studies of the industrial bourgeoisie in Brazil and Argentina, that it is possible to find ideological differences within the bourgeoisie, related to its structural position (Cardoso, 1971). Two opposing poles can be identified: the 'national-populist' orientation on the one hand; and the 'international-developmentalist' orientation on the other. Those firms which were linked to foreign capital most closely tended to approximate the latter position, while those without any foreign links (either ownership, payments abroad or the use of foreign credit) were more likely to have a national-populist ideology. Unlinked firms tended to be more favourably disposed towards an alliance with the working class as a means of promoting development than those sectors of the bourgeoisie most closely linked to foreign capital. Unlinked firms were also more likely to favour land reform as a means of expanding the internal market, through an increase in the number of consumers (rather than a more intensive exploitation of existing markets) than firms with links abroad. However, such differentiation occurred within the context of a homogeneous broader ideological framework which is élitist, favouring the cohesion of all the dominant classes (including landowners) and the strengthening of the western block.

The study by Petras and Cook on Argentina concludes that there is a convergence of attitudes towards foreign capital and US policy on the part of Argentinian executives whether they are employed in TNC subsidiaries or are members of the local bourgeoisie, and that the degree of dependence of local firms is not an important variable. This may be taken as confirmation of Cardoso's conclusion that there is an overall homogeneous ideology of the local bourgeoisie. The possible differentiation within this ideology is not brought out by the study except on a few issues, perhaps because all but two of the national firms considered depended on imported technology. It does not, however, negate the existence of the kind of differentiation to which the previous analysis points.

At certain times in some Latin American countries, this differentiation has been reflected in the institutional organisation of the bourgeoisie. Rather than one organisation representing the industrial bourgeoisie at a national level, there have in some cases been competing organisations. In Argentina, the Confederación General Económica (CGE) was created during the first Peronist Government to express the interests of 'national entrepreneurs' in opposition to the Unión Industrial Argentina (UIA), which represented industry as a whole including the subsidiaries of the TNCs. The CGE frequently adopted nationalist positions *vis-à-vis* foreign capital, and favoured an alliance with the trade unions (O'Donnell, 1978, pp. 46–51). In Mexico in the 1950s, the Cámara Nacional de la Industria de la Transformación (CANACINTRA) composed of small and medium-sized firms, and certain organizations at the level of industrial branches such as the Cámara Textil del Norte, were highly critical of foreign investment and pressurised for stricter government controls. The Confederación de Camaras Industriales, representing large firms, were much more favourably disposed towards foreign investment arguing that it should be neither discriminated against nor given privileges (Pellicer de Brody, 1974, pp. 93–101).

In conclusion then, the structural differentiation of the Latin American bourgeoisie, in terms both of its links with foreign capital and its scale of operation, particularly the control of many large firms by conglomerate economic groups, is reflected at the ideological level. Under certain conditions, and despite the broader homogeneous ideological orientation of the bourgeoisie, these differences are sufficiently strong to be reflected in the institutional representation of the industrial bourgeoisie by competing organisations. Where such a division exists, one of the main lines of division arises over the position to be adopted *vis-à-vis* foreign capital. While total exclusion of foreign capital is never an option, these divisions reflect the more general ambiguity of the local bourgeoisie towards the TNCs.

## 3 THE WORKING CLASS

Two major issues are crucial in analysing the impact of the expansion of TNCs on the formation and development of the Latin

American working class. There is a line of thought which argues that the internationalisation of capital is expanding the working class in the third world, which could become an important base for anti-capitalist struggles (Landsberg, 1979). Against this, it has been argued that TNC penetration tends to lead to a differentiation of the working class and the emergence of a 'labour aristocracy' on the one hand, and the marginalisation of the bulk of the population on the other. Both the small size of the industrial working class and its internal differentiation have been seen as sources of weakness. The first issue that needs to be addressed, therefore, is the one usually discussed under the heading of the employment effects of TNCs, with the proviso that this is not simply a quantitative question but also implies qualitative changes in the relations of production. The second issue relates to the effects on the structure of the working class, both objectively in terms of wages and productivity, and subjectively in terms of political activity and ideological orientation.

## *Employment by TNCs*

Even at the most simple level of the number of workers directly employed by foreign manufacturing firms in Latin America, there are no readily available data. The best that can be obtained is an estimate of the rough orders of magnitude. Even for US subsidiaries for which there is usually much information, we only have an estimate that the total number employed in the region came to 945 000 in 1972 (May, 1975, pp. 31–2). Employment by almost 300 West German subsidiaries came to over 220 000 in 1974, and this represented less than three-quarters of all known German manufacturing affiliates in Latin America (Fröbel *et al.*, 1980, table 11.2). If it is assumed that the US share in manufacturing employment by foreign firms is roughly the same as its share in the stock of foreign investment, than the total number employed by foreign manufacturing firms in the region in the early 1970s would have been of the order of 1.75 million.[11]

Studies of employment by TNCs in the major Latin American countries suggest that this is not way off-beam. Table 6.2 indicates that manufacturing employment by TNCs in five countries for which data could be obtained was at least 1.4 million in the early 1970s, and it is certain that the inclusion of the remaining Latin American countries would push the total past the 1.5 million mark.

TABLE 6.2 *Employment by TNCs in selected countries, early 1970s*

| Country | Year | No. employed ('000) | As % of industrial employment | As % of economically active population |
|---------|------|---------------------|-------------------------------|----------------------------------------|
| Argentina | 1972 | 200 | 11 | 2.2 |
| Brazil | 1970 | 500 | 20 | 1.7 |
| | 1974 | 635 | n.a. | n.a. |
| Colombia | 1974 | 128 | 28 | 2.5 |
| Mexico | 1973 | 402 | 16 | 3.1 |
| Peru | 1973 | 44 | 25 | 1.1 |

SOURCES Sourrouille (1976); Luiz Possas (1979); ECLA (1977a and b); ECLA/UNCTC (1979); Bernal Sahgun (1976); Vaitsos (1981).

The earlier estimate on the basis of employment by US affiliates may be taken as an upper limit and 1.5 million as a lower limit of the range within which the number directly employed by foreign capital in Latin American industry lay in the early 1970s. This implies that in aggregate, foreign manufacturing firms accounted for less than 2 per cent of the economically active population in the region.

Table 6.2 also indicates the share of TNCs in employment in the major Latin American countries. Two features stand out. Their share in industrial employment is much lower everywhere than their share in output (c.f. Table 2.2). Comparison with the total economically-active population of each country also reveals that in global terms the contribution of manufacturing TNCs to employment is marginal. The conclusion that is usually drawn from this type of figure is that in terms of solving the 'employment problem' of the Latin American countries, the TNCs are unlikely to make a major contribution. Nevertheless this may be consistent with the view that TNCs are contributing significantly to the formation of the working class in the region, both numerically and in terms of political activity, although in terms of the total population this class may be a small minority.

Two patterns can be discerned in Latin America when one looks at the dynamic impact of TNCs on industrial employment. The first, characterised by Argentina, is the situation in which employment by TNCs has grown very slowly in absolute terms, making little contribution to increasing total industrial employment. In the Argentinian case, TNCs accounted for 40 per cent of the increase in

industrial output between 1955 and 1974, but only for 7 per cent of
the increase in employment over the same period, (Sourrouille,
1976, p. 57). On the other hand Mexico is an example of very rapid
growth in TNC employment – 12.1 per cent per annum between
1965 and 1970 (Fajnzylber and Tarrago, 1975, p. 494) – where their
share in the total manufacturing labour force has increased rapidly,
and where as much as 60 per cent of the increased employment of
the period 1965 to 1970 was accounted for by such firms (Sepulveda
and Chumacero, 1973, table 18). Although no comparable data is
available on Brazil, it seems likely that the situation there is similar
to that in Mexico, in view of the rapid rate of industrial growth and
the role played by TNC-dominated sectors in this expansion.

However, before concluding that, at least in those countries in
which they have expanded most dynamically, the TNCs are
making a major contribution to creating an industrial working
class, a *caveat* is in order. The increase in employment by TNCs is
partly a result of take-overs of local firms, and since, as was shown
above, there is evidence to suggest that most acquired firms are
profitable, this part of increased TNC employment cannot be
considered as a net increase. In Mexico, once employment in
acquired firms had been discounted, the rate of growth of TNC
employment in the 1960s was cut by half (Bernal Sahgun, 1976, pp.
156–61).

In any case, to focus exclusively on the direct employment by
TNCs is too narrow an approach to answer the questions at issue.
Apart from acquisition of existing firms, there are a number of
further factors that need to be taken into account. As has been
stressed previously, the operations of TNCs in Latin America is only
an aspect of the internationalisation of capital, which affects
industrial branches other than those dominated by the TNCs and
local firms which may have no direct links with foreign capital. In
general terms, the accumulation of capital has a double and
contradictory effect on employment. On the one hand, the
expansion of the market which it implies tends to increase the
demand for labour, while on the other the incorporation of new
production techniques tends to reduce the labour required per unit
of output. At the level of the branch, the consequences for total
employment will depend on the balance between growth of output
and 'modernisation' (in the sense of increased labour productivity
and capital intensity). Two aspects of the internationalisation of
capital have tended to contribute to TNCs accounting for a
significant share of the increase in employment in both Mexico and

Brazil. The replication of international consumption patterns through the diversification of high income consumption has resulted in TNC-dominated sections enjoying the fastest rates of growth of output. But over and above this, there has been a tendency for rapid modernisation in the traditional industries which had previously been characterised by low capital-labour ratios and low productivity (Fajnzylber and Terrago, 1975, pp. 490–511 and Luiz Possas, pp. 92–3). This has frequently been associated with the import of foreign technology, as in the case of the Brazilian textile industry, which is the second most important sector in terms of number of technology contracts with national firms (Almeida Biato *et al.*, 1973, table 4.17). This has contributed to the low employment creation of these sectors in recent years.

What this evidence suggests is that it is not TNCs *per se* which are the cause of the limited expansion of the industrial proletariat in Latin America, but rather the type of industrialisation model associated with the internationalisation of capital in Latin America since the mid-1950s. This is particularly well documented for the Argentinian case, where the employment elasticity of industrial production dropped from 0.55 in the period from the beginning of the twentieth century to 1955, to 0.22 between 1955 and 1973 (Sourrouille, 1976, p. 62). The period since the mid-1950s (in Latin America) had been characterised by a new pattern of accumulation, in which the expansion of industrial output resulted from increased labour productivity rather than expanded employment (cf. Salama, 1976, pp. 130–8).

It is also apparent that in terms of the formation of a proletariat in the major Latin American countries, the period before the mid-1950s, characterised by national-populist development strategies of one kind or another, was crucial. It was in these years that the proletariat grew numerically from insignificant numbers, and in which the basic trade union organisations were created (Spalding, 1977, chapters 3 and 4). It is true that over half the industrial employment in Latin America in the early 1950s was in artesan shops rather than factories, but nevertheless in 1950 there were almost three and a half million workers employed in factories, twice the number employed by foreign firms in the early 1970s.

## TNCs and the working class

Although an established proletariat was already in existence in the most industrialised Latin American countries prior to the rapid expansion of TNCs after the mid-1950s, and their subsequent growth has not contributed to a major numerical increase in the working class, this does not negate the possibility that significant qualitative changes may have occurred. There are two contrasting views of the impact of TNCs and the internationalisation of capital on the Latin American working class. One emphasises the intense exploitation (often referred to rather imprecisely as 'super-exploitation') of Latin American workers by international capital in search of cheap labour. The other stresses the differentiation of the working class as a result of the introduction of new production processes, possibly leading to the creation of a labour aristocracy.

There is no doubt that TNC workers in Latin America often do suffer from low money wages, long hours, poor working conditions, high labour turnover, speed ups and so forth, particularly when compared to workers in the parent company. Wages paid to workers in US subsidiaries in Brazil and Mexico are a sixth or a seventh of those paid by the parent companies (Salama, 1978, p. 272). Workers are often required to do compulsory overtime and may be threatened with dismissal if they refuse, or physically prevented from leaving the plant (Juarez, 1979, pp. 235–6; de Souza, 1975, p. 15). Assembly line processes which have been superceded by less Taylorist forms of work organisation in the advanced capitalist countries continue to be used in Latin America (Hirata, 1981). Labour turnover is often high. In Brazil in 1974, the average turnover rate was 72 per cent in the motor industry and 63 per cent in the electrical/electronic and the metallurgical industries, all branches in which there is a substantial TNC presence (Marini, 1978, p. 88). A comparison of the turnover rate in a French textile subsidiary in Brazil and the parent company indicated that it was almost five times as high in Brazil (Hirata, 1981, p. 14).

A common corollary of the emphasis on the intense exploitation of workers by TNCs is a belief in the tendency for the expansion of large firms in Latin America to lead to the homogenisation of the working class (Juarez, 1979, p. 160). In contrast, the differentiation thesis stresses the relatively privileged position of workers employed by TNCs and the divisions created within the working class as a result of the internationalisation of capital. Foreign firms, because of their high levels of productivity and/or need for a stable labour force have, it is claimed, paid higher wages than the norm and tended to provide better working conditions for their labour force than the local firms.

TABLE 6.3    *Average wage and salary payments per person employed of foreign firms (national firms = 100)*

| Country | Year | Wage and salary payments | Basis |
|---------|------|--------------------------|-------|
| Argentina | 1963 | 184 | All industries in census |
| Brazil | 1970 | 142 | Four largest plants in each four digit industry |
| Colombia | 1971 | 162 | All industries in census |
| Mexico | 1970 | 170 | All industries in census |
| Peru | 1973 | 147 | All industries in census |

SOURCES   Sourrouille (1976, ch. 6, table 6); Luiz Possas (1979, table 20); Matter (1976, table 3.39); Fajnzylber and Tarrago (1975, p. 374); Vaitsos (1976).

It is a well-established fact that TNCs in Latin America tend on average to pay higher wages than local firms. Table 6.3 indicates that these differences are substantial in Argentina, Brazil, Colombia, Mexico and Peru with average wage and salary payments by foreign firms ranging from almost 50 per cent to over 80 per cent higher than for locally owned firms. The problem with such comparisons is that they are not comparing like with like. Foreign firms differ from their local counterparts in a number of significant respects. They tended to be concentrated in particular branches of industry, rather than being evenly distributed throughout the industrial structure. They tend on average to be significantly larger than local firms, as is indicated by their concentration amongst the largest firms in each Latin American country. They may also have a dissimilar distribution of the labour force between different levels of skills and manual and white-collar workers. The problem that then arises is to distinguish between the effects of foreign ownership and these other factors in explaining wage differentials.

Firm size is indeed a major cause of differences in levels of remuneration between foreign and national firms, since wage levels tend to be higher in large firms than in small ones. The most detailed evidence on the relationship between ownership, firm size and wage rates comes from Peru (Vaitsos, 1976, table 8). The conclusion reached on comparing wage and salary levels for six size groups of firms, five categories of employees and four categories of ownership (49–100 per cent foreign, 20–49 per cent foreign, 1–20 per cent foreign and 100 per cent Peruvian) was that,

"Size . . . and not 'foreignness' becomes the most relevant explanatory variable on differences in remunerations. In fact majority or wholly owned national firms often pay higher salaries or wages than foreign controlled enterprises among firms of equivalent size in the Peruvian manufacturing sector' (Vaitsos, 1976, p. 28). A less detailed analysis of average remunerations in foreign and national firms in Argentina also revealed that amongst medium and large firms, the difference between the two types of firm was relatively small (Sourrouille, 1981, graph 3).

Although differences in wage levels appear to be related more to the size of firm than to the branch in which it operates (Souza, 1978, pp. 217–8) differences in the insertion of foreign and local firms in the industrial structure may also contribute to the observed differential in wage levels. The tendency for foreign investment to be concentrated in branches paying relatively high wages appears to be general in Latin America. In Brazil there is a significant correlation between foreign penetrationn and level of average wages at the level of industrial branches (Luiz Possas, 1979, p. 88) while in Mexico, industries in which TNCs account for more than 75 per cent of production had average levels of remunerations which were over twice as high as those in which their share in production was less than 25 per cent (Fajnzylber and Tarrago, 1975, p. 409).

Contrary to the initial evidence presented, therefore, there is strong reason to believe the foreign firms do not pay higher wages than *comparable* local firms.[12] This does not, however, rule out the possibility that TNCs have tended to raise the level of wages in particular branches with competing local firms having to follow suit. It could also be argued that the internationalisation of capital since the mid-1950s involving the establishment of new modern industries in Latin America has led to the differentiation of the labour force, not along lines determined by ownership, but between employees of large, modern-sector firms and the bulk of workers employed in small-scale traditional industries. This would correspond to a dual or segmented labour market in which the large firms of the modern sector employed skilled workers, paying them high wages, while the mass of the proletariat and the industrial reserve army would be confined to the traditional sector because they lacked the requisite industrial experience and skills (Quijano, 1974).

Such an interpretation is open to several objections, however. It assumes that a high proportion of workers in large, modern firms are skilled workers, and implies that in a situation of overall skill shortage, large firms will pay high wages in order to ensure a stable labour force. However, studies of the capitalist labour process have shown that far from workers in industries in the advanced countries requiring more skills as technological progress occurs, the effect has been deskilling for the bulk of the labour force (Braverman, 1974). The separation of mental and manual labour has meant that a small group of workers have become more skilled while the majority have suffered deskilling. If this analysis is extended to Latin America, the implication is that large firms in the modern sector will not employ a high number of skilled workers but rather that the greater part of the work force will be unskilled. Moreover, as was mentioned above, far from the modern sector paying high wages in order to obtain a stable labour force, labour turnover is often high and in some cases this is the result of a deliberate strategy of labour 'rotation' followed by the firms themselves (Afonso, 1975).

The paradox is that many examples exist where large firms both pay relatively high wages and resort to the mechanisms of 'super-exploitation'. This can be explained, however, where high wages are part of a deliberate control strategy adopted by capital. Phelps noted this aspect of the relatively high wages paid by US subsidiaries in Latin America in the 1930s (Phelps, 1936, p. 273). Higher wages were paid both because more was required of the worker and because it gave the firms the pick of the best workers. This has been analysed in more detail by Humphrey (1980: forthcoming) in the context of the Brazilian motor industry. He notes that high wages are not a correlate of the use of skilled labour, since skilled workers are a relatively small proportion of the labour force and the large wage differentials compared to other firms are found in the unskilled category. In fact, high wage rates are part of the labour control strategy of the TNCs in this branch, which has relied on high labour turnover and hostility towards union organisation as a means of increasing the control exercised by capital over the labour process and ensuring the high degree of labour intensity which characterises the industry. It is the large modern firms which have the necessary technology and management systems to make this strategy of domination of capital possible.

It should be stressed, however, that this is not a universal strategy of TNC capital but one that is moulded by the particular political

and economic situation in Brazil, which in the 1970s was characterised by an authoritarian military regime and weak trade unions.
In Mexico, in contrast, the motor industry is characterised by high
wages, low turnover and comparatively strong unions. The unions
themselves, through the union leadership, play an important role in
controlling labour. The system of giving part of the work force
permanent status and maintaining the remainder on a series of
short-term temporary contracts is also an important mechanism
through which control of labour is exercised (Roxborough forthcoming; Juarez, 1979). Thus, the different nature of the Mexican
political economy leads to a rather different strategy being employed by the TNCs towards the working class in the same industry.
    Another example of these variations is the case of the world
market factories producing exclusively for exports discussed in
Chapter 5. These are characterised by the employment of predominantly female wage labour. In this case international capital is able
to take advantage of pre-existing gender subordination as part of its
control strategy to ensure valorisation (Elson and Pearson, 1980).
As in the motor industry, these firms are characterised by high
labour turnover and hostility to unions (or in the case of Mexico the
use of unions to contract labour rather than to promote the interests
of labour). A crucial mechanism by which such labour rotation is
ensured is through employment of young, unmarried women who
are dismissed when they marry or become pregnant. Another aspect
of the exploitation of gender subordination is through the hierarchy
of labour within the factory. Thus, the higher up in the structure,
the higher the ratio of male to female workers with the shop-floor
being usually exclusively female. Perhaps the most crucial aspect for
capital is its ability to appropriate female skills, usually regarded as
innate dexterity, which are in fact the result of socialisation within
the family, while treating its labour force as unskilled (because it
requires a very short training period in order to become proficient)
and paying it accordingly.
    What these examples illustrate is that, contrary to the view that
some general characteristics can be attributed to modern sector
workers employed by TNCs or large national firms such as
'privileged' or 'super exploited', the impact of the internationalisation of capital on the Latin American working class varies
according to circumstances. The only general feature is the
interaction of the valorisation of capital, mediated through strategies to organise and control labour, and the local situation

whether in terms of gender subordination, political regime or strength of the working class.

Although, as was seen above, foreign subsidiaries do not pay higher wages than similar locally owned companies on aggregate, there is some evidence to suggest that the distribution of wages within the TNCs is different from that in local firms. In Mexico, a comparison between 254 foreign subsidiaries and a small sample of thirty 100 per cent Mexican-owned firms with similar characteristics, revealed that while average per capita income was similar in the two groups, employees were much more concentrated in the middle income group for national firms (almost 70 per cent) compared to foreign firms (only 45 per cent) (Bernal Sahgun, 1976, pp. 128–37). In Brazil too, comparative data on the distribution of the work force according to income levels for foreign and national companies in the metal working and textile industries indicate a greater dispersion of wages in the case of the TNC subsidiaries (Luiz Possas, 1979, tables 42 and 43). In the Mexican case, it was suggested that this reflected differences in the structure of the labour force with the locally owned firms employing a higher proportion of labour with moderate levels of training, as a result of their more antiquated production techniques, whereas the production processes used by TNCs tended to require a larger proportion of unskilled labour on the one hand and highly specialised technicians on the other (Bernal, Sahgun, 1976, p. 137). A similar conclusion to the effect that differences in wages both between firms of different size and different ownership could be explained by occupation and/or skill classification was also drawn in the Brazilian study.

This evidence is consistent with the view that far from large modern firms, and TNCs in particular, requiring a skilled labour force, the new production processes are characterised by the deskilling of a substantial sector of the labour force because of the elimination of traditional craft skills and the concentration of skills and high wages in relatively few hands (Braverman, 1974).

*Differentiation and the question of the labour aristocracy*

The existence of structural heterogeneity in Latin American industry in terms of firm size and ownership, differential rates of growth of industrial branches and differential levels of productivity is too obvious to be denied. Nor can it be denied that to some extent this has created a sector of the working class which is privileged in terms of its income levels (although as was suggested above this is not necessarily associated with other privileges). Capitalist development is always and everywhere an uneven process and the notion of a homogeneous factor labour paid a uniform wage is only found in orthodox economic theory. Nevertheless, this has not prevented some authors from seeing a certain sector of the working class in Latin America as a labour aristocracy, and a significant proportion of this aristocracy is seen as being made up of the workers employed by TNCs.

The concept of a labour aristocracy implies the existence of a stable group of privileged workers who, as a result of their favoured position, are politically and ideologically divided from the rest of the working class.[13] As was implied above, it is not sufficient to show that some workers are economically privileged in terms of receiving higher wages, but it is also necessary to establish that these economic differences are so deep that they separate the groups on either side of the economic divide, ideologically and politically. Such a view immediately confronts the paradox that workers in large TNCs in dynamic branches, such as the motor industry, have often played a leading role in militant working class movements whose demands were not aimed at increasing their own privileged position, but represented major neivindications of the entire working class. The role of the Fiat and IKA-Renault workers in the *Cordobazo* of 1969 in Argentina and the part played by the metal workers of Sao Bernardo do Campo in the opposition to the Brazilian dictatorship since the late 1970s are two particularly notable examples (Evans, J. *et al.*, forthcoming; Humphrey, 1979).

Evidence from surveys of workers' attitudes which touch on this point suggest that although real economic differentiation does exist amongst the Latin American working class, and favoured workers are aware of their privileged position, this does not generally constitute a major obstacle to solidarity with the rest of the proletariat. Obviously, at a sectoral level the immediate demands of workers in a dynamic, capital-intensive foreign owned industry may differ from those of workers in declining traditional industries. Nevertheless, as a study of Argentina concluded, the workers, in the most modern sectors in no way tended to differentiate their interests from those of workers in other firms (quoted by Jelin, 1979, p. 248). Difference between the types of firm in which they worked (foreign, national, modern and traditional) were not reflected in a differentiation in the attitudes of the workers. Only skill levels were an important factor in the internal differentiation of the working class.

The evidence on workers' ideology tends to confirm the findings of the previous section. The presence of TNCs *per se* has not tended to create a labour aristocracy in Latin America. In so far as workers in TNCs enjoy higher wages than in other firms, this is a reflection of their size and the intensity of labour required. This does not differentiate them from the rest of the proletariat in such a way as to justify the description 'labour aristocracy'. If there is an important sector of privileged workers who can be called an aristocracy, it is the skilled workers whose privileged position derives from the overall shortage of skilled labour in Latin America rather than the penetration of these economies by TNCs.

NOTES

1. The term 'local bourgeoisie' is preferred to 'national bourgeoisie' because of the connotations of the latter discussed above.
2. Calculated from ECLA (1977).
3. For evidence of the importance of groups in other Latin American countries see Rangel (1979) on Venezuela, Melo (1974) on Colombia, Strachan (1976) on Nicaragua.
4. For evidence of this in the pharmaceutical industry see above, p. 92.
5. For more on this point, in the context of the transfer of technolocy to the Argentinian cement industry, see Pearson (1982).
6. Katz (1976, pp. 24–31) develops a theoretical model of the determination of the price of technology which is illustrative of this point.
7. Phelps (1936, p. 7) quotes an example of a US firm in Argentina which decided to use a number of local firms to supply metal parts and castings so that no one local firm would be able to produce all the parts and pose a competitive threat in the future.
8. Two-thirds of the Brazilian firms and more than half of those in Mexico made profits of over 9 per cent in the year prior to being taken over. These profit rates were calculated on the basis of the prices paid by the US parent and where this exceeded the existing value of stockholder equity, the profit rate is under-estimated (Newfarmer and Mueller, 1975, table 4.5 and 6.5).
9. In Argentina, however, there is a significant penetration of foreign capital in this sector too, particularly among the largest firms (Vitelli, 1978, ch. 3).
10. Johnson's survey was carried out in 1964–65, Petras and Cook's in 1971 and Mytelka's (1979) in 1975. In the mid-1960s the developmentalist view of the role of foreign investment discussed in Chapter 1 was only beginning to be questioned on a wide scale.
11. Calculated on the basis of a US share in the total stock of direct foreign investment in manufacturing by OECD countries of 54 per cent. This was the figure for 1967 the latest data available (ECLA, 1978, table 2).
12. This conclusion is also supported by Wilmore's findings on the basis of

comparing like pairs of foreign and locally owned firms in Costa Rica that except for administrative employees, foreign firms did not pay higher wages (Wilmore, 1976, p. 13).

13. We shall not discuss here the view that the entire industrial working class in Latin America constitutes a labour aristocracy in relation to the mass of 'marginals' and peasants, since our main concern is in the impact of TNCs in terms of the differentiation of the working class.

# 7 Transnational Corporations and the State

## I INTRODUCTION

The relationships between the state and the TNCs in Latin America are many and varied. The state lays down the conditions on which foreign capital enters and operates in Latin America. It provides the necessary infrastructure for capital in the form of transport and communications networks, certain basic inputs such as power, and a general framework of legal and economic conditions. At times, it enters into production with TNCs through the creation of joint ventures. At the same time TNCs attempt, either directly or indirectly, to persuade or to force the state to adopt policies which are consonant with their interest, including attempts to overthrow those regimes which they do not find congenial. Sometimes, these relationships appear to indicate a high degree of cooperation between the state and the TNCs, at other times the relationship appears to be primarily one of conflict. In order to make sense of the overall pattern of state–TNC relationships, it is necessary to have a clear understanding of the nature of the state in Latin America.

It was suggested in Chapter 1 that the analysis of the state was an important weakness in both the economic nationalist and dependency analyses of the TNCs in Latin America. The nationalist view of the state, with its emphasis on bargaining, assumes that the state is the embodiment of the 'national interest'. Indeed, the approach appeals to state intervention as a means of controlling and altering various aspects of TNC behaviour, such as high levels of profit remittances or restrictions on exports, which are regarded as being contrary to the interest of the host country. The emphasis on conflict of interest between TNCs and host countries leads to the latter being treated as an undifferentiated unit, and consequently to the neglect of conflict between different classes and/or groups within Latin America.

Pro-TNC critics of economic nationalism are quick to point out that the companies did not foist themselves upon unwilling host countries, but were seduced by a range of incentives offered by the Latin American governments (Behrman, 1975, p. 2). This highlights a central problem of the 'national interest' view of the state. If indeed, the effects of TNC behaviour are so contrary to the national interest, why have governments at certain times bent over backwards to attract foreign investment with little or no attempt at regulation, and then at a later date applied much more restrictive policies towards TNCs? This has been explained in terms of an 'obsolescing bargain' in state–TNC relations (Vernon, 1977, p. 151). This approach, which was initially developed to analyse the extractive industries, but also has relevance for manufacturing, implies that there is a secular tendency for a shift in bargaining power from TNCs to the host country governments in the third world. This shift comes about as TNCs become less indispensable for the host country and governments learn more about the industry, and competition increases between rival firms. As a result, TNCs are increasingly on the defensive, subject to more controls and eventual nationalisation.

The shift from extremely liberal policies towards foreign investment in Latin America in the late 1950s and early 1960s, to much greater control in the late 1960s and early 1970s has been analysed in these terms (Vaitsos, 1973). Changing international conditions, particularly increased competition between US and European capital in Latin America, it is argued, have increased the room for manoeuvre of host governments. This explanation is not entirely convincing, however, since as was indicated in Chapter 2, competition between US and European capital for the Latin American market dates back to the mid-1950s and therefore preceded the change in policies by more than a decade. Indeed, it coincided with the earlier period of extremely liberal policies towards foreign investment. A second factor, it is claimed, has been 'enhanced knowledge about the operations, effects and treatment of foreign direct investments' (Vaitsos, 1973, p. 11). Within the framework of the state as representing the national interest this is perhaps the most convincing explanation. Failure to adopt policies which are in the national interest must be ascribed either to the inability to do so (because of the international situation) or ignorance. It is not clear that conditions up to the late 1960s prevented such policies being adopted and therefore ignorance must be the explanation. While there is little doubt that research over the past two decades has greatly increased our understanding of the operations of TNCs, much of this has followed, and indeed arisen from attempts to control the TNCs. A third set of factors cited by Vaitsos are internal changes within the Latin American economies and the different pressures brought to bear on governments. This does not, however, fit well within the bargaining framework, and opens the way to a recognition that the state is not the representative of the national interest but of particular group or class interests.

The problem with some of the dependency writers' treatment of the state is quite the reverse. Far from the state being seen as embodying the national interest, 'the dependent state comes to represent the hegemony of imperialism; this takes place through its minor partners (local bourgeoisie, bureaucrats, technocrats) who are in the government but do not have political power' (de Souza, 1977, p. 38). In fact, explicit discussion of the state is very limited in these writings, reflecting the view that it is unproblematic because of the alliance of local dominant classes with international capital.[1] The difficulty with this approach is that it is unable to address the conflicts between the state and the TNCs, either denying their existence or arguing that they are of no real significance.

Another aspect of the dependency view of the state is to derive the nature of the state in Latin America from the 'needs' of international capital. Specifically, the requirements of the TNCs and the internationalisation of capital are used to explain the emergence of repressive regimes in Latin America since the mid-1960s. This, in a sense, goes even further in seeing the state not only pursuing policies which promote the interests of the TNCs, but the very nature of the state itself being determined by these requirements.

## The role of the state

What is common to these approaches is an inadequate theorisation of the state and a tendency to view the state as unproblematic. Recent developments in the Marxist theory of the state provide a number of important insights which will be useful to bear in mind in analysing state–TNC relationships in Latin America. This is not the place to go into the various debates between alternative Marxist approaches to the state.[2] Rather than attempting to construct a comprehensive position on the state in Latin America, some of the elements of the recent debates which are particularly useful in analysing the relationship between the state and TNCs in the region will be indicated. Naturally, the starting point of all Marxist analyses of the state is the view that the state is not above society and class struggle but reflects class forces within society.[3] The capitalist state, (and it will be assumed that the states of those countries with which we are primarily concerned, are capitalist) serves to maintain and expand the accumulation of capital. To do so, it not only performs certain economic functions for capital, but it also performs an ideological function in securing the cohesion of the social formation (Murray, 1975). In doing so, Latin American states intervene not only to promote the accumulation of their 'own' (i.e. national) capital, but all capital that is located within their territory.

Two points emphasised in the recent literature are of particular importance to bear in mind. The 'instrumentalist' view (Gold *et al.*, 1975) that the state apparatus is directly controlled by members of the capitalist class or those who share a common background, values etc. with capitalists, and who therefore act directly in the interests of the bourgeoisie is either rejected or regarded as unnecessary for the functioning of the capitalist state. In contrast, there is an emphasis on the 'relative autonomy' of the state in the sense that, in order to perform its functions the state must be independent of the particularistic interests of individual capitals or fractions of capital. This is not to argue that the state develops an interest of its own, although this is a view which has been put forward by some authors (for example Smith, 1977 on Mexico). The emphasis on relative autonomy provides a basis for the possibility of conflict between the state and the TNCs, in a particular situation where the individual requirements of valorisation of some, or all, TNCs contradict the requirements of expanded reproduction for capital as a whole. A concrete example of this arose in Brazil in the mid-1970s when, in the wake of the sharp increase of oil prices and the consequent deterioration of the balance of payments which was threatening the continuation of accumulation, the government attempted to restrain the expansion of the TNC-dominated motor industry which was a major consumer of imported oil (Mericle, forthcoming).

The second important feature stressed in some of the recent literature is that the state, far from being able to resolve the

competition and conflict between different capitals and class
fractions, in fact reproduces such competition within the state
apparatus itself. As Hirsch puts it, 'this means that the anarchy of
monopoly competition reproduces itself at the level of the administrative state apparatus and creates a many-branched system of
mutually independent, partly competing and contradictory activities' (quoted in Picciotto, 1978, p. 224). It has been argued that
this competition is particularly characteristic of third world states,
leading to the establishment of large numbers of public organisations each with its specific objectives and criteria and with little
prospect of collaborating among themselves to achieve common
goals (Evers, 1979, p. 169). Such fragmentation of the state
apparatus tends to be accompanied by the 'capture' of certain
sections of the state by particular interests (Evers, 1979, p. 171).
There is ample evidence within Latin America of such competing
and contradictory activities by different parts of the state apparatus,
not least in their relations with foreign capital.

In Mexico, for instance, when the state was establishing its policy
towards the development of local vehicles manufacture in the early
1960s, the two ministries primarily involved, Finance and Industry
and Commerce not only failed to coordinate policies but were also
seriously at odds during much of the period (Bennett and Sharpe,
1979a). In Brazil, it is reported that the National Institute of
Industrial Property (INPI) and the Industrial Development
Council (CDI), both autonomous organisations within the Ministry
of Industry and Commerce, have adopted diametrically opposed
attitudes towards foreign capital (Briones, 1981, p. 25).

A further point which it is necessary to bear in mind in analysing
the state in Latin America is its dual and contradictory role as both a
*national* state, whose legitimacy is posed largely in national terms
and, simultaneously, as a partner in the promotion of the internationalisation of capital (O'Donnell, 1978). To put it another way,
the role of the state in presenting the interest of capital as the
national interest is rendered particularly problematic where a large
section of that capital is foreign owned (Evers, 1979, pp. 156–7). As
a result, the state in these countries can neither be consistently
nationalist nor consistently promoters of international capital (as
some dependency writers argue). The result is likely to produce
contradictory positions both within the state apparatus at any one
point in time and oscillations in policy over time.

The implications of this view of the state can be contrasted to the 'obsolescing bargain' view of state–TNC relations. The view that TNCs in Latin America were likely to be increasingly subject to government controls, which was prevalent in the early and mid-1970s (cf. Vaitsos, 1973) has been contradicted by subsequent reversals of policy in a number of key countries. In fact, looking back over the past three decades, the pattern of TNC–government relations seems to be marked by oscillations rather than any secular trend.

## 2 ATTRACTION OF FOREIGN CAPITAL

State–TNC relationships in Latin America seem to be marked by oscillations, rather than any linear progression towards greater government control. These changing relationships have to be analysed in the context of changing patterns of accumulation and political developments in Latin America. Moreover, in view of the often inconsistent nature of state intervention in the region, at any particular point in time, a particular line towards foreign capital is likely to be dominant rather than exclusive.

From the 1930s to the 1950s, a number of Latin American countries had populist regimes whose nationalist rhetoric was explicitly hostile to foreign capital. In several cases, including the Mexican oil industry and the Argentinian railways, foreign capital was nationalised and conflict between the state and foreign capital was not uncommon. However, the bulk of foreign investment was still in the extractive industries and in public utilities at this time, and it was in these areas that conflict tended to occur. Foreign capital in manufacturing was allowed to expand without interference, although no specific efforts were made to attract investment.

Between 1955 and 1960, several Latin American countries introduced specific legislation to attract foreign investment. These included SUMOC Instruction 113 in Brazil (1955), Law 14780 in Argentina (1958) and the Estatuto de Inversionista (DFL 258) in Chile (1960). In Colombia, virtually all controls on foreign investment were abolished by Law Ia in 1959, while in Mexico, although no specific new legislation was passed after 1955, official statements, for the first time, began to present foreign investors as a group who could and should participate in the economic development of the country (Pellicer de Brody, 1974).

The policies adopted in each Latin American country were broadly similar. Generally, foreign capital was granted at least equal treatment with local capital and in some cases preferential treatment. SUMOC 113 in Brazil, for instance, granted foreign firms an advantage over their local competitors, while in Argentina it was only a number of modifications made to the original law by the Congress that prevented a similar situation from being created. Even equality of treatment between unequal forces, however, was a very dubious kind of equality. The broad common features of the policy in each country were that foreign investors were guaranteed a number of conditions which they considered vital for their operations. These were a protected market for their final products, preferential or negligible tariffs on imports of machinery and equipment, intermediate inputs and raw materials and guarantees concerning the repatriation of profits, interest etc. The tariff policies resulted in high effective rates of protection, which ensured profitability often despite inefficient production, while the absence of exchange controls or guarantees of unlimited remissions ensured that operations in Latin America could contribute to the global accumulation of the TNCs.

The analysis of the changes in policy towards foreign capital in the late 1950s must be seen in the context of the economic and political changes which preceded them. The model of accumulation based on the expanded production of non-durable consumer goods reached its limits in a number of Latin American countries in the early 1950s. In the most industrialised countries import substitution in these branches was substantially complete, while further expansion through increasing real wages and the growth of the working class was limited by the effects on profits of a falling rate of surplus value in a situation of low productivity growth. At the same time, following the Korean War boom, there was a general deterioration in external conditions reflected in a movement in the terms of trade against the Latin American countries. In this situation, as the developmentalist theory emphasised, the attraction of foreign capital could be used to establish new industries, relax the foreign exchange constraint and incorporate new technology in order to increase the level of productivity. As Cardoso and Faletto (1979) pointed out in discussing these developments:

The foregoing observations do not attach any inevitability to capitalist development through external control or participation;

nor do they imply the opposite belief that would make historica
chance the only explanation. On the contrary, this interpretatior
proposes that there are necessary structural limitations on a
nationally controlled industrial development within which various social forces operate. (pp. 153-4).

The 'appeal to foreign capital' which characterised the developmentalist strategies of the mid- and late-1950s, only came
about as a result of a process of class struggle. In Argentina and
Brazil, this was initiated under avowedly populist regimes with
Peron's unsuccessful attempt to attract foreign investment after
1953 and Kubitschek's legislation in 1955. In Argentina, the
overthrow of Peron and the defeat of the Peronist movement in 1955
opened the way to a much more liberal approach to foreign
investment, while in Brazil there was a growing divergence between
the political bases of populism under Kubitschek and the control of
economic power. The class coalition of national industrialists and
sectors of the middle and working class that had provided the basis
of support for populism broke down. Sections of the local bourgeoisie supported the opening to foreign capital, while the working
class was demobilised and/or repressed. Even in Mexico, where
there was no sharp political break to mark the change, and where
there was no new legislation of the kind passed in other Latin
American countries, there was also a political struggle over the issue
of foreign investment. Some sectors of the local bourgeoisie were
opposed to the policy of attracting foreign investment and argued
for stricter controls on foreign capital (Pellicer de Brody, 1974).
    The internationalisation of the market through the attraction of
foreign investment was also facilitated by the defeats suffered by the
working class. This was particularly marked in Argentina where the
banning of Peronism, the dismantling of the Commissiones Obreras
and the substantial reduction in real wages contributed to the
creation of a favourable climate for foreign investment. This was the
case in Brazil too, after Vargas' death moves were taken against
communist-controlled unions and union militants. In Mexico, the
control exercised over the working class through the CTM was
reinforced by the repression of the transport workers' strike in 1958-
59, and real wages appear to have deteriorated in the late 1950s.
    The encouragement of foreign investment was provided with an
ideological justification by developmentalism, which replaced the
nationalism of the populist period. This drew a sharp distinction

between the traditional type of foreign investment, which had been concentrated in the extractive and export sectors, and the new type of investment in manufacturing, which was to be encouraged. Thus, foreign investment to develop the manufacturing base of the economy was seen as serving the interest of national economic development. This type of investment 'contributes to strengthen the country's autonomy *vis-à-vis* the external factor and to a radical change in the economic structure' (R. Frigerio, economic adviser to Frondizi, quoted in Sourrouille, 1976, p. 12). The contradiction between the 'national' and the 'international' was thus conveniently swept away.

In summary, therefore, the new strategy of reliance on foreign capital which many Latin American states adopted in the mid-1950s can be seen as the outcome of a number of internal factors. The need to resolve the contradictions of the populist accumulation model which had run its course was mediated to a greater or lesser extent through class struggle and changes of political regime. The state apparatuses at the national and international level[4] provided a new ideology to legitimise the new strategy. The success of the strategy, in terms of attracting of significant inflow of foreign capital, however, also depended crucially on external conditions. As was emphasised in Chapter 2, intensified inter-imperialist rivalry between the United States and Western Europe ensured that TNCs, faced with a combination of carrots (in the form of tax incentives) and sticks (in the forms of the threat of losing the Latin American market), responded through setting up subsidiaries in the region.

## 3 CONTROL OF FOREIGN CAPITAL

The late 1960s and early 1970s saw a marked shift towards stricter control over foreign capital in most Latin American countries. Colombia began to scrutinise all new foreign investment and imposed a ceiling on profit remittances in 1967. Three years later the Andean Pact adopted Decision 24 on the 'Common Treatment for Foreign Capital, Trademarks, Patents, Licensing Agreements and Royalties'. Argentina in the early 1970s passed new more restrictive legislation on foreign investment and set up Registries for Foreign Investment and for Technology Transfer, as did Mexico.

As in the late 1950s and early 1960s, there is a striking similarity in the kinds of policies adopted towards foreign investment in different Latin American countries (with the significant exception of Brazil) in this period. The non-discrimination of the preceding period was abandoned in favour of preferential treatment for local firms either through ownership restrictions or preferential access to credit, and so on. In some countries, limits on profit repatriation and payments of royalties were imposed. There was a general move towards closer scrutiny of technology contracts through the creation of Registries for Technology Transfer. This involved the elimination of restrictive clauses in such agreements and efforts to reduce royalty payments. Why, within such a short period of time, did almost all the major Latin American countries abandon their liberal policies towards foreign capital?

*Sources of state–TNC conflict*

In order to answer this question, we shall first look at the broad socio-economic changes which led to the more critical attitude towards foreign capital of the late 1960s and early 1970s, and then consider in somewhat more detail the specific experiences of Mexico and the Andean Pact countries. One attempt to explain these developments, that of Vaitsos (1973) has already been mentioned. His interpretation, in its emphasis on increased knowledge about TNC operations and changing international conditions (especially the increased competition facing US capital) fits within the 'obsolescing bargain' interpretation of TNC–state relations. However, as was suggested above, this is not an entirely satisfactory approach.

As was argued above, one possible source of state–TNC conflict arises where the behaviour of TNCs tends to impair capital accumulation within the social formation as a whole, in other words where there is a contradiction between the valorisation of TNC capital and the expansion of the capitalist mode of production. A common manifestation of such a contradiction in the Latin American countries has been a balance of payments crisis. Such a crisis has usually been accompanied by the state resorting to IMF support which is granted in return for a government commitment to an IMF designed 'stabilisation' policy. Such stabilisation policies often result in high costs in terms of interrupting the process of capital accumulation, particularly with an import-substitution strategy which continues to depend critically on imported inputs.[5]

After the initial period of capital inflow which resulted from the attraction of foreign investment to Latin America, TNC operations began to be seen increasingly as a source of balance of payments problems. There are two reasons for this. First, repatriation of profits, royalties, and so on, soon exceeded new inflows of foreign capital, and second, the manufacturing TNCs had substantial negative trade balances since they relied to a considerable extent on imported inputs, while their outputs were almost exclusively directed towards the domestic market.

The capital flows associated with foreign investment in Latin America show a common pattern, with an initial inward flow in the period when the new investment is being made, and a subsequent outflow when repatriations exceed the continuing flow of new investment. Taking the region as a whole, the outflow of profits, interest, dividends, fees and royalties by US manufacturing firms exceeded the new inflow of capital by an annual average of US $34 million in 1966–69, and US $102.5 million in 1970–73.[6] The increasing reliance on foreign capital also gave rise to a situation in which a growing proportion of the region's export earnings were being used up to service foreign capital (Caputo and Pizarro, 1970).

Balance of payments problems associated with foreign capital were not confined to the capital account, but also arose from their export and import performance. As was seen in Chapter 5, the export performance of TNCs has in general been unremarkable in the absence of government policies to promote exports, while the fact that subsidiaries are part of a global operation has often meant that foreign inputs are preferred to local inputs. As a result, the trade balances of TNC subsidiaries are often heavily in deficit. In Mexico in the early 1970s, TNCs had a trade deficit of around US $500 million a year, equal to roughly half the country's entire trade deficit (Fajnzylber and Tarrago, 1975, p. 549). In Brazil, the largest 115 TNCs has a trade deficit of over US $2 000 million in 1974, which again was almost half the total national deficit (Newfarmer, 1980, table 10.5).

The economic and political problems caused by successive balance of payments crises forced a number of Latin American countries to search for new solutions. One of these solutions was, of course, the greater emphasis on industrial exports which became such a feature of policy in a number of countries from the mid-1960s. As well as adopting general incentive policies to encourage such exports, a number of countries used measures specifically designed to force an improved export performance by TNCs (see above

Chapter 5). At around the same time, governments also began to show concern over the balance of payments outflow caused by the profit and royalty payments of TNCs. Controls on profit repatriation were a reflection of this concern, as were the creation of registries whose evaluation of licensing agreements depended primarily on the price charged for technology (UNCTAD, 1980, p. 5).

The broad outlines of state–TNC conflicts were set in the context of the problems of continuing capital accumulation within the prevailing development model. Intervention by the state was also, in part, an outcome of conflicts between different fractions of capital, particularly between international and local capital. Whereas initially, foreign penetration in the late 1950s had occurred in new sectors which meant that there was little direct conflict between foreign and local capital, the growing interrelation of national and international capital gave rise to new conflicts over the distribution of surplus value. For instance, the increasing reliance of local capital on foreign technology made the terms of technology contracts an important factor in the distribution of surplus value. At the same time, large national capital was anxious to enter the most dynamic sectors of industry, where surplus value was being concentrated to the benefit of the TNCs, providing a basis for policies such as Mexicanisation (requiring foreign firms to share ownership with local capital), which in turn reinforced the interpenetration of capitals and the creation of new areas of conflict. The particular balance of class forces within a number of Latin American countries in the late 1960s and early 1970s (with the significant exception of Brazil) was such that those sectors of the state apparatus which favoured a more nationalist policy were able to exercise greater influence on policy.

A further element in the adoption of new policies towards TNCs in Latin America was to legitimate the existing regimes. The late 1960s and early 1970s were marked by a growth of the left in Latin America and a number of popular victories. As an ideology, developmentalism was discredited for large sectors of the population by the late 1960s. Dependency theory was in vogue. Although not the intention of most dependency writers, it could be interpreted rhetorically as an appeal to nationalist sentiments against the predatory behaviour of the transnationals. It is no accident that the regimes which instituted policies to control TNCs most strictly also appealed strongly to nationalism for legitimacy, the most clear-cut examples being Velasco in Peru, Peronism in Argentina and Echeverria in Mexico, with a particular emphasis on third worldism in the last case.[7] The importance of this factor is illustrated by the changes which occurred when these regimes were replaced. Morales Bermudez, and to an even greater extent Belaunde in Peru, have reversed the policies of Velasco. The Argentinian *junta* replaced the Peronist foreign investment law with an extremely liberal code. The Chilean *junta* left the Andean Pact as a result of a conflict over its new policy on foreign investment. Even Lopez Portillo in Mexico went out of his way to reassure foreign investment and tone down the hostility towards TNCs of the Echeverria government after his election. By the late 1970s, there was a more favourable climate for foreign investment throughout Latin America.

*Mexico*

In Mexico, as was seen above, the major changes in policy towards foreign capital were made after 1970. By the late 1960s the viability of the existing import substitution model was coming increasingly into question. The growth of agricultural production, which had been well above the rate of population growth since the 1940s and had played a major role in sustaining the industrialisation strategy, fell below the population growth rate in the second half of the 1960s. The balance of payments was deteriorating at an accelerating rate and growing sectors of the population were being marginalised. Land seizures in the urban areas and an intensified struggle for land in the countryside were a popular response to these developments. The most significant threat to the Mexican ruling class arose with the student unrest of 1968, fiercely repressed by the government.

At this time, three alternative non-revolutionary strategies were proposed by various social groups and sectors within the state apparatus (Del Campo, 1972). A 'neo-liberal' alternative was supported by the largest economic groups, which favoured a reduction in the role of the state in the economy, the promotion of manufactured exports and the attraction of new foreign investment. A second alternative, 'technocratic rationalisation' was proposed by sectors of the state apparatus who emphasised the need for the state to maintain a long-term development strategy against the pressures of particular fractions of capital. A central element of this strategy was a fiscal reform designed to increase tax revenues, reduce luxury

consumption and stimulate investment. They proposed that industrialisation should be concentrated more along the lines of comparative advantage and a coherent policy should be instituted towards
foreign capital involving the adoption of explicit criteria of which a
main one should be its technological contribution. The third 'neo-
cardenist' alternative was more nationalistic in orientation and
found support among some small and medium-sized capitals. The
agreement was that the state should restructure the internal
productive system to absorb unemployment through the promotion
of labour-intensive techniques, public works and land redistribution and redistribute income through a progressive tax system.
Stricter controls should be imposed on foreign capital, to ensure that
the productive system remains under national control.

Significantly, all three alternatives proposed involved some
change in government policy towards foreign capital. Even the neo-
liberal proposal, which advocated increased foreign investment and
an increased role for TNCs in exporting manufactures, also saw a
need for Mexicanisation policies to prevent too drastic a shift in the
balance between foreign and national capital. The other two
alternatives favoured the establishment of criteria for evaluating the
impact of foreign investment which would be more restrictive.

In the event, the more restrictive policies on foreign capital
involved both an extension of Mexicanisation and an increase in
controls over the operations of TNCs. Mexicanisation has provided
considerable benefits to private Mexican capital which has been
able to enter into a profitable association with foreign capital as a
result.[8] The introduction of controls on technology contracts has
also benefitted local capital.

> Even the largest firms, with technical capacity and vast financial
> resources, which have bought technology on world markets for
> years, find that the Law and the Registry enables them to obtain
> substantially better terms in their contracts, since their negotiat-
> ing capacity is increased through the assistance of the State.
> (Campos, 1974, p. 474)

These measures have also contributed to improving the balance of
payments with royalty payments being reduced by over US $200
million in the first two years of National Registry of Technology
Transfer operations (UNCTAD), 1980, p. 15). Other measures,
such as those applied in the motor industry (see above Chapter 3),

have been more directly aimed at improving the balance of payments performance of TNCs.

The new policies towards foreign capital were by no means entirely welcome to the TNCs, although they did not engender as much hostility as Decision 24. The US Ambassador to Mexico created a political furore by warning that the change in the 'rules of the game' could have an adverse effect on business confidence. In the final analysis, however, the policies did not threaten the essential interests of foreign capital in Mexico, nor call into question the capitalist development model in which TNCs would play a prominent role.

## *The Andean Pact countries*

The origins of the Andean Pact's Decision 24 are to be found in earlier national legislation, particularly in Colombia. What led to the sudden change in Colombian policies towards foreign capital within the space of a few years in the mid-1960s? The immediate factor which triggered the move to increase control over foreign capital was the balance of payments problems of the mid-1960s. In 1966, the Colombian government had rejected IMF advice that the *peso* should be devalued, and had instead imposed strict import and foreign exchange controls. A fundamental purpose of the new foreign investment regulations was to reduce the adverse effects of TNC activities on the balance of payments. Profit remittances minus new direct investment had increased from US $5 million in 1950–55 to US $15 million in 1956–60 and US $45 million in 1961–66 (Matter, 1976, table 3.6). Both the ceiling on profit remittances and the creation of the Comité de Regalías were intended to stem the outflow associated with foreign capital and technology.[9] The Colombian government was no longer prepared to pay the price in terms of interruptions to accumulation and the loss of political support and legitimacy which orthodox IMF deflationary policies implied.

While the overriding consideration in these policies appears to have been to reduce the balance of payments deficit, it has been suggested that the pressures of a rising industrial bougeoisie also contributed to a more restrictive policy towards foreign capital. Certainly, judging from the evidence of the surveys of industrialists' attitudes undertaken in Colombia in the mid-1970s, discussed in the previous chapter, there was considerable support for such policies from these elements. Colombian capital was facing strong competition in those sectors such as textiles and clothing which had traditionally been the preserve of local capital. The new policies certainly benefitted local capital by increasing its bargaining power *vis-à-vis* the TNCs.

The experience of the Latin American Free Trade Association, where, many commentators felt, the principal beneficiaries of regional cooperation had been the TNCs (Teubal, 1968; Vaitsos, 1978, ch. 5), put the treatment of foreign capital high up on the agenda of the Andean Pact countries when they formed the integration scheme. Decision 24 was never intended to impede the flow of direct foreign investment to the region (Mytelka, 1979, p. 64), but it was intended to ensure that accumulation would occur at the regional level and to avoid the pitfalls of particularistic interests which would threaten to tear the Pact apart. In other words, a common policy on foreign capital was necessary in order to avoid the member countries competing among themselves to attract foreign investment.

Although the creation of a larger regional market was not against the interests of TNCs, the specific measures adopted towards foreign capital generated considerable hostility and pressures were brought to bear first to prevent the adoption of Decision 24, and then to modify it. The Council of the Americas played a leading role in coordinating foreign pressures. It prepared a critical report on Decision 24 and the economic instability which it would allegedly create, which was sent to presidents and ministers in the Andean Pact countries and to influential members of the US Congress. The Council also declared that business interests were very adversely affected and that a number of new investment projects were held up because of the adoption of Decision 24. Colombia was selected as the weak link in the Andean Pact chain to be subject to particular pressures. The Council of the Americas warned the President of Colombia that 'if he did not withdraw his support of the Common Code, he would be responsible for a violent revolution not only in Colombia but also in 'other countries of the Americas'' ' (Wionczek, 1971, p. 131). TNCs also made use of their local contacts in the Andean Pact countries. A representative of foreign interests attempted to have the Cartagena Agreement, which created the Andean Pact, declared unconstitutional in the Colombian courts. There was a bitter conflict within ANDI, the industrialists association in Colombia, which had initially given strong support to Decision 24, culminating in a change of president in the association, and a call for modifications in the policy towards foreign capital.

Some TNCs, however, saw the possibilities of deriving positive benefits from the regional integration scheme despite the controls on foreign investment. As Mytelka notes, 'Where the oligopoly market power of existing US affiliates had impeded the penetration of the Andean market in the past by non-US-based firms, regional industrial programs, for example, might be viewed by these firms as opportunities to gain a foothold in the Andean market' (Mylelka, 1979, p. 107). Firms which saw the Andean Pact as an opportunity to attempt to gain ground on the competition included Volvo, Bayer and Massey-Ferguson (Vaitsos, 1978, p. 129). As a result, the TNCs were unable to act as a monolithic block in opposition to the Pact's policy.

The fact that the design and implementation of policy occurred at two different levels, the international and the national, gave the opponents of Decision 24 ample scope for attempting to modify its content. As already indicated, Colombia was first identified as a weak link in the chain. Later, after the overthrow of the Popular Unity Government, Chile became a focus of pressure. Although Chile withdrew from the Andean Pact in October 1976 a number of modifications to Decision 24 were agreed by the remaining members on the following day. These modifications 'substantially altered the thrust of these Andean regulations. From a mechanism designed to favour national firms over multi-national corporations, Decision 24 has become a device advantaging above all the joint venture, whether between state and international capital or national private and international capital' (Mytelka, 1979, p. 73). The relaxation of some of the most restrictive measures such as the limit on access to local credit, and the increased ceiling on repatriation from 14 per cent to 20 per cent reflects the limits of autonomy of the Andean Pact Junta and the national states. By the mid-1970s it was clear that the most restrictive policies lacked the necessary basis of political support. The weakness of the local bourgeoisie in Bolivia and Ecuador and the fear of the expansion of the state sector and state control over private investment in Peru meant that these sectors preferred to ally themselves with the TNCs rather than support more independent state policies.

## 4 STATE CAPITAL AND THE TNCS

So far, state–TNC relationships have been considered only from the point of view of specific government policies affecting foreign investment. But, as was indicated at the beginning of this chapter, this is only one aspect of the interaction of state and TNCs. The state in Latin America plays an important direct role in production and capital accumulation. In 1970, the state sector accounted for an average of 18 per cent of GDP and 40 per cent of gross fixed capital formation in the seven major Latin American economies (Fitzgerald, 1977, pp. 73–4). Moreover, state enterprises enjoy a prominent role amongst the largest non-financial corporations in most Latin Americans countries. In Brazil, 74 per cent of the assets of the largest hundred firms are controlled by state enterprise (Evans, 1979, p. 224). In Chile in 1966 before the take-over of the copper industry, state firms accounted for 25 per cent of the assets of the largest 193 non-financial corporations.[10] In Mexico, 30 of the largest hundred non-financial firms were state-owned (Newfarmer and Mueller, 1975, table 3.4). In Brazil, Chile, Mexico and Peru, at least, there is also a significant participation of state enterprises amongst the largest firms in the manufacturing sector (see Table 2.5 and Bitar, 1977, ch. 5, table 1). Indeed, the share of state firms in the manufacturing sector appears to have increased sharply in the late 1960s and early 1970s.

The growing importance of the state sector in Latin America raises the question of the nature of its role in the economy. Do the state, and state firms in particular, develop their own independent interests, or do they support capital accumulation in the private sector? More specifically do state firms represent a countervailing force for TNC penetration in Latin America or do they support accumulation by foreign capital? A large part of public investment and the operations of state enterprises have traditionally been, and continue to be, the provision of infrastructure for private capital particularly transport, communications and public utilities. In recent years there has, however, been an extension of state ownership in two directions, namely into the primary sector through the nationalisation of foreign owned export industries and into manufacturing. Although the take-over of foreign oil and mining companies may involve conflicts between the state and the TNCs to be nationalised, it is still possible to view such nationalisation as being aimed at facilitating local capital accumulation where this has been impeded by inadequate earnings from a key export sector. In fact, in many cases nationalisation was the culmination of numerous attempts by the state to increase the integration between the export sector and the rest of the economy.

'hus, the key area for analysing the implications of growing state
ctivity must be the manufacturing sector.

For some authors, the increased role of the state in manufacturing
an be interpreted simply by broadening the definition of infra-
tructure to include such general inputs as steel and petrochemicals
which can be analysed in the same terms as, for instance, electricity.
'avares and Serra (1973) discussing Brazil argue that there exists 'a
ivision of labour where the state took up the heavier responsibility
f supplying the domestic market at low costs with basic inputs and
xternal economies which were used by MNCs for their own
xpansion, both domestically and in export markets' (quoted by
Evans, 1979, p. 22). This would appear to be supported by the
distribution of public enterprises in the manufacturing sector which
hows that they are highly concentrated in a small number of
ectors, especially in intermediate goods.

However, the sectoral distribution of state enterprises is not
ufficient to prove that they act as handmaidens for the expansion of
private, especially international, capital. The crucial question is the
nature of the relationship between state and private capital. Do
tate enterprises constitute an autonomous sphere of accumulation
or is their role primarily to subsidise private capital? The low
profitability of state enterprises, sometimes interpreted as an
ndicator of inefficiency, may in fact reflect a tendency for prices to
be kept low in order to support private capital accumulation. The
etting up of state enterprises which are sold off to private capital
once they are well established also lends support to the view that
tate intervention is primarily in support of private capital.

On the other hand, the growth of state enterprises amongst the
argest firms in some Latin American countries has led to their being
seen as 'an alternative and countervailing economic power to
MNCs in the Mexican economy' and 'the principal force countervailing MNC penetration in the Brazilian economy' (Newfarmer and
Mueller, 1975, pp. 55, 111). This is certainly true in a purely
statistical sense, in that the share of local capital amongst the largest
firms has only been maintained by the increased share of state firms
offsetting the fall in the share of private national capital. However,
the crucial question is whether state capital can be seen as an
independent force whose interests are opposed to that of private
capital generally and the TNCs in particular.

While there is little doubt that individual state firms, like other
capitals, have their own particular interest, this is not sufficient to

justify the identification of a distinct class interest. Even where the managements of state enterprises have a considerable degree of autonomy from central government, they do not necessarily constitute a separate class. In particular the ideological cohesiveness which would justify their characterisation as a class is lacking. This is not to deny the possibility of particular state enterprises which pursue their own interests, being seen as a threat by private capital. In practice, however, the dominant relationship is complementary rather than competitive. One manifestation of this is the 'tri-pé' in Brazil, the alliance between state, multinational and national capital which is particularly characterised by the development of the local petrochemical industry. As Evans (1979) concludes 'overall, the tri-pé in the petrochemical industry has succeeded in involving multinational capital in a nationalist agenda for the local accumulation of capital, while at the same time allowing them considerable leeway to exploit those areas of the industry in which they have the strongest leverage and expertise' (p. 248).

### The Proquivemex case

Conflict between state enterprises and TNCs arise when the latter go beyond their complementary functions and begin to threaten the very existence of foreign capital. An illustration of this is the conflict between the Mexican state firm Proquivemex and six TNC producers of steroid hormones in Mexico.[12] These firms had set up plants in Mexico to process a local root, *barbasco*, which is the basic natural raw material for diosgenin used in steroid hormone production. Most of their production was for the export market. In 1974, in a period when nationalist feeling against TNCs had been encouraged by the measures of the previous year, these firms came under criticism from student groups and in the press, for exploiting the peasants from whom they bought *barbasco* by paying excessively low prices. The following year, a state firm Productos Quimicos Vegetales Mexicanos S.A. de C.V. (Proquivemex) was created, to control all transactions related to the gathering, processing and sale of *barbasco*. The conflict broke out when Proquivemex insisted that the TNCs pay a higher price for *barbasco* – the state firm was now the sole supplier – and that they devote a certain part of their capacity to produce finished steroid hormones for Proquivemex to sell. The six TNCs refused to buy *barbasco* on the new terms. This led to an intensification of the conflict, and it was broadened beyond the normal scope of state–TNC conflicts.

Proquivemex decided to mobilise mass support from the peasants, in order to try and break the deadlock with the TNCs. The demand now was not for higher prices but for nationalisation. This broadening of the conflict to threaten private property and to incorporate the peasantry in the dispute was going too far. The government reacted by negotiating directly with the TNCs, bypassing Proquivemex. When Proquivemex went even further, and charged that the TNCs had defrauded both the peasants by failing to pay *derechos de monte* (surface exploitation rights) and the exchequer through transfer pricing, the TNCs were able to unite the private sector (both national and foreign) behind them. The Confederación de Camaras Industriales accused Proquivemex of agitating the peasants and creating conflict in the countryside to the detriment of the private sector as a whole. The National Chamber of Chemical–Pharmaceutical Laboratories criticized Proquivemex for threatening private laboratories through 'disloyal competition'. The dispute was finally settled in favour of the TNCs after the new government came to power in 1977.

The case of Proquivemex and the steroid TNCs is instructive in that it brings out the limits within which state enterprises operate in Latin America. When state firms pose a threat to the entire pattern of accumulation and the role of TNCs within it, international and national capital close ranks, find allies within the state apparatus and bring the firms back into line. The view of state enterprise as a countervailing force to the expansion of international capital tends to exaggerate the autonomous aspect of state capital. In fact state enterprises, like the state itself, are in a highly contradictory position, caught between a tendency to reproduce themselves as capital and their role in supporting accumulation, including accumulation by TNCs.

## 5 TNCS AND THE NEW AUTHORITARIANISM

The reversal of the policies to control foreign capital in a number of countries, discussed in Section 3, followed the overthrow of the elected governments which had instituted controls. This was the case with the 1964 coup in Brazil, the overthrow of the Popular Unity government in Chile in 1973 and of the Argentinian government in 1976. These regimes, together with the Ongania government in Argentina (1966–70) and post-1973 Uruguay have been characterised as a new form of authoritarianism, sometimes termed bureaucratic authoritarianism.[13]

## The new international division of labour

Attempts to explain the emergence of these regimes in Latin America have emphasised a number of key factors which are related in one way or another to the internationalisation of capital. The most direct link is established by those who give primary importance to the restructuring of the capitalist world economy as a cause of the rise of authoritarianism in Latin America (and elsewhere). 'The exigencies of the process of capital accumulation and the international division of labour, world-wide and in the underdeveloped countries themselves, thus become the principal determinants of the role and the form of the State in the Third World' (Frank, 1979, p. 1). The major feature of this restructuring of the world economy, as far as the Latin American countries are concerned, is a reorientation of production and employment towards the world market. Such a reorientation is necessary because of the crisis of accumulation in the advanced capitalist countries, which is being resolved through the establishment of a new international division of labour, the major feature of which is the relocation of production processes and product lines in the third world.

   This new international division of labour breaks the link between the accumulation of capital and the development of the domestic market which characterises import-substituting industrialisation. 'The wages and income of workers in manufacturing, mining agriculture, public and private service become no more than costs that must be reduced through real wage cuts and unemployment' (Frank, 1979, p. 26). This comes about because relocated production within the new international division of labour is primarily for the markets of the advanced capitalist countries. 'In other words, while capitalist production is geographically *decentralized*, consumer markets are increasingly *centralized* in the Western industrialized countries' (Chossudovsky, 1979, p. 17). The division of labour involves the production of commodities and products (within internationally dispersed production processes) which make intensive use of unskilled labour in the third world, while high technology, high skill requirement activities are concentrated in the developed countries. This is seen as contributing to a bi-polar state structure, with socio-democratic welfare states in the West providing for the necessary well-trained, well-fed, healthy labour force required, while authoritarian states in the third world provide the cheap, unskilled labour required there (Chossudovsky, 1979, pp. 23–6).

This line of reasoning is extremely appealing at first sight. Clear evidence exists of a link between a move towards authoritarianism in Latin America and more liberal economic policies. Sheahan (1980), has established a positive correlation between the degree of shift towards market orientation between the late 1950s and late 1960s in six Latin American countries and the level of repression in the late 1960s. Developments in the 1970s would seem to reinforce such a correlation. Nevertheless, the thesis as presented above is unsatisfactory on a number of counts.

Empirically, the argument that a new international division of labour has emerged since the 1960s, in which the Latin American countries have specialised in the production of labour-intensive manufactures for export, is untenable. As was seen in Chapter 5 above, the bulk of industrial production in the major Latin American countries continues to be directed to the *domestic* market, despite the rapid growth of manufactured exports in recent years. Moreover, these exports are not exclusively, or even mainly composed of labour-intensive products. In many cases, government subsidies far outweigh low labour costs in making these exports internationally competitive.

At a more theoretical level, this approach continues the dependency emphasis on the external determination of state structures in Latin America. The state is seen as the instrument of foreign capital and the armed forces as the true 'political party of the multinational corporations' (Petras, quoted in Serra, 1979, p. 100). Such an approach explicitly denies the relative autonomy of the capitalist state in Latin America. It also implies that the logic of capital accumulation is always enforced, tending to downplay the importance of the local class struggle, which is seen merely as a reflection of world accumulation whose outcome is predetermined. This leads to a completely undialectical approach, presenting only the unfolding of the logic of accumulation, which, as was argued above, is misinterpreted.

*Super-exploitation*

A somewhat different attempt to relate the emergence of authoritarianism in Latin America to the dynamic of accumulation arising
from the internationalisation of capital is that of Marini (1973).
Starting from a very abstract analysis of capitalist accumulation, he
argues that super-exploitation (defined as lenghtening the working
day, increasing the intensity of labour and depressing wages below
the value of labour power) is a necessary condition for capitalist
development in Latin America. Central to his argument is the
assumption that manufactured goods do not enter into the value of
labour power because they do not constitute a significant element in
workers' consumption. Thus, increases in labour productivity in
manufacturing do not increase the rate of surplus value.
Furthermore, as with export production, the fact that workers are
not an important market for the goods which they produce means
that wages are purely a cost for capital and not a factor in
realisation.

In these circumstances, the main sources of growth for capitalism in Latin America derive from luxury consumption, state
expenditure (particularly military expenditure) and exports.
Authoritarianism is required in order to ensure that wages are
depressed below the value of labour power, and to prevent the
working class from organising to limit the length of the working day
and the intensity of labour. Sub-imperialism, the strategy of export
expansion in association with TNCs emerges as a way of overcoming the restrictions of the internal market. This provides a point of
convergence with the analysis of the changing international division
of labour and the reorientation of Latin American production
towards the world market.

A major problem with this thesis is that the theoretical arguments
for the necessity of super-exploitation are not convincing (see the
critiques of Cardoso and Serra, 1978 and Serra, 1979). The key
assumption that manufactured goods do not enter the value of
labour power is unfounded. Moreover, although the coming to
power of authoritarian regimes in Latin America in recent years has
been followed by a significant fall in real wages, this is by no means
sufficient to show that super-exploitation is necessary for accumulation to continue. Even if it were accepted that super-exploitation
was a necessity, it is not clear that this can only be guaranteed by
authoritarian regimes. Since some of the conditions identified as

requiring super-exploitation are so general that they could apply not only anywhere in Latin America, but also virtually anywhere in the third world, the range of countries covered becomes so broad that the definition of authoritarianism loses its specific characteristics. What this reflects are the dangers of deriving iron laws from abstract categories, without passing through the necessary mediations in order to approximate a concrete analysis. Although starting from accumulation within Latin America, Marini's thesis has much in common with the approach which starts from international accumulation, above all a tendency to derive political conclusions in a linear fashion from a mistaken analysis of the accumulation process.

## 'Bureaucratic authoritarianism'

A third interpretation of the emergence of authoritarianism in Latin America in recent years, which is much more deeply rooted in a concrete analysis of developments in the region, is O'Donnell's explanation of what he terms 'Bureaucratic Authoritarianism' (O'Donnell, 1978b). He argues that the populist period in Latin America coincided with the 'easy' phase of import substitution, based on the production of consumer goods in the most industrialised countries. The ending of this initial phase created a number of economic problems including limited scope for further industrial expansion, increased dependence on imported intermediate and capital goods, growing foreign indebtedness and inflation. This undermined the class alliances on which populism was based, and led to the formulation of a programme for the 'deepening' of industrialisation through import substitution in intermediate and capital goods. Since these industries were both capital-intensive and used advanced technology, attempts were made to attract foreign capital (see above). To provide favourable conditions for the TNCs, 'orthodox' development policies were adopted of the kind favoured by international monetary institutions. However, the growth of the industrial working class and urban white-collar workers during the populist period created a force able to pose a powerful challenge to such policies, leading to successive crises and frequent reversals in economic policy. This is paralleled by the growth of civilian and military technocrats who form a '*coup* coalition' to put an end to political and economic instability through the institution of Bureaucratic Authoritarian rule.

O'Donnell's original formulation has been questioned on a number of empirical grounds. It has been shown that he has over-emphasised the concern for 'deepening', which has not been an important problem or strategy except in the specific case of Argentina (Serra, 1979). It has also been argued that the emergence of technocratic roles was not everywhere a prerequisite for bureaucratic authoritarianism (Kaufman, 1979). The exact relationship between the emergence of authoritarian regimes and a particular phase of industrial development has also been questioned. Nevertheless, despite criticism and questioning on points of detail, many of the critics are agreed in wanting to reformulate rather than reject the analysis.[14]

One of the most appealing features of O'Donnell's analysis is that although he sees bureaucratic authoritarianism as functional for international capital and oligopolistic accumulation, he stresses that changes in the type of regime are not the result of any irreducible logic of capital but 'pass through the sieve of class struggles and through the accidents of history' (Cardoso and Faletto, 1979, p. 205). This is particularly evident in the use he makes of the concept of the perception of threat to the existing economic and political order in explaining the emergence of authoritarianism and variations between the pattern in different countries. The attack on the working class which followed the institution of bureaucratic authoritarianism is not simply an economic attack, aimed at reducing wages in order to make the country more competitive in the international market for production sites or to increase absolute surplus value; it is also fundamentally a political attack aimed at demobilising and depoliticising the working class by dismantling their economic and political organizations.

The emergence of authoritarianism cannot be related directly to the internationalisation of capital in any simple way. However, the transition from the initial phase of import substitution which gave a new strategic significance to TNC penetration of the Latin American economies from the 1950s has led to an intensification of certain contradictions, the resolution of which has been attempted in an authoritarian way in some countries. This does not imply that authoritarianism is a necessary consequence of these developments in Latin America, nor obviously does it mean that economic logic will determine a continuation of authoritarian rule where it has been instituted until overthrown through a socialist revolution.

# 6 CONCLUSION

The relationship between the state and the TNCs can be characterised as consisting of islands of conflict within a sea of cooperation
and mutual accommodation. Government policies towards TNCs
and the role of state enterprises in the Latin American economies
have been marked by sharp reversals over short periods of time,
laying traps for those who attempt to project the latest trend. Such
vicissitudes reflect changes in the balance of class forces within each
social formation, the ambivalent position of certain classes and the
reproduction of competition and conflict within the state apparatus
itself. Nevertheless, despite these changes the broad limits of TNC–
state relationships are well defined. The state does not question the
continuing role of TNCs as a whole within the national economy.
When parts of the state apparatus do question this role, then the
TNCs are able to call on the support of the economically dominant
sectors of the local bourgeoisie, other sectors of the state apparatus
and of course the state of their home country. The recalcitrant part
of the state apparatus is then isolated and brought into line or even
disbanded.[15] Where, as in the case of Brazil, the state is increasingly
entering into joint ventures with the TNCs, a further material basis
is being established for a correspondence of interests. This does not,
however, mean that the Latin American state is reduced to serving
the interests of international capital and its position as both a
national state and a promoter of accumulation by TNCs will remain
contradictory.

## NOTES

1. It should be pointed out that Cardoso and Faletto (1979) is a notable
   exception to this tendency.
2. For useful summaries of these debates see Gold *et al.* (1975), Jessop (1977) and
   Holloway and Picciotto (1977).
3. This is not to deny the possible existence of a 'Bonapartist' state in which, as a
   result of a balance of forces between different classes, the state enjoys a high
   degree of autonomy.
4. Recall the significance of the United Nations Economic Commission for Latin
   America in developing and propagating the developmentalist theory.
5. It is sometimes argued that these stabilisation policies might run counter to the
   interests of domestic capital but not those of foreign capital (Fitzgerald, 1977,
   p. 71). For a discussion of the shifting position of oligopolistic capital (including foreign subsidiaries) over the cycle, see O'Donnell (1978a).

6. Calculated from US Department of Commerce, *Survey of Current Business* (August 1979, pp. 24–5).
7. A somewhat different case, Chile under the Popular Unity government, combined socialism with its appeal to nationalism.
8. Bennett *et al.* (1978, p. 266). The authors state that there is no evidence (one way or the other) that the state acted at the behest of private interest and suggest an alternative explanation of Mexicanisation. Their evidence does not however contradict the interpretation put forward here.
9. The Comité de Regalías had considerable success in this respect, reducing royalty payments by about 40 per cent between 1967 and 1971, a saving of US $8 million (Vaitsos, 1974, p. 129).
10. Ratcliff and Zeitlin (1976, table 6). Had the copper companies been included under state ownership, the share of state enterprises would have increased to over 45 per cent of total assets.
11. See Evans (1979, pp. 267–8), for a discussion of this point in Brazil.
12. For a full discussion see Gereffi (1978).
13. Mexico is also sometimes included in this category.
14. This is certainly the thrust of the contributions in the volume edited by Collier (1979).
15. See the discussion of CEME in Brazil and its relationships to the pharmaceutical TNCs in Evans (1979).

# Part IV
# The Total Perspective

# 8 TNCs and the Internationalisation of Latin American Industry

The extension of TNC control over industrial production is an aspect of the internationalisation of capital which has increasingly integrated the Latin American economies into the international circuits of capital. It has led to transformations, both in production and circulation, which have tended to eliminate national idiosyncracies (cf. Vernon, 1977, pp. 3–5), replacing them by a homogeneous international norm, around which individual firms pursue their strategies of competitive differentiation. Some aspects of this process have already been illustrated in Chapters 3 and 4, particularly the way in which international industrial structures and competitive strategies and consumer patterns have been reproduced in Latin America. In this chapter the transformations in production and circulation will be discussed at a more general level, to bring out the homogenising tendencies of the internationalisation of capital. In the last part of the chapter, the consequences of these tendencies in the specific socio-economic context of Latin America will be analysed.

## 1 THE TRANSFORMATION OF PRODUCTION

The internationalisation of capital has played a major role in the introduction of new labour processes and the transformation of existing ones in Latin America. In the most advanced sectors of industry, TNCs are introducing the Fordist techniques applied in the United States in the inter-war period and shortly afterwards in Europe. Such techniques are characterised by the application of

Taylorist principles of dividing conception from execution, and the subdivision of tasks, with the introduction of two further principles, the conveyor belt and a new form of control over labour power (Palloix, 1976, pp. 59–60). A crucial element is the transition from human-paced operations to machine-paced operations, which removes a major element of worker autonomy and control over the labour process.

The introduction of Fordism in Latin America is by no means universal. In many branches of industry the constraint of market size poses a limit on the introduction of automatic processes because the heavy fixed investment required is only justified if production is on a large scale (Mathias, 1978, pp. 44–7). Adaptation to the smaller size of the Latin American markets frequently involves the use of universal machine tools in place of automatic transfer lines with specialised machines. This gives rise to restricted modernisation of the labour processes with only some branches, or even some stages of the production process using automatic machinery.

Where market size is not a constraint, however, it is possible to introduce Fordist techniques. Indeed, whereas in the advanced capitalist countries workers' resistance has led to a modification of Fordism through job-enrichment schemes, job recomposition and the creation of semi-autonomous groups, sometimes referred to as Neo-Fordism (Palloix, 1976, pp. 62–5), TNCs which have abandoned Fordism in the factories of the home country, apply it in Latin America (Hirata, 1981). The industries which are most closely integrated into the international economy are those which seem particularly likely to adopt Fordist or Taylorist labour processes. The motor industry in Brazil is a clear example of Fordism (Humphrey, 1980), while export-oriented industries of the *maquiladora* type are generally characterised by Taylorism, that is fragmented and repetitive jobs not linked by automated machinery (Lipietz, 1982, pp. 41–2).

These changes in the labour process tend to be accompanied by increases in the level of mechanisation, that is, in the capital employed per worker. Production techniques in the advanced capitalist countries have tended to become more mechanised, and the introduction of these techniques together with the displacement of labour-intensive artisan production have tended to increase the capital intensity of Latin American manufacturing (ILPES, 1974). Foreign subsidiaries do little to adapt imported technology in a labour intensive direction, as opposed to adapting to the smaller scale of Latin American markets.[1] Moreover, local firms seeking to compete with the TNCs, and also often importing foreign technology to modernise their plants, use similarly capital-intensive techniques.[2] Large firms, whether foreign or national, which are in the best position to apply Fordist techniques, tend to have the highest levels of fixed capital per worker (see for instance, Vaitsos, 1976, table 3 on Peru; Newfarmer and Marsh, 1981, ch. 3, table 6 on Brazil).

The industrial branches dominated by TNCs, – those which have been implanted during the recent phase of internationalisation of capital and which have experienced the most dynamic growth – tend to be far more capital intensive than those branches dominated by local capital. In Brazil the capital–labour ratio was 83 per cent higher in those sectors in which the four largest plants were controlled by TNCs than in those where all four were owned by national firms (Luiz Possas, 1979, table 21). In Mexico, the capital–labour ratio was over three times as high in branches in whuch TNCs accounted for more than 75 per cent of output as in those where their share was below 25 per cent (Fajnzylber and Tarrago, 1975, p. 396). The shifts in the relative importance of different branches of manufacturing have also tended to increase the overall capital intensity of production.

## TNCs and agriculture

The transformation of production brought about by the internationalisation of capital extends far beyond those activities directly under TNC control. One area in which this is particularly marked is agriculture, where direct production by TNCs is limited with the notable exception of some plantation crops. Nevertheless, in recent years large areas of Latin American agriculture have been transformed and TNCs have been involved in a major way, both as suppliers of agricultural inputs (machinery, fertiliser, pesticides and seeds) and as purchasers of crops both for export and for processing for the domestic market.

Increasingly agriculture in Latin America is becoming subordinated to industry. One manifestation of this is the increasing proportion of agricultural output which is subject to subsequent processing.[3] Increasing industrialisation of agricultural crops has been accompanied by changes in the composition of agricultural output away from basic food crops (such as wheat and maize) towards agro-industrial crops, such as sorghum and soya, and fruits and vegetables.

The increasing domination of agriculture by industry has not resulted in any single pattern being adopted by food-processing TNCs to obtain supplies of agricultural raw materials. In some areas, TNCs give preference to capitalist farmers, who can cover part of the costs of agricultural inputs themselves and who can supply relatively large volumes of the crop. This is the general pattern in the Mexican fruit and vegetable industry (Rama and Vigorito, 1979, p. 186). In other cases, the TNCs take advantage of non-capitalist producers such as the *ejidatarios* who are the principal suppliers of strawberries in Mexico (Rama and Vigorito, 1979, p. 190) or the dairy producers of Southern Peru (Lajo, 1979).

Whether production is by peasants or capitalist farmers, it is geared to the requirements of the food processors. The most extreme expression of this subordination of agriculture is the contract farming system whereby, although landownership remains formally in the hands of the farmer, key production decisions are made by the TNCs and their agronomists. The TNCs also provide inputs, machinery and credit to cover part of the farmer's costs, with payment being deducted from the price paid when the crop is harvested (Rama and Vigorito, 1979, ch. 5; Burbach and Flynn, 1980, ch. 9).

The activities of the food TNCs have not only contributed to major changes in the composition of output, but also to changes in land-owning and production relations. In those areas where capitalist agriculture has been favoured, there has been a tendency for the size of farms to increase and small peasant producers to be marginalised. In the Mexican Bajio, the average acreage of Del Monte's suppliers increased by 150 per cent between 1964 and 1977 (Burbach and Flynn, 1980, p. 186). In the Cauca Valley in Colombia, the arrival of a number of US food-processing TNCs in the 1960s led to the displacement of many of the existing small peasants (UNCTC, 1980, p. 133), and an increase of 12 per cent in holdings of over 50 *hectares*. Where, in contrast, peasants are used as suppliers, the independent nature of peasant production is radically altered.

On the input side, TNCs have been active in providing agricultural machinery, fertiliser and pesticides, often with credit facilities provided by host governments or international agencies (Burbach and Flynn, 1980, pp. 110–8). These have supported the increasingly intensive nature of production which is often required by food processing TNCs. They have reinforced the tendency for the new type of agro-industrial development to benefit medium and large farmers who are able to meet the capital expenditures required by the new pattern of agriculture. They also contribute to the displacement and marginalisation of peasants and share-croppers unable to participate in the new expansion, who find their opportunities of wage employment are limited by mechanisation. For instance, the introduction of tractors, produced mainly by TNC subsidiaries, was estimated to have cost as many as 2.5 million jobs in Latin American agriculture by the late 1960s (Jenkins and West, forthcoming). The Inter-American Development Bank has concluded that 'It would appear that if current mechanization policies and trends, in many Latin American countries continue the outcome will be greater concentration of land use in the hands of a few, greater unemployment in the rural areas and probably little, if any, increases in food production levels' (IADB, 1978, p. 35).

It is not only in agriculture that TNCs make use of non-capitalist relations in order to obtain inputs for their own production. The existence of sub-contracting relationships between capitalist firms and artisan type workshops is another example. Here, there are examples both of TNCs directly transforming artisans into out-workers which supply them or carry out certain production processes for them, and of small and medium local capitals often faced with competition from large national and international capital, using outworkers as a means of reducing labour costs and avoiding heavy investment (Schmukler, 1977).

## 2 CONCENTRATION AND CENTRALISATION

One of the general features of capitalist development has been the concentration and centralisation of capital, as a small number of firms come to dominate many industrial branches, and a few hundred firms to account for a significant share of industrial production in all capitalist countries. Amongst the most significant consequences of this concentration and centralisation of capital in the advanced capitalist countries have been the increasingly social nature of production, the increasing productivity of labour, and the tendency for non-price forms of competition to substitute for price competition.

*The prevalence of oligopolies*

In contrast to the countries of the centre, where most industries
evolved to their present oligopolistic structures as a result of a long
drawn-out competitive process, major branches of Latin American
industry, particularly those which developed in the post-war
period, have been oligopolistic or monopolistic from the outset. The
prevalence of oligopoly in Latin America is illustrated by Table 8.1.
Similarly, at an aggregate level, despite the existence of a considerable number of small and medium firms, the largest hundred
account for between a quarter and a half of industrial production in
Argentina, Chile, Colombia, Mexico and Peru (Sourrouille, 1976,
table 9; Misas, 1973, p. 83; Cinta, 1972, table 9; INP, 1976, table
17), a situation that is probably reproduced in the other Latin
American countries.[4]

TABLE 8.1    *Share of industrial production accounted for by oligopolistic industries*

| Country | Date | Share of production | Definition of oligopolistic industry |
|---|---|---|---|
| Argentina | 1963 | 59% | 8 firms account for over 50% of production |
| Brazil | 1968 | 37% | 4 establishments account for over 50% of production |
| Chile | 1967 | 34% | 4 firms account for over 50% of production |
| Colombia | 1968 | >53% | 4 firms account for over 50% of production |
| Mexico | 1970 | 40% | 4 establishments account for over 50% of production |

SOURCES    CICSO (n.d., pp. 13–4); Fajnzylber (1970, table 3. 1); CORFO (1971) own
elaboration; Misas (1973); Fajnzylber and Tarrago (1975, p. 305).

Data for Argentina also indicates that there was a rapid increase
in oligopoly during the period of internationalisation of the late
1950s and early 1960s. The share of oligopolistic branches in
manufacturing output rose from 31.4 per cent to 43 per cent
between 1953 and 1963, and the number of branches in which eight
firms accounted for more than 50 per cent of output increased from
52 to 64 over the same period (CICSO, n.d., pp. 54–5). The same
tendency was also evident at the level of the industrial sector as a
whole, where the share of the largest 100 firms increased from 18 per
cent in 1956 to 26 per cent in 1969 (CICSO, n.d., p. 79).
    The internationalisation of capital has contributed to concentra-

tion and centralisation in a number of ways[5]. The introduction of production techniques and capital goods developed for the much larger markets of the advanced capitalist countries tends to lead to oligopolistic structures in third world countries (cf. Merhav, 1969). This tendency may be attenuated by a scaling-down of plant, fewer multi-plant firms and excess capacity as firms build plants ahead of demand, but nevertheless there does appear to be a tendency for small national markets to be associated with higher levels of concentration than larger markets.[6] It is not surprising, therefore, to find that on average, concentration ratios tend to be higher in Latin America than in the United States. For example, it has been estimated that the average four-firm concentration ratios for comparable products in 1972 was 69 per cent in Brazil, 71 per cent in Mexico and 50 per cent in the United States (Connor, 1977, table B.1). It has also been found that the ranking of sectors according to concentration is broadly similar in different countries lending support to the view that internationalisation of production techniques is taking place (Tavares and Facanha, 1981, pp. 354–5).

Concentration and centralisation of capital is not, however, determined purely by technological factors. Corporate strategies such as advertising (which create barriers to entry to the industry) or acquisitions and mergers also contribute to the creation of oligopolistic structures. In some branches which have well-established, relatively tight oligopolies on an international scale, the creation of 'spheres of influence' is an important element in determining the oligopolistic nature of Latin American markets (see Newfarmer, 1980, ch. 4, for the example of heavy electrical equipment). Thus, the internationalisation of capital transfers not only commodities, capital and technology but also certain industrial structures (Newfarmer and Marsh, 1981, ch. 2).

Paradoxically, as the case studies of Chapters 3 and 4 illustrated, the transfer of industrial structures may lead to less concentrated oligopolistic structures in Latin America than in the advanced capitalist countries. In these cases, there is a tendency for the *international* market structure to be reproduced within each Latin American country. Apart from cars and pharmaceuticals, there is evidence of such a pattern in record players and TV sets and electrical appliances in Mexico (Fajnzylber and Tarrago, 1975, p. 335) and household appliances in Brazil (Connor, 1977, table B.1). In other words, it appears to be a pattern found exclusively in some consumer-good industries where competition is based on product differentiation, advertising and the introduction of new models or products.

Concentration and centralisation is, moreover, a cumulative phenomenon because of the advantages enjoyed by oligopolistic branches and large firms. The mechanisms of surplus transfer between sectors enable the most concentrated branches of industry to expand at a faster rate than manufacturing as a whole. The existence of impediments to the equalisation of the rate of profit has been recognised by Marxists since the beginning of the century and more recently, by orthodox economists (Hilferding, 1963, ch. 2; Bain, 1956). The most important of these barriers are the large absolute amounts of capital required to initiate production under modern conditions; the high minimum scale of production required to take advantage of economies of scale in relation to the size of existing markets; the technological advantages of existing producers; and the product-differentiation advantages of existing firms.

These barriers enable certain branches of industry to appropriate a higher share of surplus value than their share of capital, reflected in a higher rate of profit. The empirical relationship between concentration and profitability is well established for the advanced capitalist economies,[7] however much less data is available for the Latin American economies. What evidence there is confirms that the same relationship holds in the region. Using census data for Mexico in 1970, it was found that a proxy for the rate of profit (value added minus remunerations as percentage of capital invested) was over 40 per cent higher in the most concentrated branches than in manufacturing as a whole (Fajnzylber and Tarrago, 1975, p. 418). Detailed analyses of the impact of market structure on profitability for US subsidiaries in Brazil and Mexico (Connor, 1977, ch. 5) and for a sample of foreign and national firms in Brazil (Newfarmer and Marsh, 1981, ch. 5), confirmed that profitability was positively related to the level of concentration in an industry. While these results must be treated with caution because of the possibility that a part of the profit of TNC subsidiaries is hidden by transfer pricing, they do confirm expectations.

*Access to funds*

The financial system may also contribute to concentration and centralisation, through the access of some capitals to credit on preferential terms. Large capitals, both national and foreign, located in oligopolistic branches are naturally most likely to enjoy this privileged access. Foreign capital has preferential access both to international and local sources of finances. Local firms which belong to the large groups enjoy preferential access to the groups' financial institutions (Strachan, 1976, pp. 70–3). By using sources of funds external to the firm, it is possible to raise the rate of return on capital invested. This is particularly true in Latin American countries, where the rate of interest has often been negative in real terms, that is, less than the rate of inflation (Sheahan, 1980). Those firms which have privileged access to credit are thus in a position to raise their rate of profit at the expense of other firms and branches and *rentiers*. In Argentina in 1970, almost half of the credit from private and official banks went to the most concentrated branches of industry (CICSO, n.d., p. 66). In Mexico, it has been noted that there is a positive correlation between size of firm and access to outside finance (Quijano, 1979). In Venezuela, almost 80 per cent of all credit went to the 'Gran Industria', defined as firms employing more than a hundred workers (CORDIPLAN, 1971, table 57).

The tendency for TNC subsidiaries to be amongst the largest firms in each Latin American country, and to be located in the most oligopolistic branches of industry, as well as the backing which they receive from parent companies, leads to a situation in which they have considerable advantages in terms of access to local credit, as well as foreign sources of funds. This is reflected in the tendency for TNC subsidiaries in Latin America to make greater use of external sources of funds and to be more highly geared than their local competitors, that is, to have a higher ratio of debt to equity in their capital structure (see Table 8.2). There are several advantages of

TABLE 8.2 *Debt–equity ratio of foreign and national firms*

| Country | Date | Foreign | National | Foreign ÷ National (%) |
|---|---|---|---|---|
| Argentina | 1963–68 | 1.83 | 1.30 | 141 |
| Brazil[1] | 1970–73 | 1.11 | 1.03 | 108 |
| Colombia[2] | 1968 | 0.77 | 0.67 | 115 |

[1] Refers to 318 large firms.
[2] Refers to a sample of 53 foreign firms, and to 298 firms which accounted for 80% of manufacturing sales. The figure under national firms in the Table therefore includes both foreign and local firms.
SOURCES Sourrouille (1976); von Doellinger and Cavalcanti (1975); Chudnovsky (1974, tables 18 and 19).

local borrowing for TNC subsidiaries. As for local firms, there is the possibility of increasing the rate of return on own capital through increased borrowing, where the real rate of interest is low or negative. Second, the use of local sources of funds avoids exchange risks for TNC subsidiaries if there is a possibility of a devaluation. Third, local borrowing enables the parent company to keep control of a growing subsidiary without having to commit further capital, which would not be the case if shares were sold locally.

There is considerable evidence that the ability of foreign subsidiaries to have a higher debt–equity ratio than local firms enables them to increase the rate of return on their own capital and may be a major factor accounting for the higher profitability of foreign firms. In Argentina, for instance, despite very similar profit margins on sales, TNC subsidiaries had a rate of return on net worth of almost 30 per cent more than national firms in the 1960s (Sourrouille, 1976, p. 73). Chudnovsky (1974) concludes after a detailed study of the financial behaviour of firms in Colombia 'We have established clearly the tremendous advantage which indebtedness represents in increasing the profits which foreign firms can obtain on their own capital' (p. 167). There is further evidence that the level of gearing has a positive effect on profitability from econometric studies of samples of foreign subsidiaries in both Colombia and Mexico. These found that gearing was a significant determinant of the rate of profit on net worth in multiple regressions in which the profit rate was taken as the dependent variable (Chudnovsky, 1974, pp. 162–9, 180–4; Connor, 1977, pp. 187, 200).[8]

The implications of this analysis are that both the oligopolistic structure of industry and the nature of the financial system in Latin America facilitate transfers of surplus value to the benefit of TNCs and the large local economic groups. These transfers tend to be at the expense of small local capital located in the competitive sectors of industry and also of *rentiers*, and contribute to further concentration and centralisation of capital.

## 3 THE TRANSFORMATION OF CONSUMPTION

The internationalisation of capital implies transformations, not only in the sphere of production, but also in the sphere of circulation. The tendency towards standardisation of products on a world scale was clearly seen in the discussion of the motor industry in Chapter 3. The internationalisation of consumption norms characterises other branches as well. In the tobacco industry for instance, there has been an expansion of consumption of 'light' tobaccos of the American type relative to the traditional 'dark' tobaccos in a number of Latin American countries since the mid-1960s. Moreover, this trend has been accompanied by a shift to even more specific types of product forms developed by TNCs, namely longer-length, filter cigarettes (Shepherd, forthcoming). National product idiosyncrasies tend to be eliminated with the creation of an international product. The process is never complete and minor variations to local conditions do continue to exist. However, the logic is one of variations in the same basic product and not the production of completely different products in different markets. The reversal of the neo-classical flow of information from the consumer via the market to the producer which Galbraith has emphasised (Galbraith, 1975), is nowhere more clearly brought out than in the way in which the internationalisation of capital is transforming comsumption patterns.

## Competitive strategies

TNCs contribute to this transformation by the introduction of the same competitive strategies which they developed in their countries of origin. As the case studies in Chapter 3 and 4 illustrated, these include product differentiation, the introduction of new products and the provision of consumer credit. These all have implications for the pattern of consumer expenditure, serving to channel demand towards TNC dominated sectors, and TNC products. At the same time, large local firms which attempt to compete with TNC subsidiaries are forced to adopt similar strategies in order to maintain their position in the market.

The great majority of TNCs producing consumer goods in Latin America operate in markets characterised by a high degree of product differentiation. In addition to vehicles and pharmaceuticals, these include branded processed foods, drinks, tobacco, soaps, cosmetics and electrical appliances. In all these branches, competition is based on the promotion of brand names and trademarks through large scale advertising and other techniques. It is not surprising, therefore, that the internationalisation of industrial capital in these branches has been accompanied by an enormous overseas expansion of advertising agencies, particularly US agencies since the 1960s. By the late 1970s, five of the ten top US agencies had over half of their revenue outside the United States (UNCTC, 1979a). Within the third world, Latin America has been a prime area for expansion by these agencies. In the mid-1970s foreign advertising agencies accounted for more than 60 per cent of total billings in Argentina, Brazil and Mexico (Chudnovsky, 1979a, table 4). The importance of advertising in transforming consumption patterns in the region is illustrated by the high proportion of GNP spent on advertising, particularly in the more industrialised countries. In Argentina and Brazil, advertising represents 1.4 per cent of GNP, levels exceeded by only two countries in the world, the United States and Bermuda. Amongst the other Latin American countries, Venezuela and Colombia had similar ratios of advertising to GNP to France, Peru ranked just behind West Germany and Mexico and Chile followed Belgium (UNCTC, 1979a).

It is clear that TNC subsidiaries are major customers of the transnational advertising agencies in Latin America. This is reflected in the high levels of advertising by such firms. US subsidiaries spent 2.4 per cent of total sales on advertising in Mexico and 1.4 per cent in Brazil (Newfarmer and Mueller, 1975 appendix, tables 15 and 19), while in Argentina, 99 foreign subsidiaries (with over 80 per cent foreign shareholding) spent 3.4 per cent of sales on advertising (INTI, 1974, table 2). However, product differentiation is by no means confined to foreign firms. Often, the acquisition of foreign trademarks through licensing agreements is an important element in the competitive strategy of local capital (Sercovich, 1974). Such firms also engage in heavy sales promotion of licensed products, and may even spend more on advertising than their foreign competitors, as in the case of the Argentine pharmaceutical industry (see Chapter 4).

### Effects of advertising

The sales promotion strategies of TNCs have a number of significant consequences for consumption patterns in Latin America. Heavy promotion of TNC product forms, both by TNCs and local firms, leads to a shift in demand away from traditional substitutes. The shift in demand for cigarettes towards 'light' tobacco in Argentina in the late 1960s was brought about by a sharp increase in advertising expenditure. It has also been suggested that less orthodox techniques, such as smuggling, have been used to establish TNC brands in a number of Latin American markets (Shepherd, forthcoming). Another example which has acquired notoriety is the shift away from breast milk to bottle-feeding promoted through heavy advertising by TNCs (Bader, 1980).

As well as affecting the distribution of demand between 'international' and 'traditional' product forms, advertising may serve to increase the market for particular products. In Argentina, heavy cigarette advertising in the late 1960s was accompanied by a rapid increase in consumer demand (Shepherd, forthcoming). Since the sectoral pattern of advertising in Latin America is very similar to that found in the United States (see Connor and Mueller, 1977, for comparisons between Brazil, Mexico and the US), this tends to reproduce the US pattern of consumption in Latin America.

From the standpoint of individual capital, advertising has a considerable effect on the rate of profit. In Colombia, Brazil and Mexico, the level of advertising expenditure was an important factor in explaining the rate of profit of foreign subsidiaries (Chudnovsky, 1974, pp. 131–7, 145–6; Connor, 1977). Not only was the impact on profitability statistically significant but, over the relevant range of advertising levels, an increase of 1 per cent in the ratio of advertising to sales led to an increase of at least 1 per cent in the rate of profit.

In addition to the effects of advertising on the pattern of consumer demand in Latin America, and on the profit of individual capitals, it should also be noted that the growth of advertising is essentially unproductive. Such expenditures, in so far as they have any function at all for capital as a whole (and do not serve simply to redistribute surplus value between branches and capitals) are required in order to realise surplus value. The paradox of such large sums being spent to overcome realisation problems in countries where large sectors of the population do not even have the basic necessities of life should require no underlining.

Product differentiation has been accompanied by the introduction of new products, as a· major element in the competitive strategies of capitals in the advanced capitalist countries. It is not surprising, given the continuous flow of new products generated by the parent companies, that TNC subsidiaries in Latin America have also adopted this strategy. The introduction of new products can take a number of forms. It may involve diversification into new fields, it may be the introduction of a new product within the same line of business, as in the case of pharmaceuticals, or it may simply be the introduction of new models, as in the motor industry. The extent to which TNCs in Latin America have resorted to the last two was amply illustrated in Chapters 3 and 4. More generally, there has been a tendency for TNCs to introduce a large number of new product lines into the region. This process accelerated rapidly in Latin America in the 1950s and 1960s. The number of new product lines introduced by 187 US TNCs in the region increased from 195 in 1940–50 to 435 in 1951–59 and 675 in 1960–67 (Vernon, 1973, table 3.3).

The emphasis on the introduction of new products has tended to lead to the intensive exploitation of the upper income sector of the market, rather than a rapid diffusion of products to lower income groups. There is a tendency for products to become increasingly sophisticated rather than cheaper – an emphasis on more for the same price rather than the same for a lower price. This strategy also militates against the achievement of long production runs which might lead to lower prices, by making it necessary to change products at frequent intervals. In brief, the result is that both the nature of the products being introduced (increasingly advanced specifications) and the consequences of product changes, even when these do not involve any substantive improvement, tend to make acquisition by the bulk of the population more difficult (but not necessarily impossible).

Another important development in the sphere of circulation has been the rapid growth of consumer credit in Latin America, both directly tied to the financing of sales of consumer durables and the increasing use of credit cards. The most important kind of consumer durable for which credit is extended is of course the motor car. Since the early 1960s, there has been a massive growth of credit to finance car sales, and an increasing proportion of sales come to be made for credit. The transnational motor manufacturers were extremely active in setting up finance companies in order to provide consumer credit. By the early 1970s the proportion of new cars sold on credit had reached 70 per cent or more in Argentina, Brazil and Venezuela, figures which compare with 74 per cent of all new cars being sold on credit in the United States, the home of hire purchase (AMDA, 1973).

The significance of the growth of consumer credit is illustrated by the case of Brazil, where finance houses, which were mainly engaged in giving loans to purchase consumer durables, increased their share of total loans from the financial system to the private sector from 3.3 per cent in 1963 to 15.1 per cent ten years later (De Oliveira and Travolo Popoutchi, 1979, table 86). In the early 1970s vehicles accounted for anything up to three-quarters of the total financial resources devoted to consumer credit (De Oliveira and Travolo Popoutchi, 1979, table 88).

The growth of credit cards has been spectacular in the region. In Mexico for instance, by the early 1970s, as many as 600 000 consumers had credit cards and 66 000 shops were affiliated (Guillén Romo, 1974). The expansion of consumer credit has enabled the oligopolistic branches producing consumer durables to maintain a rate of expansion otherwise constrained by the limited proportion of the population with a sufficiently high income to constitute an effective market.

## 4 INTERNATIONALISATION OF CAPITAL AND UNEVEN DEVELOPMENT

The major aspects of internationalisation of capital described in this chapter are world-wide phenomena. These include the homogenisation of production processes, the subordination of industry to agriculture, the concentration and centralisation of capital, the redistribution of surplus value towards oligopolistic branches of industry, the application of similar competitive strategies and the homogenisation of consumption patterns. These tendencies which operate internationally raise particular questions in the context of the specific socio-economic formations of Latin America.

### Employment

Changes in the sphere of production leading to increasing capital intensity, limit the expansion of employment in manufacturing (see Chapter 6). This is not reflected necessarily in the numbers employed directly by TNCs, which may increase, but in the overall employment implications of the kind of model of accumulation in which the TNCs play a leading role. As a result, industrialisation makes little impact on the large-scale unemployment and under-employment which characterises most of Latin America. However, it is important to stress this is not merely a result of the introduction of modern technology, but also of the capitalist relations of production within which such technology is applied. It is not technology *per se* that creates marginality, but the fact that it is introduced in order to produce maximum profit, and not to fulfil human needs, that is at the root of the problem (Quijano, 1974, p. 426).

## Distribution

The transfer of production processes and industrial structure to Latin America has major consequences for the distribution of net output. The introduction of more productive techniques in oligopolistic situations has meant that relative prices in those branches in which the process has been most marked have not fallen to the full extent of the increase in productivity. As a result, a part of the gain in productivity is retained in the form of higher profits or higher wages within the branch concerned (Sylos-Labini, 1962, 6; Salama, 1976). In Latin America, the pressure of the industrial reserve army on wages is such that increased profits are more likely to result than increased wages. This is reflected in the tendency for the differential productivity of TNCs *vis-à-vis* local firms to be much greater than the wage differential. As a result, the share of wages in value added of TNCs and TNC-led sectors is considerably lower than for national firms and the sectors which they dominate. Data from Argentina, Mexico and Peru indicate that the share of wages is between 20 and 30 per cent higher for national firms (Sourrouille, 1981, table 12; Fajnzylber and Tarrago, 1975, p. 377; Vaitsos, 1981, appendix, table 1). Moreover, in Argentina and Peru the higher share of wages of national firms held, irrespective of firm size. The view that this is accounted for by the ability of firms in the most concentrated branches of industry to maintain favourable price levels is confirmed by the clear negative relationship between the share of wages and the level of concentration in industry (see CICSO, n.d., p. 65 on Argentina, and Fajnzylber and Tarrago, 1975, p. 379 on Mexico) and the fact that it is the most highly concentrated branches which tend to show the most significant falls in the share of wages in value added over time.[9]

These relationships lead to the conclusion that, in a period of concentration and centralisation of capital and rapid denationalisation such as occurred in Latin America from the mid-1950s, there would be a tendency for the share of wages in industrial value added to fall. This is indeed borne out by the data for five Latin American

TABLE 8.3  *Share of wages in manufacturing value added*

|  |  | Initial year | End year |
|---|---|---|---|
| Argentina | (1953–63) | 25.7% | 17.0% |
| Brazil | (1959–70) | 26.1% | 23.1% |
| Mexico | (1960–67) | 42.0% | 31.5% |
| Chile | (1960–68) | 42.2% | 36.5% |
| Peru | (1963–73) | 26.1% | 24.1% |

SOURCES  CICSO (n. d., p. 65); IBGE (1979); Perzabal (1979, appendix, tables 12 and 13); Aranda and Martinez (1970, table 10); INP, (1976, table 17).

countries presented in Table 8.3. Moreover, there was clearly a similar trend in Colombia where productivity grew faster than real wages in most branches of industry between 1958 and 1968 (Misas, 1973).

The introduction of Fordist or Taylorist techniques, where it does take place, implies also changes in the composition of the labour force. As was seen above, in Chapter 6, there is evidence that TNCs which are most likely to apply such techniques tend to have a more heterogeneous labour force than similar local firms. This is consistent with the separation of conception from execution implicit in both Taylorist and Fordist principles. As studies in the advanced capitalist countries indicate, this gives rise to the emergence of a group of skilled workers involved in maintenance, planning of production processes and so on, and the deskilling of those involved in the immediate production process.

The tendency for the internationalisation of capital to produce an internal differentiation of the working class is reflected in the distribution of wage incomes. In Latin America, massive unemployment and underemployment together with a shortage of skilled labour mean that wage differentials between skilled and unskilled workers are generally between 60 per cent and 100 per cent, far greater than those found in the advanced capitalist countries (Gregory, 1974). There is a tendency for TNC subsidiaries to have a much greater spread of wages than similar local firms, reflecting the bipolar structure of skills amongst their workers.

Although there is no simple relationship between the functional distribution of income and the personal distribution, and although wage incomes in manufacturing are only a small part of total incomes in Latin America, nevertheless the concentration of income towards profits and within wages both tend to contribute to increasing income inequality. The most successful of the Latin American countries in terms of industrial expansion led by international capital, Brazil and Mexico, have both been characterised by significant increases in income inequality during the period of rapid internationalisation and concentration and centralisation (Tavares and Serra, 1973; Hernandez Laos and Cordova Chavez, 1979).

Of the other larger Latin American countries for which data is available, Peru and Venezuela were both characterised by increasing income inequality during the 1960s (Chenery *et al.*, 1974. Table 2.1). In Argentina, the share of the poorest 40 per cent of the population declined in the 1960s, although the main beneficiaries were the middle income groups (ECLA, 1969; Chenery *et al.*, 1974, table 1.1). Only in Colombia did the poorest 40 per cent in fact increase their share of national income (Chenery *et al.*, 1974, table 2.1). This suggests that, although one cannot deduce any hard and fast law concerning income inequality, there is a tendency for the model of industrialisation led by international capital to be associated with increasing inequality, with a significant sector of the population being marginalised at least in relative terms.

*Competition and accumulation*

The oligopolisation of Latin American industry affects both the form and the intensity of competition in manufacturing. In differentiated oligopolies non-price competition predominates. This has a double effect. It tends to reinforce reliance on the upper income segment of the market, by emphasising the prestige of owing the newest product and the latest model. At the same time, it enables the consumer ethic to penetrate lower income groups, creating new demands through advertising and permitting their satisfaction to a certain degree through the extension of consumer credit, although this may be at the expense of purchases of basic necessities.

The diffusion of consumption of durable goods to lower income groups is dependent on credit, which makes it subject to the limits of the financial system, and disproportionate expansion would threaten to lead to financial collapse. The barriers to further expansion have led to a typical profile of demand for consumer durables in Latin America characterised by a rapid initial growth and premature saturation, after which further growth in demand depends on the expansion of the economy as a whole, and cannot therefore play a leading role in dynamising the accumulation process. The introduction of new products thus becomes an important way of revitalising accumulation (Felix, 1968, pp. 18–30).

In concentrated oligopolies, which tend to characterise those branches dominated by TNCs which produce intermediate goods and capital goods, a different pattern prevails. The relatively large scale of plant compared to the size of the local market is such that barriers to entry are effective even against rival TNCs, unless they are prepared to suffer losses over a lengthy period of time. The behaviour of these industries is characterised by price rigidity, since reductions in costs do not lead to lower price, as under competitive conditions (Sylos-Labini, 1962, ch. 6). As a result gains from technical progress in these branches are not generalised to the rest of the economy through lower price which would encourage accumulation in other branches.

A tendency to mutual restraint in TNC-dominated oligopolistic markets in Latin America is also facilitated by the relatively limited proportion of the TNCs' total resources which every individual country represents. Apart from a few exceptional cases (Volkswagen in Brazil is an obvious example), any one Latin American country accounts for less than 5 per cent of *world-wide* sales for the TNCs (Sourrouille, 1976, ch. 2, table 9; von Doellinger and Cavalcanti, 1975, table 3. 12). It is, therefore, unlikely to be worthwhile unleashing an intense competitive struggle to eliminate TNC competitors when these could draw on vast resources, relative to the size of the local operation, if the need arose. Intra-TNC competition will therefore be decided at the international level and not within individual Latin American countries.

Thus, the behaviour of firms in both differentiated and concentrated oligopolies tends to retard the accumulation process. It should be emphasised, however, that this is only a tendency, and does not imply that the internationalisation of capital leads to stagnation in Latin America. There are important counteracting factors which maintain the dynamic of accumulation, such as the growth of advertising and credit and the intervention of the state.

## Balance of payments

The accumulation process tends also to be constrained by the increasing balance of payments deficit associated with the model. The tendency for the production structure to shift in favour of the most concentrated, foreign dominated branches is associated with both an increasing import content of industrial production as a whole, and an increasing proportion of foreign exchange earnings being taken up in servicing foreign capital.

The initial inflow of foreign capital is relatively short-lived. Foreign firms are able to earn high profits in the early stages of the development of an industry, either because they are competing with local firms with less efficient production techniques and are therefore able to earn super-profits, or because in the case of an entirely new industry, demand may exceed supply, providing very favourable market conditions. These high profits can then be re-invested to meet further expansion with no additional inflow of foreign capital required. In addition, as was seen above, TNCs also enjoy preferential access to local sources of funds. The tendency, therefore, is for each new investment to become self-financing within a relatively short period of time and to begin to generate a net flow of profits and dividends abroad (cf. Chudnovsky, 1981).

The branches of industry which show the most rapid rates of growth tend to be relatively import intensive. Moreover, one of the few clear and consistent differences observed in comparisons between national and foreign firms in Latin America has been the tendency of the latter to rely much more heavily on imported inputs. In Mexico, the ratio of intermediate inputs to output for TNCs was 7.8 per cent, compared to only 3.4 per cent for local firms (Fajnzylber and Tarrago, 1975, p. 520). In Peru, the equivalent ratios were 20.7 per cent and 16.6 per cent (Vaitsos, 1981, appendix, table 4). Although similar comprehensive data does not exist for other countries, the situation appears to be similar. In Argentina, foreign firms had an import coefficient of 11.3 per cent compared to 9.4 per cent for local firms with technology contracts – which are likely to be the local firms which make most use of imported inputs (INTI, 1974, table 2). In Brazil, the average import propensity of TNCs was 15.6 per cent compared to 8.8 per cent for local firms in a large sample (Newfarmer and Marsh, 1981, ch 4, table 1). There is also evidence to suggest that foreign firms have a greater propensity to import in Colombia and Chile (Matter, 1976, p. 246; Acevedo and Vergara, 1970).

It is true, of course, that the concentration of TNCs in dynamic sectors of the economy, which also tend to be import intensive, will naturally show up in a higher overall share of imports in production. Nevertheless, this is not likely to explain the entire difference in import intensity since foreign firms tend to have a higher propensity to import in most (but not all) branches. A study of nine electrical industries in Brazil found that ownership is highly significant in explaining import ratios, but the industry is barely significant (Newfarmer, 1980, table 10.8). Only one study has failed to find a difference in terms of import behaviour, that of Wilmore (1976) in Costa Rica.

The restructuring of consumption and the increased penetration of foreign capital both tend to increase the overall import intensity of production. In Argentina, for instance, comparisons of the input–output tables of 1953, 1963 and 1970 revealed a continuous and general increase in the intermediate import content of final demand. Moreover, in 1970, the import content of the dynamic branches of industry were significantly higher than those of the traditional industries (13.5 per cent as opposed to 8 per cent) (Sourrouille, 1981, p. 335). In Brazil, the share of imports in the total supply of industrial goods increased sharply from 6.8 per cent in 1965 to 17.1 per cent in 1974 (Serra, 1979, table 3). In Colombia, the share of imports in intermediate inputs for manufacturing as a whole increased from 21.5 per cent in 1953 to 24.3 per cent in 1969, despite a reduction in the import intensity of most branches (Matter, 1976, table 3.30). In Mexico, the net import substitution of the 1960s was reversed from around 1970, with a rise in the ratio of imports to manufacturing output (ECLA, 1976, table 3). The characteristic pattern, at least for the most industrialised Latin American countries, is that an initial phase of reduced import dependence as a result of the import-substituting strategy is then reversed with the growing weight of both import-intensive branches of industry and TNC subsidiaries within the industrial structure.

## Consumption

The internationalisation of consumption patterns has implications for the whole lifestyle associated with this model of development. Chapters 3 and 4 gave two examples of this, the restructuring of transport towards private rather than public transport, and the emphasis of health care systems on drug-intensive curative medicine rather than preventive medicine. The transfer of consumption patterns characteristic of advanced capitalism to Latin America has to be seen in the context of the region's income levels and income distribution.

It is sometimes argued that, given the low per capita income in Latin America relative to the countries of origin of most TNCs, such firms have a vested interest in an inegalitarian income distribution, without which there would be no local market for their products. Evidence for both Brazil and Mexico indicates that a more unequal income distribution does tend to contribute to a faster rate of growth of demand for those sectors dominated by foreign capital, but that it is by no means necessary for these sectors to grow. In Brazil, it was found that the share of foreign firms in manufacturing was likely to increase whatever the assumption made about changes in distribution, but that the extent of the change was small even though it would be greater for a more regressive distribution (Morley and Smith, 1973). There are three main reasons for this. In the first place, different patterns of final demand associated with changes in income distribution tend to give rise to very similar structures of production of intermediate and capital goods which are well developed in Brazil. Second, foreign capital is not exclusively located in those branches characterised by a high income elasticity of demand. Although this is the case for the motor industry, income elasticity is less than one in some foreign dominated branches, particularly tobacco and pharmaceuticals. Finally, the diffusion of many consumer durable goods (other than cars) to groups below the richest 10 per cent of the population, and the saturation of the market at the highest income levels means that demand for such goods tends to increase more rapidly when the redistribution of income is not to the benefit of the highest income groups.

In Mexico the situation is broadly similar. The growth of the modern sector (defined as rubber, machinery, motor vehicles and other manufactures) in which TNCs account for more than half of total production, is favoured by increasingly regressive distribution of income (Lustig, 1979). However, it was also concluded that increasing inequality is not a necessary condition for expanding the market for these types of commodities, and that for domestic appliances the saturation of the market at the upper end of the income scale implies that a less regressive distribution is more favourable. A static comparison of gross output of branches in which TNCs accounted for more than 50 per cent of production, under the prevailing Mexican distribution of income and the more egalitarian British distribution, indicated that the share of these branches would only be marginally reduced by a more progressive income distribution (Jenkins, 1979, pp. 187–9). Again, this comes about because changes in gross output are considerably less marked than changes in final demand and because for some TNC-dominated branches (again notably tobacco and pharmaceuticals) the income elasticity is well below one.

The extent to which demand for consumer durables other than cars depends on sectors of the population below the highest income groups, in contradiction to some stagnationist theories, is a vivid indicator of the success of TNCs in restructuring consumption patterns in Latin America. Indeed, it appears that in some cases, at least, capital has been so successful in diffusing consumer durables to the working class and lower income groups in the urban areas generally, that they have been acquired at the expense of commodities conventionally regarded as basic necessities, particularly food. In Brazil, there was a significant increase in the share of working-class household expenditure on domestic appliances in Sao Paulo during the 1960s at the expense of food consumption. Since real incomes remained roughly constant, this involved a fall in physical food consumption and an absolute deterioration in nutrition levels (Wells, J., 1977, pp. 269–70). A similar phenomenon, of substituting consumer durables for necessities, characterised as the 'empty refrigerator' syndrome, is also at work in Mexico (Lustig, 1979, p. 541).

When it comes to differentiated non-durable goods, the possible displacement of low-cost basic goods by high-cost branded products affects even the poorest groups. The substitution of bottle feeding for breast feeding is a vivid example of the disasterous effects which the reproduction of the consumption patterns of developed countries by the poor in Latin America can have (Bader, 1980; Ledogar, 1975, ch. 9). Similarly, heavy promotion of differentiated food and drink products have led to changes of diet which are detrimental nutritionally (Montes de Oca and Escudero, 1981).

## CONCLUSION

In the areas of employment, distribution, accumulation, balance of payments and consumption, the internationlisation of capital combines with specific local socio-economic structures in Latin America, themselves the outcome of previous phases of internationalisation of capital, to create new problems and new possibilities of resolving them. The model of industrial growth is not necessarily undynamic, although in some cases it has been (for example in Argentina). It is, however, highly uneven in terms of the distribution of benefits. The main beneficiaries are undoubtedly the TNCs themselves and those sections of local capital which are able to adapt to the exigencies of the internationalisation of capital, primarily the large economic groups. The losers are those who are marginalised both as producers and consumers, and those who are incorporated in unskilled jobs, and subject to a regime of intense labour exploitation.

NOTES

1. See Sourrouille (1981, pp. 292–3) on Argentina; Morley and Smith (1977b) on Brazil and Von Bertrab (1968) quoted in Wionczek *et al.* (1971) on Mexico.
2. It is, of course, true that in aggregate, foreign firms are more capital intensive than local firms (see Fajnzylber and Tarrago, 1975 on Mexico; Vaitsos, 1981, appendix, table 1 on Peru). However the importance of ownership, as opposed to other factors such as firm size or branch of industry, is not clear. See Vaitsos (1981); Wilmore (1976) on Costa Rica; Lall and Streeten (1977) on Colombia; Morley and Smith (1977a) and Newfarmer and Marsh (1981, ch. 3) on Brazil for different views.
3. In Mexico, it is estimated that this proportion increased from 25 per cent to 43.7 per cent between 1960 and 1970 (Montes de Oca and Escudero, 1981, p. 999).
4. The figures compare with those found in advanced capitalist countries such as the United States, where a hundred firms accounted for a third of industrial output in the 1960s (Baran, 1973, p. 73) and Britain, where the same number controlled over 40 per cent of production (Hannah and Kay, 1977, fig. 1.1).
5. It has been argued in some quarters that penetration by foreign capital serves to eliminate monopoly positions (cf. Weeks, 1977). Clearly, this can only be true when TNCs enter existing branches rather than creating new ones, and if they do so through establishing new firms rather than taking over existing ones. In any case, even if these conditions are satisfied and there is an initial reduction in concentration, in the long term the outcome may be the recreation of monopoly positions. Weeks' finding that monopoly was reduced in Peru in the period 1957–62 is based on a highly-aggregated analysis which cannot distinguish between increased competition for existing firms and the development of new branches which may be highly concentrated. For a survey of the literature on this issue, see Newfarmer, forthcoming.
6. On the relationship between market size and concentration in advanced industrial countries see Pryor (1973). On the relationship in Latin America, see Meller *et al.* (1976).
7. It has however been suggested that since barriers to entry are also often barriers to exit (i.e. they inhibit capital mobility generally) the positive correlation between profit rates and barriers to entry may be reversed in times of recession (Semmler, 1982).

8. Connor failed, however, to find a statistically significant relationship between profitability and gearing in Brazil. This may be due to the fact that, whereas in Colombia and Mexico the discount rate was below the rate of inflation at the time of the studies, in Brazil the reverse was true.

9. See CICSO (n.d., p. 65) on Argentina and Misas (1973, p. 54) on Colombia. There is evidence from Argentina to suggest that the least concentrated sectors are second in terms of a falling wage share, but in this case it is a result of an absolute fall in real wages rather than rapid increases in productivity.

# 9 TNCs and Latin American Industrialisation

It was suggested at the outset that the operations of TNCs should not be treated in isolation but seen as part of a wider process of internationalisation of capital, of which they themselves are primary protagonists. It was seen in the last chapter that the homogenisation of production and consumption patterns is a characteristic of the internationalisation of capital everywhere, but that in the socio-economic context of Latin America, it has effects which are very different from those in the advanced capitalist countries. Most of the so-called 'distortions' which are identified in Latin America are the result of the internationalisation of capital interacting with the specific, local socio-economic structure to generate patterns which are in significant ways different from those found in the advanced capitalist countries.

Given their importance in the world economy today, it is not surprising that TNCs should play a leading role in the internationalisation of capital. This should not lead to an excessive concern with the institutional form adopted, as opposed to the process of internationalisation itself. Such an approach leads to a number of dangers. It underestimates the extent and significance of the internationalisation of capital, identifying it only with that part of production which is under the direct control of TNCs. It also implies that local or foreign ownership is a crucial variable in determining the nature and behaviour of capital. Throughout this book it has been argued, however, that large local firms, often operating with licences from abroad, behave in most respects in ways which are very similar to the TNCs. They employ similar capital-intensive production techniques, carry out very limited local R & D and modifications to production processes, have similar competitive strategies and are also overwhelmingly oriented towards the domestic market. In some cases, large Latin American firms have themselves begun to become TNCs.

Manufacturing TNCs in Latin America play a crucial role in the promotion of international patterns of production and consumption. They are able to do so because they occupy leadership positions within the most dynamic sectors of industry (see Chapter 2). Many local firms are then forced to adapt to the production norms and product standards set by TNCs. In order to compete successfully with TNC subsidiaries, local firms adopt imitative strategies, as in the case of the Argentinian pharmaceutical industry where the very successful local firms have based their strategy largely on heavy sales promotion, product differentiation and the introduction of new products, often produced under licence from abroad (see Chapter 4). Also, the key positions occupied by TNCs within much broader systems of inter-industry relationships (industrial complexes) enable them to have a major influence on the production of a broader range of goods. The motor industry provides a classic illustration of this pattern, with the terminal sector being totally dominated by a handful of TNCs which can exercise considerable control over the parts industry, much of which is in local hands (see Chapter 3). As a result, major local part manufacturers produce international products to the terminals' specification.

The model of accumulation in Latin American manufacturing since the mid-1950s is characterised by a number of contradictions. As was seen in the last chapter, the oligopolistic structure of industry and the relatively small scale of TNC operations in Latin America tend to limit the rate of capital accumulation. This is reinforced by the tendency of the balance of payments to deteriorate as a result of a growing outflow of profits, royalties and technical assistance payments, and of the import-intensive nature of TNC activities. A model which offers little or no benefit for the mass of the population, whose opportunities of employment are severely restricted, while at the same time concentrating the gains in the hands of TNCs and large local economic groups has major social and political implications. There is also a contradiction between the legitimacy of the *national* state and its objective role in promoting the internationalisation of capital.

The question of the state is of central importance in this context because it plays a major role in revitalising the accumulation process. The growth of the state sector and particularly the state productive sector has characterised a number of Latin American countries (Fitzgerald, 1977). The state also plays a role in attempting to attract new waves of foreign investment. It intervenes in order to loosen the balance of payments constraint, both by its general export promotion policies and specific measures aimed at reducing the trade deficit of TNCs (see Chapter 5). A further important way in which capital accumulation is maintained despite continuing balance of payments deficits is through growing external indebtedness.

The state is involved in a delicate balancing act. Expanding its role in production, it must not be seen to threaten the private sector. Attempting to attract new inflows of foreign capital, it must not be seen to threaten the position of local capital. While attempting to reduce the adverse balance of payments impact of TNCs it must not be seen as threatening the position of foreign capital, otherwise new foreign investment will dry up. Even in Brazil, the alliance between state, foreign and private local capital is subject to many strains (Evans, 1981).

Finally, the model of accumulation is affecting class structure in Latin America in a number of ways. The local bourgeoisie is becoming increasingly differentiated between those large local groups and other sectors of local capital which are closely involved in the internationalisation of capital, and other sectors which find themselves restricted to low growth, low profit activities in the most competitive sectors of manufacturing. Both groups may find themselves in conflict with foreign capital over issues such as levels of royalty payments and export restrictions, or the spheres reserved for local capital. Nevertheless, such conflicts were relatively minor and do not extend to advocacy of the wholesale exclusion of foreign capital (see Chapter 6).

There is also a certain differentiation of the working class associated with the spread of Fordist labour processes and the accompanying bipolar skill structure (see Chapter 6). Politically, however, this is less important that the relatively slow growth of the industrial proletariat under the prevailing model of accumulation. The result is that the industrial working class remains a relatively small share of the labour force, and that with rapid population growth marginality increases. On the other hand, the effects of the internationalisation of capital in agriculture is leading to pro-letarianisation or semi-proletarianisation of peasants in a number of

Latin American countries, which is expanding the size of the rural working class and posing a new threat to political stability.

## TNCs AND ALTERNATIVE DEVELOPMENT PATHS

It should be clear from the tenor of this study that measures to restrict foreign capital and to give preference to local firms do not offer a significant alternative to the present model. Studies which show the superior performance of local firms in terms of certain development criteria, such as more labour-intensive production processes are often based on a fallacious methodology which does not compare like with like (Ingles and Fairchild, 1977). When similar firms are compared, there is often little difference between foreign and local capital, and other variables such as firm size or industry are more important in explaining apparent differences. Thus, substituting local for foreign ownership may have very little effect on most aspects of firm behaviour.[1] Measures for increasing local share ownership, far from being intended to alter the behaviour of firms as has sometimes been implied (Weinert, 1977) are, in fact, primarily a way of ensuring the local bourgeoisie's share of the fruits of economic growth (cf. Chapter 7).

Restricting the spheres of operation of TNCs is unlikely to alter the fundamental problems because these derive from the internationalisation of capital rather than from the presence of TNCs *per se*. Is there, then, an alternative in the shape of national capitalist development of the kind which historically characterised Japan, independent of the internationalisation of capital? To sustain such a thesis it would be necessary to abstract from the specific historical and geo-political characteristics of the development of Japanese capital. In particular, the internationalisation of capital, and the development of the forces of production in transport and communications which have made it possible, were much less advanced in the late nineteenth century. It should also not be forgotten that imperial expansion played an important part in the development of Japanese capitalism, while it is highly unlikely that this could be repeated in Latin America in the late twentieth century.

A more active role for the state in production and in the control of foreign capital is unlikely to alter the pattern of accumulation significantly. The capitalist state is not an independent agent able to construct a socially more rational development strategy, but itself reproduces in its interior the conflicts and contradictions of the capitalist mode of production. The role of the state in production is restricted by the prime objective of promoting capital accumulation. Moreover, state capital itself tends to reproduce the patterns of behaviour of private capital as individual state firms seek to free themselves from their obligation as *state* capital and realise their nature as *capital*.

The fundamental problem with all these alternatives is that they do not question the capitalist nature of production relations. The internationalisation of capital is a social process involving the extension and strengthening of capitalist relations of production. It is not surprising that a model of accumulation based on the valorisation of capital does not lead to the full utilisation of human resources. It is only by changing the main purpose of production and adopting different criteria that the latter objective can be fulfilled. Thus, ultimately, human needs must be the purpose of production. It is the failure of the internationalisation of capital to fulfil these needs that is its major indictment. The success of Cuba in this respect shows the possibilities which a socialist transormation offers.

Can and should TNCs have a part to play in a socialist development strategy in Latin America? A socialist strategy will undoubtedly reduce the scope for TNC operations, as for example public transport replaces private transport or preventive health care increases relative to intensive promotion of drugs. Similarly, those areas in which the competitive advantage of TNCs lies in the creation of demand through advertising branded products could be substituted by undifferentiated basic products (Hymer, 1979, p. 254). Nevertheless, the TNCs do make a real technological contribution in many branches and local alternative technologies may not exist. It is, therefore, likely that even socialist regimes in Latin America could resort to the TNCs for technological inputs. There would, however, have to be a major effort at local adaptation not simply to the different local conditions in Latin America, but also to the socialist nature of the new relations of production. Clearly, such a strategy is by no means free from problems, but the solution is not to refuse to maintain any relations with TNCs. The crucial question is whether TNCs are involved as leading elements in the internationalisation of capital, which determines a particular model of accumulation, as occurs at present, or whether the model of accumulation is directed towards fulfilling the needs of the mass of the population, and the TNCs are permitted a certain degree of involvement in fulfilling these needs.

NOTE

1. See, for example, the case of Clemente Jacques, sold by the TNC United Brands to the Grupo Alfa in Mexico (Rama and Vigorito, 1979, p. 213).

# Bibliography

Acevedo, E. and Vergara H. (1970) 'Concentración y Capital Extranjera en la Industria Chilena', *Economía y Administración*, no. 15.

Afonso, C. (1975) 'A Note on the Exploitation of Labour in the "Brazilian" Automobile Industries', in M. Arruda *et al.*, *Multinationals and Brazil: the Impact of Multinational Corporations in Contemporary Brazil* (Toronto: Brazilian Studies Latin America Research Unit).

Alfaro Lara, C. *et al.* (1977) 'Las Transnacionales y el Costo de los Medicamentos en Costa Rica', *Comercio Exterior*, vol. 27, no. 8.

Allende, S. (1972) 'Speech to the United Nations', in H. Radice, *International Firms and Modern Imperialism* (Harmondsworth: Penguin, 1975).

Almeida Biato *et al.* (1973) *A Transferência de Tecnologia no Brasil*, Série Estudos para o Planejamento 4 (Brasilia: IPEA).

AMDA (1973) *La Comercializacion Automotriz*, Associación Mexicana de Distribuidores de Automoviles (México: DF).

AMIA (1976) *La Industria Automotriz de México en Cifras* (Mexico City: Asociación Mexicana de la Industria Automotriz).

Anaya Franco E. (1974) *Imperialismo, Industrialización y Transferencia de Tecnología en el Peru* (Lima: Editorial Horizonte).

Aranda, S. and Martinez, A. (1970) 'Estructura Económica: Algunas Características Fundamentales', in A. Pinto *et al.*, *Chile, hoy* (Santiago de Chile: Siglo XXI).

Bader, M. (1980) 'Breast Feeding: the Role of Multinational Corporations in Latin America', in K. Kumar (ed.), *Transnational Enterprises: their impact on Third World Societies and Cultures* (Boulder: Westview Press).

Baer, W. and Samuelson L. (eds), (1977) 'Latin America in the Post Import Substitution Era', *World Development*, vol. 5, no. 1/2.

Bain, J. (1956) *Barriers to New Competition* (Cambridge, Mass.: Harvard University Press).

Baklanoff, E. N. (1966) 'Foreign Private Investment and Industrialization in Brazil', in E. N. Baklanoff (ed.), *New Perspectives on Brazil* (Nashville: Vanderbilt University Press).

Balassa, B. (1973) 'La Política Comercial de México: Análisis y Proposiciones', in L. Solis (ed.), *La Economía Mexicana, Vol. I Análisis por Sectores y Distribución* (Mexico City: Fondo de Cultura Económica).

Balassa, B. (1978) 'Export Incentives and Export Performance in Developing Countries: A Comparative Analysis', *Weltwirtschaftliches Archiv*, vol. 114, 1978.

Balli, F. (n.d.) *La Industria de la Maquila en México: Estudio Monográfico* (Mexico City: El Colegio de México, mimeo).

Bambirra, V. (1974) *El Capitalismo Dependiente Latinoamericano* (Mexico: Siglo XXI).

238

Baran, P. (1973) *The Political Economy of Growth* (Harmondsworth: Penguin).

Baranson, J. (1969) *Automotive Industries in Developing Countries* (Washington: World Bank Staff Occasional Paper, no. 8).

Barkin, D. (1973) 'Automobiles and the Chilean Road to Socialism', in D. L. Johnson (ed.), *The Chilean Road to Socialism* (New York: Anchor Press/ Doubleday).

Barnet, R. and Muller, R. (1974) *Global Reach: the Power of the Multinational Corporations* (New York: Simon & Schuster).

Behrman, J. (1975) *Review of 'Multinational Corporations in Brazil and Mexico: Structural Sources of Economic and Non-economic Power'*, (New York: Council of the Americas).

Bennett, D., Blachman, M. and Sharpe, K. (1978) 'Mexico and the Multinational Corporations: an Explanation of State Action', in J. Grunwald (ed.), *Latin America and World Economy: a Changing International Order* (Beverly Hills: Sage).

Bennett, D. and Sharpe K. (1979) 'Export Promotion and the Mexican Automobile Industry', *International Organization*, Spring 1979.

Bennett, D. and Sharpe, K. (1979a) 'Agenda Setting and Bargaining Power: the Mexican State vs. Transnational Automobile Companies', *World Politics* no. 32, (1).

Bergsten, F., Horst, T. and Moran, T. (1978) *American Multinationals and American Interests* (Washington: The Brookings Institution).

Bernal Sahgun, V. (1976) *The Impact of Multinational Corporations on Employment and Income: the Case of Mexico* (Geneva: International Labour Office).

Bernal Sahgun, V. (1979) 'Las Empresas Transnacionales y el "Desarrollo" de la Industria de la Salud en México', in J. Alvarez Soberanes *et al.*, *Foro Sobre Empresas Multinacionales y Transferencia de Tecnología en el Ramo de la Industria Químico Farmacéutica* (Mexico City: Universidad Autonoma Metropolitana-Xochimilco).

Bertrero, C. (1972) *Drugs and Dependency in Brazil. An Empirical Study of Dependency Theory: the Case of the Pharmaceutical Industry* (Cornell University: Latin American Studies Program Dissertation Series, no. 36).

Bhaskar, K. (1980) *The Future of the World Motor Industry* (London: Kogan Page).

Bitar, S. (1977) *Corporaciones Multinacionales y Autonomia Nacional* (Caracas: Monte Avila Editores).

Bitar, S. and Moyano, E. (1972) 'Redistribución del Consumo y Transición al Socialismo', *Cuadernos de la Realidad Nacional*, no. 11.

Bitar, S. and Troncoso, E. (1981) *Venezuela y América Latina: Industrialización Comparado* (paper presented to the first congress of the Asociación de Economistas de America Latina y el Caribe, Caracas, mimeo).

Boatler, R. (1973) *Trade Theory Prediction and the Growth of Mexico's Manufactured Exports* (Cornell University, Ph.D. Thesis).

Booth, D. (1975) 'Andre Gunder Frank: an Introduction and Appreciation', in I. Oxaal, T. Barnett and D. Booth (eds), *Beyond the Sociology of Development* (London: Routledge & Kegan Paul).

Braverman, H. (1974) *Labour and Monopoly Capital* (New York: Monthly Review Press).

Briones, A. (1981) *Entre el Conflicto y la Negociación: Los Funcionarios Públicos frente a las Empresas Transnacionales*, mimeo (Paris: Institute for Research on Multinationals).

Brooke, P. (1975) *Resistant Prices: a Study of Competitive Strains in the Antibiotic Markets* (New York: Council on Economic Priorities).

Buarque, C. (1981) *Diretrizes a un Estudo de Alternativas para a Indústria Automobilística* (mimeo).

Bueno, G. (1971) 'La Industria Siderúrgica y la Industria Automotriz' in Instituto de Investigaciones Sociales, UNAM, *El Perfil de México en 1980*, vol. 2 (Mexico City: Siglo XXI).

Burbach, R., and Flynn, P. (1980) *Agribusiness in the Americas* (New York: Monthly Review Press/NACLA).

Campos, M. (1974) 'La Política Mexicana sobre Transferencia de Tecnología: Una Evaluación Preliminar', *Comercio Exterior*, vol. 24, no. 5.

Campos, M. (1981) 'La Industria Farmacéutica en México', in F. Fajnzylber (ed.) *Industrialización e Internacionalización en la América Latina*, vol. 2 (Mexico City: Fondo de Cultura Económica).

Caputo, O. and Pizarro, R. (1970) *Desarrollismo y Capital Extranjero* (Santiago de Chile: Ediciónes de la Universidad Tecnica del Estado).

Cardoso, F. H. (1971) *Ideologias de la Burguesía Industrial en Sociedades Dependientes (Argentina y Brasil)* (Mexico City: Siglo XXI).

Cardoso, F. H. (1973) 'Associated Dependent Development: Theoretical and Practical Implications', in A. Stepan (ed.) *Authoritarian Brazil: Origins, Policies and Future* (New Haven: Yale University Press).

Cardoso, F. H. and Faletto, E. (1979) *Dependency and Development in Latin America* (Berkeley and Los Angeles: University at California Press).

Cardoso, F. H., and Serra, J. (1978) 'Las Desventuras de la Dialéctica de la Dependencia', *Revista Mexicana de Sociología*, numero extraordinaria.

Caves, R. (1971) 'International Corporations: the Industrial Economics of Foreign Investment', in J. Dunning (ed., 1972), *International Investment* (Harmondsworth: Penguin).

Chang, Y. S. (1971) *The Transfer of Technology: Economics of Offshore Assembly: the Case of Semi-conductor Industry* (New York: United Nations Institute for Training and Research).

Chavez, E. (n.d.), 'Las Empresas Matrices de las Maquiladoras Mexicanas. Dos Estudios de Caso de la Industria del Vestido', in *Lecturas del CEESTEM, Maquiladoras*.

Chenery, H. B., *et al.* (1974) *Redistribution with Growth* (Oxford: Oxford University Press).

Chilcote, R., and Edelstein, J. (1974) *Latin America: the Struggle with Dependency and Beyond* (New York: John Wiley and Sons).

Chossudovsky, M. (1979) *Transnationalization and the Development of Peripheral Capitalism* (Ottowa: University of Ottawa, Faculty of Social Sciences, Department of Economics, research paper no. 7903, 1979).

Chudnovsky, D. (1974) *Empress Multinacionales y Ganancias Monopólicas en una economía Latinoamericana* (Buenos Aires: Siglo XXI).

Chudnovsky, D. (1979) 'The Challenge by Domestic Enterprises to the Transnational Corporations' Domination: a Case Study of the Argentine Pharmaceutical Industry', *World Development*, vol. 7, no. 1.

Chudnovsky, D. (1979a) 'Las Marcas Extranjeras en los Paises en Desarrollo', *Comercio Exterior*, vol. 29, no. 12.

Chudnovsky, D. (1981) *Las Subsidiarias en América Latina y el Financiamiento de la*

*Inversión de las ET Manufacturas de EUA* (Mexico City: ILET, DEE/D/59/e).

CICSO (n.d.) *El Poder Económico en la Argentina* (Buenos Aires: Centro de Investigaciones en Ciencias Sociales).

CIFARA (1970) *Estudio Técnico-Económico de la Industria Nacional de Transporte* Buenos Aires: Camara Industrial de Fabricantes de Autopiezas de la República Argentina).

Cinta, R. (1972) 'Burguesía Nacional y Desarrollo', in Instituto de Investigaciones Sociales, UNAM, *El Perfil de México en 1980*, vol. 3 (Mexico City: Siglo XXI).

Collier, D. (ed., 1979) *The New Authoritarianism in Latin America* (Princeton: Princeton University Press).

CONADE (1966) *La Industria Automotriz (Analísis Preliminar)* (Buenos Aires: Consejo Nacional de Desarrollo).

Connor, J. M. (1977) *The Market Power of Multinationals* (New York: Praeger).

Connor, J. M., and Mueller, W. F. (1977) *Market Power and Profitability of Multinational Corporations in Brazil and Mexico* (Report to the Subcommittee on Foreign Economic Policy of the Committee on Foreign Relations, US Senate, Washington).

Cooper, C., and Clark, N. (1972) *The Transfer of Technology to Latin America (Summary)* (mimeo, Science Policy Research Unit, University of Sussex).

Cordero, S., and Santin, R. (1977) *Los Grupos Industriales: una Nueva Organización Económica en México* (Mexico City: Centro de Estudios Sociologicos, Cuaderno no. 23, Colegio de México).

CORDIPLAN (1971) *3 Encuesta Industrial 1971* (Caracas: Oficina Central de Coordinación y Planificación).

CORFO (1970) *Comportamiento de las principales empresas industriales acogidas al DFL 258* (Santiago de Chile: Corporación de Fomento de la Producción, publicación no. 9 A/70).

CORFO (1971) *Principales Empresas Manufactureras* (Santiago de Chile: Corporación de Fomento de la Producción, publicación no. 58 a/71).

CORFO (1971a) *Datos Basicos Sector Industrial Manufacturero: Periodo 1960–1970* Santiago de Chile: Corporación de Fomento de la Producción, publicación no. 22 A/71).

Cypher, J. (1979) 'The Internationalization of Capital and the Transformation of Social Formations: a Critique of the Monthly Review School', *The Review of Radical Political Economics*, 11.4.

Dahse, F. (1979) *El Mapa de la Extrema Riqueza* (Santiago: Editorial Aconcagua).

Derossi, F. (1971) *The Mexican Entrepreneur* (Paris: OECD).

Davies, W. (1967) *The Pharmaceutical Industry* (Oxford: Pergamon Press).

De Oliveira, F., and Travolo Popoutchi, M. A. (1979) *El Complejo Automotor en Brasil* (Mexico: DF. ILET/Nuevo Imagen).

Del Campo, J. (1972) 'Los Grupos Dominantes Frente a las Alternativas de Cambio', in Instituto de Investigaciones Sociales, UNAM, *El Perfil de México en 1980*, vol. 3 (Mexico City: Siglo XXI).

Diaz Alejandro, C. (1976) *Foreign Trade Regimes and Economic Development: Colombia* (New York: National Bureau of Economic Research).

Diaz Alejandro, C. (1977) 'Foreign Direct Investment by Latin Americans', in T. Agmon and C. P. Kindleberger (1977) *Multinationals from Small Countries* (Cambridge, Mass: MIT Press).

DNEI [Dirección Nacional de Estudios Industriales] (1969) *Situación Actual y*

*Perspectivas de Mercado de Automóviles en la República Argentina* (Buenos Aires: Ministerio de Economía y Trabajo).

von Doellinger, C. and Cavalcanti, L. (1975) *Empresas Multinacionais na Indústria Brasileira* (Rio de Janeiro, IPEA Coleçao relatorios de pesquisa).

Dorfman, A. (1970) *Historia de la Industria Argentina* (Buenos Aires: Hachett).

Dos Santos, T. (1968a) 'The Changing Structure of Foreign Investment in Latin America', in J. Petras and M. Zeitlin (eds), *Latin America: Reform or Revolution?* (Greenwich: Fawcett Publications).

Dos Santos, T. (1968b) 'Foreign Investment and the Large Enterprise in Latin America: the Brazilian Case', in J. Petras and M. Zeitlin (eds), *Latin America: Reform or Revolution?* (Greenwich: Fawcett Publications).

Dos Santos, T. (1974) 'Brazil', in R. Chilcote and J. Edelstein, *Latin America: the Struggle with Dependency and Beyond* (New York: John Wiley and Sons).

ECLA [Economic Commission for Latin America] (1965) *External Financing in Latin America* (New York: United Nations).

ECLA (1969) *La CEPAL y el Análisis del Desarrollo Latinoamericano* (Santiago de Chile: Editorial Universitaria).

ECLA (1969a) *Economic Development and Income Distribution in Argentina* (New York: E/CN. 12/802).

ECLA (1973) *Perspectivas y Modalidades de Integracion Regional de la Industria Automotriz en América Latina* (Santiago: ECLA/DI/DRAFT/92, División de Desarrollo Industrial).

ECLA (1976) *La Exportacion de Manufacturas en México y la Política de Promoción* (Mexico City: CEPAL/MEX/76/10/Rev. 1).

ECLA (1976a) *Las exportaciones de manufacturas en America Latina: informaciones estadísticas y algunas consideraciones generales* (Santiago: E/CEPAL/L.128).

ECLA (1977a) *Las Empresas Transnacionales entre los Mil Mayores Empresas de Brasil* (Santiago: División de Desarrollo Económico, Dependencia Conjunta CEPAL/CET, documento de Trabajo no. 5).

ECLA (1977b) *Statistical Yearbook for Latin America 1976* (UN Publication Sales no. SIE 78 II, G2, New York).

ECLA (1978) *Tendencias y Cambios en la Inversión de las Empresas Internacionales en los Países en Desarrollo y Particularmente en América Latina* (Santiago: División de Desarrollo Económico, Dependencia Conjunto CEPAL/CET, Documento de Trabajo no. 12).

ECLA (1980) *Economic Survey of Latin America* (Santiago: UN).

ECLA/NAFINSA (1971) *La Política Industrial en el Desarrollo Económico de México* (Mexico City: Nacional Financiera).

ECLA/UNCTC (1979) *Foreign Participation in Colombian Development: the role of TNCs* (Santiago: Economic Commission for Latin America/Centre for Transnational Corporations Joint Unit).

EEC (1975) *A Study of the Evolution of Concentration in the Pharmaceutical Industry for the United Kingdom* (Luxemburg: Commission of the European Communities).

Elson, D. and Pearson, R. (1980) *The Latest Phase of the Internationalization of Capital and its Implications for Women in the Third World* (University of Sussex: Institute of Development Studies, DP 150).

Evans, J., James, D., and Hoffel, P. (forthcoming) 'Labour in the Argentine Motor Vehicle Industry', in R. Kronish and K. Mericle (eds.), *The Political Economy of the Latin American Motor Vehicle Industry* (Cambridge, Mass: MIT Press).

Evans, P. (1976) 'Foreign Investment and Industrial Transformation: A Brazilian Case Study', *Journal of Development Economics*, no. 3.

Evans, P. (1977) 'Direct Investment and Industrial Concentration', *Journal of Development Studies*, vol. 3, no. 4.

Evans, P. (1979) *Dependent Development: the Alliance of Multinational, State and Local Capital in Brazil* (Princeton: Princeton University Press).

Evans, P. (1981) *State, Multinational and Local Capital in Brazil: the Prospects for the Stability of the Triple Alliance in the Eighties* (paper presented to the Millenium Conference on Political Development in Latin America, London School of Economics).

Evans, P. and Gereffi, G. (1979) 'Foreign investment and Dependent Development', in S. Hewlett and R. Weinert (eds), *Brazil and Mexico: Patterns in Late Development* (Philadelphia: Institute for the Study of Human Issues, 1982).

Evers, T. (1979) *El Estado en la Periferia Capitalista* (Mexico City: Siglo XXI).

Fajnzylber, F. (1970) *Sistema Industrial y Exportación de Manufacturas* (Rio de Janeiro: Comisión Económica para América Latina).

Fajnzylber, F. and Martinez Tarrago, T. (1975) *Las Empresas Transnacionales, Expansión a Nivel Mundial y Proyeccion en la Industria Mexicana (versión preliminar)* (Mexico City: CIDE/CONACYT).

Fajnzylber, F., and Martinez Tarrago, T. (1976) *Las Empresas Transnacionales* (Mexico City: Fondo de Cultura Económica).

Fajnzylber, F., and Tavares, M. C. (1974) *Inversión Extranjera e Industrialización: Comparación México y Brasil (esquema preliminar de investigación)* (paper presented to the Seminar on Foreign Investment and External Financing in Latin America, Cambridge).

Felix, D. (1968) *Industrialización sustitutiva de importaciones y exportación industrial en la Argentina*, 2nd edition (Buenos Aires: Instituto Torcuato Di Tella, Centro de Investigaciones Economicas, Documento de Trabajo, 22).

Felix, D. (1974) 'Industrial Structure, Industrial Exporting and Economic Policy', in D. Geithman (ed.), *Fiscal Policy for Industrialization and Development in Latin America* (Florida: Florida University Press).

Ffrench-Davis, R., and Pinera Echenique, J. (1976) *Colombia Export Promotion Policy* (Santiago: ST/CEPAL/Conf. 59/L.3, 1976).

Fitzgerald, E. V. K. (1977) 'On State Accumulation in Latin America', in E. V. K. Fitzgerald, E. Floto and A. D. Lehmann (eds.), *The State and Economic Development in Latin America* (Cambridge: Cambridge University Press).

Frank, A. G. (1979) *Economic Crisis and the State in the Third World* (Norwich: University of East Anglia, Development Studies Discussion Paper no. 30).

Friedman, A. (1977) *Industry and Labour: Class Struggle at Work and Monopoly Capitalism* (London: Macmillan).

Fröbel, F., Heinrichs, J., and Kreye, O. (1980) *The New International Division of Labour* (Cambridge: Cambridge University Press).

Fung, S., and Cassiolato, J. (1976) *The International Transfer of Technology to Brazil through Technology Agreements – Characteristics of the Government Control System and the Commercial Transactions* (Centre for Policy Alternatives, MIT).

Furtado, C. (1976) *Economic Development of Latin America* (Cambridge: Cambridge University Press).

Galbraith, J. K. (1962) *The Affluent Society* (Harmondsworth: Penguin).

Galbraith, J. K. (1975) *Economics and the Public Purpose* (Harmondsworth: Penguin).

Galeano, E. (1969) 'The Denationalization of Brazilian Industry', *Monthly Review*, vol. 21, no. 7.

Gambrill, M. C. (n.d.) 'La Fuerza de Trabajo en los Maquiladoras, Resultados de una Encuesta y Algunas Hipotesis Interpretativas', in *Lecturas de CEESTEM, Maquiladoras*.

Garcia, H. A. (1978) *La Política de Desarrollo de los Exportaciones de Manufacturas en Brasil* (Santiago: E/CEPAL/1046/Add 4).

Gassic, G. (1971) *Concentración, Entrelazamiento y Desnacionalización en la Industria Manufacturera* (Santiago: Documento de Trabajo, CESO).

Gereffi, G. (1978) 'Drug Firms and Dependency in Mexico: the Case of the Steroid Hormone Industry', *International Organization*, vol. 32, no. 1.

Gereffi, G. (forthcoming) 'The Global Pharmaceutical Industry and its Impact in Third World Countries', in R. Newfarmer (ed.), *International Oligopoly and Development: Studies of International Industries and their Growth in Latin America*.

Ginsberg, C. (1973) *An Historical Analysis of the Multinationalization Process of the US Pharmaceutical Industry* (New York: New School for Social Research, Ph.D. Thesis).

Gold, D., Lo, C., and Wright, E. (1975) 'Recent Developments in Marxist Theories of the Capitalist State', *Monthly Review*, vol. 27, nos 6–7.

Gregory, P. (1974) 'Wage Structures in Latin America', *Journal of Developing Areas*, July.

Guillén Romo, H. (1974) 'Les Problèmes de Réalisation de Plus-value dans la Phase Avancée du 'Sous-development': le Cas Mexique', *Critique de l'Economie Politique*, nos. 16 & 17.

Guimaraes, E. (1981) *The Brazilian Passenger Car Industry* (paper presented to the International Conference on the Incidence of the External Environment on the Global Automotive Industry, Breau-sans-Nappe).

Hannah, L., and Kay, J. A. (1977) *Concentration in Modern Industry* (London: Macmillan).

Helleiner, G. K. (1975) 'The Role of Multinational Corporations in the Less Developed Countries' Trade in Technology', *World Development*, vol. 3, no. 4.

Helleiner, G. K. (1978) unpublished tables.

Heller, T. (1977) *Poor Health, Rich Profits: Multinational Drug Companies and the Third World* (Nottingham: Spokesman Books).

Hernandez, M. (1975) *Consideraciones Económicas y Sociales sobre la Industria Famacéutica en México* (UNAM, Escuela Nacional de Economía, Thesis).

Hernandez Laos, E., and Cordova Chavez, J. (1979) 'Estructura de la Distribución del Ingreso en México', *Comercio Exterior*, vol. 29, no. 5.

Hilferding, R. (1963) *El Capital Financiero* (Madrid: Editorial TECNOS).

Hirata, H. (1981) *Firmes Multinationales au Bresil: Technologie et Organisation du Travail* (paper presented to 2nd Seminario Internacional, Crisis, Nuevas Tecnologías y Procesos de Trabajo, UNAM, Mexico City).

Hirschman, A. O. (1969) 'How to Divest in Latin America and Why', *Essays in International Finance*, no. 76. (Princeton: Princeton University Press).

Holloway, J., and Picciotto, S. (1977) 'Introduction: Towards a Marxist Theory of the State', in J. Holloway and S. Picciotto (eds.), *State and Capital: A Marxist Debate* (London: Edward Arnold).

Horst, T. (1974) *At Home and Abroad* (Cambridge, Mass: Ballinger Publishing Company).

Humphrey, J. (1979) 'Auto Workers and the Working Class in Brazil', *Latin American Perspectives*, no. 23 (winter).

Humphrey, J. (1980) 'Labour Use and Labour Control in the Brazilian Automobile Industry', *Capital and Class*, no. 12, (winter).

Humphrey, J. (forthcoming) 'Labour in the Brazilian Motor Vehicle Industry', in R. Kronish and K. Mericle, *The Political Economy of the Latin American Motor Vehicle Industry* (Cambridge, Mass: MIT Press).

Hushloff, J. (1979) 'Analísis de Perspectivas para los Paises en Desarrollo Dentro del Campo de la Industria Químico Famacéutica: El Caso de Peru', in J. Alvarez Soberanes *et al.*, *Foro sobre Empresas Multinacionales y Transferncia de Tecnología en el Ramo de la Industria Químico Farmacéutico* (Mexico City: Universidad Autonoma Metropolitana).

Hushloff, J. (1979a) 'El Consumo de Medicamentos en el Altiplano de Bolivia y la Sierra Central de Peru', in J. Alvarez Soberanes *et al.*, *Foro sobre Empresas Multinacionales y Transferencia de Tecnología en el Ramo de la Industria Químico Farmacéutico* (Mexico City: Universidad Autonoma, Metropolitana).

Hymer, S. (1976) *The International Operations of National Firms: A Study of Direct Foreign Investment* (Cambridge, Mass: MIT Press).

Hymer, S. (1979) *The Multinational Corporation: A Radical Approach* (papers by S. Hymer, edited by R. Cohen, N. Felton, M. Nkosi and J. van Liere) (Cambridge: Cambridge University Press).

IADB [Inter-American Development Bank] (1978) *Agro-mechanical Technologies in Latin America: a Survey of Applications in Selected Countries* (Washington: IADB, Economic and Social Development Department Agricultural Economics Section).

IBGE [Fundaçao Instituto Brasileiro de Geografía e Estatística] (1979) *Anuário Estatístico do Brasil* (Rio de Janeiro: Secretaria de Planejamento de Presidência da República).

IKA, 1963. *La Industria Automotriz Argentina* (Buenos Aires: Industrias Kaiser Argentina).

ILPES [Instituto Latinoamericano de Planifacación Económica y Social] (1974) 'La Estrategia de Industrialización en la América Latina', in M. Nolff (ed.), *El Desarrollo Industrial Latinoamericano* (Mexico City: Fondo de Cultura Económica).

Imaz, J. L. (1964) *Los Que Mandan* (Buenos Aires: Editorial Universitaria de Buenos Aires).

Ingles, J., and Fairchild, L. (1977) 'Evaluating the Impact of Foreign Investment: Methodology and Evidence from Mexico, Colombia and Brazil', *Latin American Research Review*, vol. 12, part 3.

INP [Instituto Nacional de Planificación] (1976) *Concentración de la Producción y Estructura de Propiedad* (Lima: Oficina de Investigaciones de Planificacion).

INTI [Instituto Nacional de Tecnología Industrial] (1974) *Aspectos Económicos de la importación de Tecnología en la Argentina en 1972* (Buenos Aires: INTI).

Jelin, E. (1979) 'Orientaciones e Ideologías Obreras en América Latina', in R. Katzman and J. L. Reyna (eds.), *Fuerza de Trabajo y Movimientos Laborales en América Latina* (Mexico City: El Colegio de Mexico).

Jenkins, R. (1976a) *International Oligopoly and Dependent Industrialization in the Latin American Motor Industry* (Norwich: University of East Anglia, Development Studies Discussion Paper no. 13).

Jenkins, R., (1976b) *Multinational Corporations and the Denationalization of Latin American Industry: the Case of the Motor Industry*, Norwich: University of East Anglia, Development Studies Discussion Paper no. 14.

Jenkins, R. (1977) *Dependent Industrialization in Latin America* (New York: Praeger).

Jenkins, R. (1979) 'Transnational Corporations and their Impact on the Mexican Economy', in J. Carrière (ed.) *Industrialization and the State in Latin America* (Amsterdam: CEDLA Incidentele Publicaties 14).

Jenkins, R. (1979a) 'The Export Performance of Multinational Corporations in Mexican Industry', *Journal of Development Studies*, vol. 15, no. 3.

Jenkins, R. (1979b) *Foreign Firms, Exports of Manufacturers and the Mexican Economy* (Norwich: University of East Anglia, Development Studies Monograph, no. 8).

Jenkins, R. (forthcoming) 'The Rise and Fall of the Argentinian Motor Vehicle Industry', in R. Kronish and K. Mericle, *The Political Economy of the Latin American Motor Vehicle Industry* (Cambridge, Mass: MIT Press).

Jenkins, R., and West, P. (forthcoming) 'The International Tractor Industry and its Impact in Latin America', in R. Newfarmer (ed.), *International Oligopoly and Development: Studies of International Industries and their Growth in Latin America*.

Jessop, B. (1977) 'Recent Theories of the Capitalist State', *Cambridge Journal of Economics*, no. 1.

Johnson, D. L. (1972) 'The National and Progressive Bourgeoisie in Chile', in J. D. Cockroft, A. G. Frank and D. L. Johnson, *Dependence and Underdevelopment* (New York: Anchor).

Juarez, A. (1979) *Los Corporaciones Transnacionales y los Trabajadores Mexicanos* (Mexico City: Siglo 21).

Junta del Acuerdo de Cartagena (1979) *Transferencia de Tecnología de Empresas Extranjeras Hacia el Grupo Andino* (Lima: Junta del Acuerdo de Cartagena).

Katz, J. (1973) *La Industria Famacéutica Argentina. Estructura y Comportamiento* (Buenos Aires: Instituto Torcuato di Tella, Centro de Investigaciones Económicas, Documento de Trabajo 67).

Katz, J. (1976) *Importación de Tecnología, Aprendizaje e Industrialización Dependiente* (Mexico City: Fondo de Cultura Económica).

Katz, J. and Ablin, R. (1978) *Technology and Industrial Exports: A Micro-economic Analysis of Argentina's Recent Experience* (Buenos Aires: IDB/ECLA Research Programme in Science and Technology, Working Paper no. 2).

Kaufman, R. (1979) 'Industrial Change and Authoritarian Rule in Latin America: A Concrete Review of the Bureaucratic-Authoritarian Model', in D. Colier (ed.), *The New Authoritarianism in Latin America* (Princeton: Princeton University Press).

Kindleberger, C. (1969) *American Business Abroad* (New Haven: Yale University Press).

Knickerbocker, F. (1973) *Oligopolistic Reaction and Multinational Enterprise* (Cambridge, Mass: Havard Graduate School of Business Administration).

König, W. (1975) *Towards an Evaluation of International Subcontracting Activities in Developing Countries: Interim Report upon Completion of Field Work on 'Maquiladoras' in Mexico* (Mexico City: United Nations Economic Commission for Latin America).

Krueger, A. *et al.* (1981) *Trade and Employment in Developing Countries* (Chicago: University of Chicago Press).

Lajo, M. (1979) *Transnational Enterprises and Food: A Case Study of Milk in Peru* (Norwich: University of East Anglia, Development Studies Reprint no. 96).

Lall, S. (1980) *The Multinational Corporation Nine Essays* (London: Macmillan).

Lall, S. (1980a) 'The International Automotive Industry and the Developing World', *World Development*, vol. 8.

Lall, S. and Streeten, P. (1977) *Foreign Investment, Transnationals and Developing Countries* (London: Macmillan).

Landsberg, M. (1979) 'Export-led Industrialization in the Third World: Manufacturing Imperialism', *The Review of Radical Political Economics*, vol. 11, no. 4.

Laurell, A. C. *et al.* (1979) 'El Desarrollo Urbano y los Patrones de Consumo de Productos Farmacéuticos', in J. Alverez Soberanes *et al.*, *Foro sobre Empresas Multinacionales y Transferencia de Tecnología en el Ramo de la Industria Químico Farmacéutico* (Mexico City: Universidad Autonoma Metropolitana).

Ledogar, R. (1975) *Hungry for Profits: US Food and Drug Multinationals in Latin America* (New York: IDOC).

Leff, N. (1978) 'Industrial Organization and Entrepreneurship in the Developing Countries: The Economic Groups', *Economic Development and Cultural Change*, vol. 26, July.

Lenicov, J. (1973) 'Algunos Resultados de la Política Desarollista (1958–64): El Caso de la Industria Automotriz', *Económica*, vol. 19, no. 3.

Lifschitz, E. (1979) *El Complejo Automotor en México* (México DF).

Lipietz, A. (1982) 'Towards Global Fordism?', *New Left Review*, no. 132.

Luiz Possas, M. (1979) *Employment Effects of Multinational Enterprise in Brazil* (Geneva: Research on Employment Effects of Multinational Enterprise, ILO, Working Paper No. 7).

Lustig, N. (1979) 'Distribución del Ingreso, Estructura del Consumo y Caracteristicas del Crecimiento Industrial', *Comercio Exterior*, vol. 29, no. 5.

Marini, R. M. (1972) 'Brazilian Subimperialism', *Monthly Review*, vol. 27, no. 9.

Marini, R. M. (1973) *Dialéctica de la Dependencia* (Mexico City: Nueva Era).

Marini, R. M. (1978) 'Las Razones del Neodesarrollismo (repuesta a F. H. Cardoso y J. Serra)', *Revista Mexicana de Sociología*, numero extraordinaria.

Mathias, G. (1978) 'La Internacionalizacion del Capital en la Postguerra (Incidencias Sobre la Estructura Técnica y el Proceso de Trabajo en la Industria Brasileña)', *Criticas de la Economía Política*, Edición Latinoamericana, no. 9.

Matter, K. (1976) *The Effects of Foreign Private Enterprise on Development: the Case of Colombia* (Saint Gall: Saint Gall Graduate School of Economics, Business and Public Administration, Doctoral Thesis).

May, H. (1970) *Impact of US and Other Foreign Investment in Latin America* (New York: Council of the Americas).

May, H. (1975) *Multinational Corporations in Latin America* (New York: Council of the Americas).

May, H., and Fernandez Arena (1970) *Impact of Foreign Investment in Mexico* (New York: Council of the Americas).

Meller, P., Leniz, S., and Swinburn, C. (1976) 'Comparaciones Internacionales de Concentración en América Latina', *Ensayos Eciel*, no. 3.

Melo, H. (1974) 'Observaciones sobre el Papel del Capital Extranjero y sus Relaciones con los Grupos Locales de Capital en Colombia', in L. G. Izquierdo and Stanzick, K. H. *Contribución del Empresario Nacional al Desarrollo Socio-

*Económico de América Latina* (Quito: Instituto Latinoamericano de Investigaciones Sociales).

Merhav, M. (1969) *Technological Dependence, Monopoly and Growth* (New York: Pergamon Press).

Mericle, K. (forthcoming) 'The Political Economy of the Brazilian Motor Vehicle Industry', in R. Kronish and K. Mericle, *The Political Economy of the Latin American Motor Vehicle Industry* (Cambridge, Mass: MIT Press).

Minian, I. (1981) *Progreso Técnico e Internationalización del Proceso Productivo: el Caso de la Industria Maquiladora de Tipo Electronica* (Mexico City: Ensayos del CIDE).

Misas, G. (1973) *Contribución al Estudio del Grado de Concentración en la Industria Colombiana* (Santiago de Chile: ILDIS Estudios y Documentación, no. 26).

Mohar, O. (1979) 'Panoramo del Consumo de Medicamentos en México', in J. Alvarez Soberanes *et al.*, *Foro sobre Empresas Multinacionales y Transferencia de Tecnología en el Ramo de la Industria Químico Farmacéutica* (Mexico City: Universidad Autonoma Metropolitana).

Montes de Oca, R., and Escudero, G. (1981) 'Las empresas transnacionales en la industria alimentaria mexicana', *Comercio Exterior*, vol. 31, no. 9.

Moran, T. (1974) *Multinational Corporations and the Politics of Dependence – Copper in Chile* (Princeton: Princeton University Press).

Morley, S. and Smith, G. (1973) 'The Effect of Changes in the Distribution of Income on Labour, Foreign Investment and Growth in Brazil', in A. Stepan (ed.), *Authoritarian Brazil* (New Haven: Yale University Press).

Morley, S. and Smith, G. (1977a) 'Limited Search and the Technology Choices of Multinational Firms in Brazil', *Quarterly Journal of Economics*, vol. 91, no. 2.

Morley, S. and Smith, G. (1977b) 'The Choice of Technology: Multinational Firms in Brazil', *Economic Development and Cultural Change*, vol. 25, no. 2.

Morrison, T. K. (1975) 'Case Study of a "Least Developed Country" Successfully Exporting Manufactures: Haiti', *Inter-American Economic Affairs*, Summer.

Moya, J. L. (1979) 'Medicamentos Utilizados para el Tratamiento de la Ambiasis', in J. Alvarez Soberanes *et al. Foro sobre Empresas Multinacionales y Transferencia de Tecnología en el Ramo de la Industria Químico Farmacéutica* (Mexico City: Universidad Autonoma Metropolitana).

Muller R. and Moore, D. (1978) *Case One: Brazilian Bargaining Power Success in BEFIEX Export Promotion Program with the Transnational Automotive Industry* (paper prepared for UN Centre on Transnational Corporations, New York).

Munk, B. (1969) 'The Welfare Costs of Content Protection: The Automotive Industry in Latin America', *Journal of Political Economy*, no. 77.

Murray, R. (1975) 'The Internationalization of Capital and the Nation State', in H. Radice (ed.), *International Firms and Modern Imperialism* (Harmondsworth: Penguin).

Mytelka, L. (1979) *Regional Development in a Global Economy* (New Haven: Yale University Press).

NACLA (1975) 'US Runaway Shops on the Mexican Border', *Latin America and Empire Report*, vol. 9, no. 5.

NACLA (1977) 'Electronics: the Global Industry', *Latin America and Empire Report*, vol. 9, no. 4.

NACLA (1979) 'Car Wars', *NACLA Report*, July/August.

NAF INSA (1960) *Elementos para una Política de Desarrollo de la Fabricación de Vehiculos Automotrices en México* (Mexico City: Nacional Financiera).

Nakase, T. (1981) 'Some Characteristics of Japanese-type Multinational Enterprises Today', *Capital and Class*, no. 13.

Nayyar, D. (1978) 'Transnational Corporations and Manufactured Exports from Poor Countries', *Economic Journal*, vol. 88, March.

Newfarmer, R. (1977) *Multinational Conglomerates and the Economics of Dependent Development* (Madison: University of Wisconsin–Madison, Ph.D. Thesis).

Newfarmer, R. (1978) *TNC Take-overs in Brazil: The Uneven Distribution of Benefits in the Market for Firms* (University of Notre Dame, Department of Economics, Working Paper).

Newfarmer, R. (1980) *Transnational Conglomerates and the Economics of Dependent Development* (Greenwich, Conn: JAI Press).

Newfarmer, R. (forthcoming) 'International Industrial Organization and Development: A Survey', in R. Newfarmer (ed.), *International Oligopoly and Development: Studies of International Industries and their Growth in Latin America*.

Newfarmer, R., and Marsh, L. (1981) *Industrial Interdependence and Development: A Study of International Linkages and Industrial Performance in Brazil* (Mimeo).

Newfarmer, R., and Mueller, W. (1975) *Multinational Corporations in Brazil and Mexico: Structural Sources of Economic and Non-economic Power* (Report to the Subcommittee on Multinational Corporations of the Committee on Foreign Relations, United States Senate, Washington, US Government Printing Office).

Newton, J. and Balli, F. (1979) *Mexican In Bond Industry* (paper presented to UNCTAD Seminar on North South Complementary Intra-Industry Trade, Mexico).

Nixon, R. (1972) 'Economic Assistance and Investment Security in Developing Nations', quoted in P. E. Sigmund *Multinationals in Latin America: the Politics of Nationalization* (Madison: University of Wisconsin for the Twentieth Century Fund, 1980).

O'Brien, P. (1974) 'Developing Countries and the Patent System: An Economic Appraisal', *World Development*, vol. 2, no. 9.

O'Brien, P. (1975) 'A Critique of Latin American Theories of Dependency', in I. Oxaal, T. Barnett and D. Booth *Beyond the Sociology of Development* (London: Routledge and Kegan Paul).

Ocampo, C. (1980) *The Semi-conductor Industry: A Critique of Neo-Smithian Marxism* (University of East Anglia, School of Development Studies, MA Dissertation).

O'Donnell, G. (1978) *Burguesía Local, Capital Transnacional y Aparato Estatal: Notas para su Estudio* (Mexico City: ILET).

O'Donnell, G. (1978a) 'State and Alliances in Argentina, 1956–1976', *Journal of Development Studies*, vol. 15, no. 1.

O'Donnell, G. (1978b) 'Reflections on the Patterns of Change in the Bureaucratic-Authoritarian State', *Latin American Research Review*, vol. 12, no. 1.

Palloix, C. (1975) *Las Firmas Multinacionales y El Proceso de Internacionalización* (Madrid: Siglo XXI).

Palloix, C. (1976) 'The Labour Process: from Fordism to Neo-Fordism', in CSE Pamphlet no. 1, *The Labour Process and Class Struggle*.

Palloix, C. (1978) *La Internacionalizacion del Capital* (Madrid: H. Blume Ediciones).

Paredes Lopez, O (1977) 'Consideraciones sobre la Actividad de las Empresas Farmacéuticas en México', *Comercio Exterior*, vol. 27, no. 8.

Patel, S. (1974) 'The Patent System and the Third World', *World Development*, vol. 2, no. 9.

Pearson, R. (1976) *Discussion Paper on Maquiladora Project*, Mimeo (Mexico City: CIDE).

Pearson, R. (1979) *Women Workers in Mexico's Border Industries* (Mimeo).

Pearson, R. (1982) *Technology Transfer and Technological Dependency: A Case Study of the Argentine Cement Industry, 1875–1975* (University of Sussex, D. Phil. Thesis).

Pellicer de Brody, O. (1974) 'El Llamado a las Inversiones Extranjeras, 1953–1958', in B. Sepulveda, *et al. Las Empresas Transnacionales en México* (Mexico City: El Colegio de Mexico).

PEP (1950) *Motor Vehicles: A Report on the Organization and Structure of the Industry, its Products and its Market Prospects at Home and Abroad* (London: Political and Economic Planning).

Peralta Ramos, M. (1972) *Etapas de Acumulación y Alianzas de Clases en la Argentina (1930–1970)* (Buenos Aires: Siglo XXI).

Perzabal, C. (1979) *Acumulación Capitalista Dependiente y Subordinada: el Caso de Mexico (1940–1978)* (Mexico City: Siglo XXI).

Petras, J., and Cook, T., (1973) 'Dependency and the Industrial Bourgeoisie: Attitudes of Argentine Executives Toward Foreign Economic Investments and US Policy', in J. Petras (ed.), *Latin America: From Dependence to Revolution* (New York: John Wiley & Sons).

Phelps, D. M. (1936) *The Migration of Industry to South America* (New York: McGraw-Hill).

Picciotto, S. (1978) 'Firm and State in the World Economy', in J. Faundez and S. Picciotto (eds), *The Nationalization of Multinationals in Peripheral Economies* (London: Macmillan).

Polit, G. (1968) 'The Argentinian Industrialists', in J. Petras and M. Zeitlin (eds.), *Latin America: Reform or Revolution?* (Greenwich, Conn.: Fawcett Publications).

Prebisch, R. (1950) 'The Economic Development of Latin America and its Principal Problems', reprinted in *Economic Bulletin for Latin America*, vol. 7, no. 1, 1962.

Prebisch, R. (1969) 'The System and the Social Structure of Latin America', in I. Horowitz, J. de Castro and J. Gerassi, *Latin American Radicalism* (New York: Vintage Books).

Pryor, F. L. (1973) 'An International Comparison of Concentration Ratios', in B. S. Yamey (ed.) *Economics of Industrial Structure* (Harmondsworth: Penguin).

Quijano, A. (1974) 'The Marginal Pole of the Economy and the Marginalised Labour Force', *Economy and Society*, vol. 3, no. 4.

Quijano, J. M. (1979) 'México: Credito y Desnacionalización', *Economía de América Latina*, no. 3.

Rama, R. and Vigorito, R. (1979) *El Complejo de Frutas y Legumbres en México* (Mexico City: ILET/Editorial Nueva Imagen).

Ramirez de la O, R. (1981) 'Las Empresas Transnacionales y el Comerico Exterior de México. Un Estudio Empírico del Comportamiento de las Empresas', *Comercio Exterior*, vol. 31, no. 10.

Rangel, D. (1979) *La Oligarquía del Dinero* (Valencia, Venezuela: Vadell Hermanos Editores).

Reekie, W. D. (1975) *The Economics of the Pharmaceutical Industry* (London: Macmillan).

Rhys, D. G. (1972) *The Motor Industry: An Economic Survey* (London: Butterworth).

Robinson, H. J. and Smith, R. G. (1976) *The Impact of Foreign Private Investment on the Mexican Economy* (Mexico City: Stanford Research Institute for the American Chamber of Commerce of Mexico).

Rodriguez, O. (1980) *El Analísis del Subdesarrollo de la CEPAL* (Mexico: Siglo XXI).

Rosales, M. (1977) *La Tecnología y la Inversión Extranjera en la Industria Farmacéutica de Guatemala* (Guatemala: Instituto de Investigaciones Económicas y Sociales, Universidad de San Carlos).

Rosenthal, G. (1975) *The Expansion of Transnational Enterprise in Central America: Acquisition of Domestic Firms* (paper presented to the CONACYT–CIDE Symposium on Transnational Enterprise, Queretaro, Mexico).

Rowthorn, R. (1975) 'Imperialism in the 1970s – Unity or Rivalry?', in H. Radice (ed.), *International Firms and Modern Imperialism* (Harmondsworth: Penguin).

Rowthorn, R. (1979) 'Introduction to Part 3', in S. Hymer, *The Multinational Corporation: A Radical Approach* (Cambridge: Cambridge University Press).

Roxborough, I. (1979) *Theories of Underdevelopment* (London: Macmillan).

Roxborough, I. (forthcoming) 'Labour in the Mexican Automobile Industry', in R. Kronish and K. Mericle, *The Political Economy of the Latin American Motor Vehicle Industry* (Cambridge, Mass: MIT Press).

Rubin, A. (1977) *Foreign Production for the US Market in Apparel Goods: A Critique of the 'Interdependence' between the United States and Mexico* (University of Sussex, Institute of Development Studies, M.Phil Dissertation).

Salama, P. (1976) *El Proceso de 'Subdesarrollo'* (Mexico City: Ediciones Era).

Salama, P. (1978) 'Specificités de l'Internationalisation du Capital en Amérique Latine', *Revue Tiers Monde*, vol. 19, no. 74.

Schmukler, B. (1977) *Relaciones Actuales de Producción en Industrias Tradicionales Argentinas: Evolución de las Relaciones no Capitalistas* (Buenos Aires: CEDES, Estudios Sociales no. 6).

Schwartzman, D. (1976) *Innovation in the Pharmaceutical Industry* (Baltimore: The Johns Hopkins University Press).

Schydlowsky, D. M. (1972) 'Latin American Trade Policies in the 1970s, A Prospective Appraisal', *Quarterly Journal of Economics*, vol. 86, 1972.

Segall, M. (1975) *Pharmaceuticals and Health Planning in Developing Countries* (Institute of Development Studies, Communication 119).

Semmler, W. (1982) 'Theories of Competition and Monopoly', *Capital and Class*, 18, Writer.

Sepulveda, B., and Chumacero, A. (1973) *La Inversión Extranjera en Mexico* (Mexico City: Fondo de Cultura Económica).

Sercovich, F. (1974) 'Dependencia Tecnologica en la Industria Argentina', *Desarrollo Económico*, vol. 14, no. 53.

Serra, J. (1973) 'The Brazilian "Economic Miracle"', in J. Petras (ed.), *Latin America: From Dependence to Revolution* (New York: John Wiley and Son).

Serra, J. (1979) 'Three Mistaken Theses Regarding the Connection between Industrialization and Authoritarian Regimes', in D. Collier (ed.), *The New Authoritarianism in Latin America* (Princeton: Princeton University Press).

Sheahan, J. (1980) 'Market-oriented Economic Policies and Political Repression in Latin America', *Economic Development and Cultural Change*, vol. 28, no. 2.

Shepherd, P. L. (forthcoming) 'Transnational Corporations and the International Cigarette Industry', in R. Newfarmer (ed.) *International Oligopoly and Development: Studies of International Industries and their Growth in Latin America*.

SIC (n.d.) *Zonas Fronterizas de México, Perfil Socio-Económica* (Mexico City: Secretaría de Industria y Comercio).

Silberston, A. (1965) 'The Motor Industry, 1955–64', *Bulletin of the Oxford University Institute of Statistics*, vol. 27, no. 4.

Silverman, M. (1976) *The Drugging of the Americas: How Multinational Drug Companies Say One Thing about their Products to Physicians in the United States, and Another Thing to Physicians in Latin America* (Berkeley: University of California Press).

Silverman, M. and Lee, P. (1974) *Pills, Profits and Politics* (Berkeley: University of California Press).

Slatter, S. (1977) *Competition and Marketing Strategies in the Pharmaceutical Industry* (London: Croom Helm).

Smith, P. H. (1977) 'Does Mexico Have a Power Elite?', in J. L. Reyna and R. Weinert *Authoritarianism in Mexico* (Philadelphia: Institute for the Study of Human Issues).

Smith, S. and Toye, J. (1979) 'Introduction: Three Stories about Trade and Poor Economies', in S. Smith and J. Toye (eds.), *Trade and Poor Economies* (London: Frank Cass).

Society of Motor Manufacturers and Traders (1961) *The Motor Industry of Great Britain, 1961* (London: SMMT).

Sourrouille, J. (1976) *El Impacto de las Empresas Transnacionales, sobre el Empleo y los Ingresos: El Caso de Argentina* (Geneva: ILO World Employment Programme Research Working Paper WEP 2–28/WP7).

Sourrouille, J. (1980) *El Complejo Automotor en Argentina* (Mexico City: ILET/ Editorial Nueva Imagen).

Sourrouille, J. (1981) 'La Presencia y el Comportamiento de las Empresas Extranjeras en el Sector Industrial Argentino', in F. Fajnzylber (ed.), *Industrialización e Internacionalización en la América Latina*, vol. I (Mexico City: Fondo de Culture Económica).

Souza, H. de (1975) 'The Multinationals and the Exploitation of the Working Class', in M. Arruda, *et al. Multinationals and Brazil: The Impact of Multinational Corporations in Contemporary Brazil* (Toronto: Brazilian Studies, Latin America Research Unit).

Souza, H. (1977) *An Overview of Theories of Multinational Corporations and the question of the State in Latin America* (Toronto: Brazilian Studies Latin America Research Unit, Working Paper 19).

Souza, P. R. (1978) 'Wage Disparities in the Urban Labour Market', *CEPAL Review*, first half.

Spalding, H. (1977) *Organized Labor in Latin America: Historical Case Studies of Urban Workers in Dependent Societies* (New York: Harper Torchbooks).

Stobaugh, R. B. (1971) 'The Neo-Technology Account of International Trade: the Case of Petrochemicals', in L. T. Wells (ed.), *The Product Life Cycle and International Trade* (Cambridge, Mass: Harvard Graduate School of Business Administration).

Strachan, H. (1976) *Family and Other Business Groups in Economic Development: the Case of Nicaragua* (New York: Praeger).

Sunkel, O. (1969) 'National development policy and external dependence in Latin America', *Journal of Development Studies*, vol. 6, no. 1.

Sunkel, O. (1971) 'Capitalismo Transnacional y Desintegración Nacional', *El Trimestre Económico*, April–June.

# Bibliography 253

Sunkel, O. (1972) 'Big Business and "Dependencia": A Latin American View', *Foreign Affairs*, vol. 50, no. 3, 517–31.

Sylos-Labini, P. (1962) *Oligopoly and Technical Progress* (Cambridge, Mass: Harvard University Press).

Tavares, M. C., and Façanha, L. O. (1981) 'La Presencia de las Grandes Empresas en la Estructura Industrial Brasilena', in F. Fajnzylber (ed.), *Industrialización e Internationalización en la América Latina*, vol. I (Mexico City: Fondo de Cultura Económica).

Tavares, M. C. and Serra, J. (1973) 'Beyond Stagnation: A Discussion on the Nature of Recent Developments in Brazil', in J. Petras (ed.), *Latin America: from Dependence to Revolution* (New York: John Wiley and Sons).

Teubal, M. (1968) 'The Failure of Latin America's Economic Integration', in J. Petras and M. Zeitlin, *Latin America: Reform or Revolution?* (Greenwich, Conn.: Fawcett Publications).

Tokman, V. (1973) 'Concentration of Economic Power in Argentina', *World Development*, vol. 1, no. 10.

Tomasini, R. (1977) *Acuerdos de Complementación de ALALC y la Participación de las Empresas Transnacionales: los Casos de Maquinas de Oficina y Productos Electronicos* (Santiago: División de Desarrollo Económico, Dependencia conjunta CEPAL/CET, Documento de Trabajo, no. 3).

Trajtenberg, R. (1977) *Un Enfoque Sectorial para el Estudio de la Penetración de empresas Transnacionales en América Latina* (Mexico City: ILET).

Tyler, W. G. (1973) 'Manufactured Export Promotion in a Semi-industrialized Economy: the Brazilian Case', *Journal of Development Studies*, vol. 10, no. 1.

Tyler, W. G. (1976) *Manufactured Export Expansion and Industrialization in Brazil* (Tübingen: Mohr).

UNCTAD (1974) [United Nations Conference on Trade and Development] *Major Issues arising from the Transfer of Technology: a Case Study of Chile* (Geneva: IO/UN/IID/TD/B/AC.11).

UNCTAD (1975) *Major Issues in Transfer of Technology to Developing Countries: A case Study of the Pharmaceutical Industry* (Geneva: TD/B/C.6/4).

UNCTAD (1980) *Legislation and Regulations on Technology Transfer: Empirical Analysis of their Effects in Selected Countries. The Implementation of Transfer of Technology Regulations: A Preliminary Analysis of the experience of Latin America, India and Philippines* (Geneva: TD/B/C.6/55).

UNCTAD (1980a) *Technology Policies in the Pharmaceutical Sector in Cuba* (Geneva: UNCTAD/TT/33).

UNCTAD (1981) *Examination of the Economic, Commercial and Developmental Aspects of Industrial Property in the Transfer of Technology to Developing Countries: Review of Recent Trends in Patents in Developing Countries* (Geneva: TD/B/C.6/Ac. 5/3).

UNCTAD (1981a) *Examination of the Economic, Commercial and Developmental Aspects of Industrial Property in the Transfer of Technology to Developing Countries: Trade Marks and Generic Names of Pharmaceuticals and Consumer Protection* (Geneva: TD/B/C.6/Ac. 5/4).

UNCTAD (1981b) *Examination of the Economic, Commercial and Developmental Aspects of Industrial Property in the Transfer of Technology to Developing Countries: the Role of Trade Marks in the Promotion of Exports from Developing Countries* (Geneva: TD/B/C.6/Ac. 5/2).

UNCTC [United Nations Centre on Transnational Corporations] (1979) *Transnational Corporations and the Pharmaceutical Industry* (New York: United Nations).

UNCTC (1979a) *Transnational Corporations in Advertising* (New York: ST/CTC/8. United Nations).

UNCTC (1980) *Transnational Corporations in Food and Beverage Processing* (New York: United Nations).

UNIDO [United Nations Industrial Development Organisation] (1972) *The Motor Vehicle Industry* (Vienna: ID/78).

UNIDO (1978) *The Steps involved in Establishing a Pharmaceutical Industry in Developing Countries* (Vienna: ID/WG. 267/3).

UNIDO (1979) *World Industry since 1960: Progress and Prospects* (New York: United Nations).

Urquidi, V. (1965) 'The Implications of Foreign Investment in Latin America', in C. Veliz (ed.), *Obstacles to Change in Latin America* (Oxford: Oxford University Press).

US Department of Commerce, *Survey of Current Business* (Washington: Bureau of Economic Analysis, various issues).

US Senate (1973) *Hearings of the Subcommittee on International Trade of the Committee on Finance* (Washington).

US Senate, Committee of Finance (1973) *Implications of Multinational Firms for World Trade and Investment and for U.S. Trade and Labour* (Washington).

USTC [United States Tariff Commission] (1970) *Economic Factors affecting the Use of Items 807.00 and 806.30 of the Tariff Schedules of the United States* (Washington).

Vaitsos, C. (1971) 'The Process of Commercialization of Technology in the Andean Pact', in H. Radice (ed.), *International Firms and Modern Imperialism* (Harmondsworth: Penguin).

Vaitsos, C. (1972) 'Patents Revisted: Their Function in Developing Countries', in C. Cooper (ed.), *Science, Technology and Development* (London: Frank Cass).

Vaitsos, C. (1973) *The Changing Policies of Latin American Governments Towards Economic Development and Direct Foreign Investment* (paper presented to the Conference on Latin American–US Economic Interactions, The University of Texas at Austin).

Vaitsos, C. (1974) *Inter-country Income Distribution and Transnational Enterprises* (Oxford: Clarendon Press).

Vaitsos, C. (1976) *Employment Problems and Transnational Enterprises in Developing Countries: Distortions and Inequality* (Geneva: International Labour Office).

Vaitsos, C. (1978) *The Role of Transnational Enterprises in Latin American Economic Integration Efforts: Who Integrates, and With Whom, How and for Whose Benefits?* (paper presented to UNCTAD Round Table on the Role of Transnational Enterprises in the Latin American Integration Process, Lima).

Vaitsos, C. (1981) 'Los Problemas del Empleo y las Empresas Transnacionales en los Paises en Desarrollo: Distorsiones y Desigualdad', in F. Fajnzylber (ed.), *Industrialización e Internacionalización en la América Latina*, vol 2 (Mexico City: Fondo de Cultura Económica).

Vaupel, J., and Curhan, J. (1969) *The Making of Multinational Enterprise: A Sourcebook of Tables based on a Study of 187 major US Manufacturing Companies* (Cambridge: Harvard University Graduate School of Business Administration).

Vaupel, J., and Curhan, J. (1973) *The World's Multinational Enterprises,*

(Cambridge: Harvard University, Graduate School of Business Administration).

Vernon, R. (1973) *Sovreignty at Bay* (Hermondsworth: Penguin).

Vernon, R. (1977) *Storm over the Multinationals: the Real Issues* (London: Macmillan).

Vilas, C. M. (1974) *La Dominación Imperialista en Argentina* (Buenos Aires: EUDEBA).

Vitelli, G. (1978) *Competition, Oligopoly and Technological Change in the Construction industry: the Argentine Case* (Buenos Aires: IDB/ECLA Research Programme in Science and Technology, Working Paper no. 3).

Von Bertrab, H. (1968) *The Transfer of Technology: a Case Study of European Private Enterprises having operations in Latin America with special emphasis on Mexico* (University of Texas, Austin, Ph.D. Thesis).

Vuskovic, P. (1979) 'América Latina ante Nuevos Terminos de la División Internacional del Trabajo', *Economía de América Latina*, no. 2, Marzo, 1979.

Weaver, F. S. (1980) *Class, State and Industrial Structure: the Historical Process of South American Industrial Growth* (Westport, Conn.: Greenwood).

Weeks, J. (1977) 'Backwardness, Foreign Capital and Accumulation in the Manufacturing Sector of Peru, 1954–1975', *Latin American Perspectives*, 14, vol. 4, no. 3.

Weinert, R. (1977) 'The State and Foreign Capital', in J. L. Reyna and R. Weinert, *Authoritarianism in Mexico* (Philadelphia: Institute for the Study of Human Issues).

Wells, J. (1977) 'The Diffusion of Durables in Brazil and its Implications for Recent Controversies Concerning Brazilian Development', *Cambridge Journal of Economics*, no. 1.

Wells, L. (1977) 'The Internationalization of Firms from Developing Countries', in T. Agmon and C. P. Kindleberger, *Multinationals from Small Countries* (Cambridge, Mass: MIT Press, 1977).

White, L. J. (1971) *The Automobile Industry since 1945* (Cambridge, Mass: Harvard University Press).

White, L. J. (1977) 'The Automobile Industry', in W. Adams (ed.), *The Structure of American Industry*, 5th edition (New York: Collier–Macmillan).

Wilmore, L. (1976) 'Direct Foreign Investment in Central American Manufacturing', *World Development*, vol. 4, no. 6.

Wionczek, M. (1971) *Inversión y Tecnología Extranjera en América Latina* (Mexico City: Cuadernos de Joaquin Mortiz).

Wionczek, M. Bueno, G. and Navarrette, J. (1971) *La Transferencia Internacional de Tecnología al Nivel de Empresa: El Caso de México* (New York: United Nations, ESA/FF/AC.2/10).

Wogart, J. P. (1978) *Industrialization in Colombia: Policies, Patterns, Perspectives* (Tübingen: Mohr).

Wortzel, L. (1971) *Technology Transfer in the Pharmaceutical Industry* (New York: United Nations Institute for Training and Research UNITAR Research Report, no. 14).

Zeitlin, M. and Ratcliff, R. (1976) 'The Concentration of National and Foreign Capital in Chile, 1966', in A. Valenzuela and J. S. Valenzuela, (eds), *Chile: Politics and Society* (New Brunswick, Transaction Books).

# Index